Space, Place, and Gender

# Space, Place, and Gender

Doreen Massey

University of Minnesota Press
Minneapolis

First published in 1994 by Polity Press
in association with Blackwell Publishers.

Published simultaneously in 1994 in the United States by
University of Minnesota Press
2037 University Avenue Southeast
Minneapolis, MN 55455-3092

Printed in Great Britain

**Library of Congress Cataloging-in-Publication Data**

Massey, Doreen B.
    Space, place, and gender  /  Doreen Massey.
        p.  cm.
    Includes bibliographical references (p.    ) and index.
    ISBN 0-8166-2616-2 (hc   :   acid-free paper). — ISBN 0-8166-2617-0
(pbk.  :  acid-free paper)
    1. Human geography.  2. Spatial behavior.  3. Space and time.
4. Sex role.  5. Social interaction.  6. Personal space.
7. Feminist theory.  I. Title.
GF95.M37   1994
304.2'3--dc20                                          94-10955
                                                          CIP

The University of Minnesota is an
equal-opportunity educator and employer.

# Contents

# Acknowledgements

'Industrial restructuring versus the cities', written with Richard Meegan, first appeared in *Urban Studies* (1978), vol. 15, pp. 273–88, and is published by kind permission of Carfax Publishing Company. 'In what sense a regional problem?' first appeared in *Regional Studies* (1979), vol. 13, pp. 233–43, and is published by kind permission of the Regional Studies Association. The paper was originally presented to a Regional Studies Association conference entitled 'The death of regional policy'. 'The shape of things to come' first appeared in *Marxism Today*, April 1983, pp. 18–27. 'Uneven development: social change and spatial divisions of labour' first appeared in *Uneven Re-Development: Cities and Regions in Transition* edited by Doreen Massey and John Allen and published by Hodder & Stoughton in association with the Open University (1988), pp. 250–76; it is published here by kind permission of Hodder & Stoughton and the Open University. 'The political place of locality studies' first appeared in *Environment and Planning A* (1991), vol. 23, pp. 267–81, and is published by kind permission of Pion Press Limited. 'A global sense of place' first appeared in *Marxism Today*, June 1991, pp. 24–9. 'A place called home?' first appeared in *New Formations* (1992) no. 17, pp. 3–15, and is published by kind permission of Lawrence & Wishart. 'Space, place and gender' forms part of a public lecture delivered at the London School of Economics Gender Institute, which was first published in the *LSE Magazine*, spring 1992, pp. 32–4. 'A woman's place?', written with Linda McDowell, first appeared in *Geography Matters: a reader* edited by Doreen Massey and John Allen and published by Cambridge University Press in association with the Open University (1984), pp. 128–47; it is published here by kind permission of Cambridge University Press and the Open University. 'Flexible sexism' first appeared in *Environment and Planning D: Society and Space* (1991) vol. 9, pp. 31–57, and is published by kind permission of Pion Press. 'Politics and space/time' first appeared in *New Left Review* (1992) no. 196, November–December, pp. 65–84, and is published by kind permission of *New Left Review*. I should particularly like to thank Richard Meegan and Linda McDowell for agreeing to my including articles which were written jointly with them.

The articles collected here cover a considerable period. Over those years I have worked with and learned from a large number of people, both inside and beyond academe. I should especially like to thank Richard Meegan with whom much of the earlier work was done, when we were both working at the Centre for Environmental Studies, and my colleagues in geography at the Open University. A number of the articles were written in the context of courses for the OU, either directly as part of a course, or emerging from the constantly provocative discussions in 'course-team meetings'.

The period over which the articles were written (the late seventies to the present) was as a whole a fairly turbulent one. What is pleasing is that, from the early skirmishings with neo-classical location theory, through the debates over locality studies, to the more recent exchanges over post-modernism and feminism, disagreements in print have not overwhelmed personal friendships.

Finally, I should like to thank Rebecca Harkin of Polity for encouraging me to undertake this project, and Doreen Warwick of the Open University for her help with its physical production.

# General Introduction

The terms space and place have long histories and bear with them a multiplicity of meanings and connotations which reverberate with other debates and many aspects of life. 'Space' may call to mind the realm of the dead or the chaos of simultaneity and multiplicity. It may be used in reference to the synchronic systems of structuralists or employed to picture the n-dimensional space of identity.[1] Likewise with place, though perhaps with more consistency, it can raise an image of one's place in the world, of the reputedly (but as we shall see, disputed) deep meanings of 'a place called home' or, with much greater intimations of mobility and agility, can be used in the context of discussions of positionality.

The papers in this collection pull out a few threads from the enormous complexity of this field and put the case for a particular way of thinking of space and place. It is not the only way in which they can be thought about; both concepts are incredibly mobile and I have no wish to take issue with that in principle. Nor are the views advanced here simply incompatible with all others. There are other lines of debate about space and place which derive their impetus from different questions and which concentrate on different issues. The conceptualizations presented here do not pretend to be exhaustive. What the papers collected here do is focus on particular aspects of the ways in which space and place are commonly conceptualized, in daily and political life as well as in academe. The arguments emerge from particular debates and respond to issues which I see as having lent to space and place especially problematical readings in recent years. This does mean, therefore, that there are some ways of thinking of space and place which I do want to argue against. The aim is to put forward alternative readings which are appropriate to these times.

The central thread linking the papers is the attempt to formulate concepts of space and place in terms of social relations. Throughout, there is an assumption that one aspect of those relations which is likely to be important is that of class. It was from work on the class relations within industrial geography that the arguments emerged. There is another focus developed here, however, and that is the intricacy and profundity of the connection of space and place with gender and the construction of gender relations. Some of this connection works through the actual construction of, on the one hand, real-world geographies and, on the other, the cultural specificity of definitions of gender. Geography matters to the construction of gender, and the fact of geographical variation in gender relations, for instance, is a significant element in the production and reproduction of both imaginative geographies and uneven development. The papers here, and the introductions to Parts I, II and III, draw out some of these interconnections.

But there are also other levels at which space, place and gender are interrelated: that is, in their very construction as culturally specific ideas – in terms both of the conceptual nature of that construction and of its substantive content – and in the overlapping and interplaying of the sets of characteristics and connotations with which each is associated. Particular ways of thinking about space and place are tied up with, both directly and indirectly, particular social constructions of gender relations. My aim is to unearth just some of these connections (other writers have highlighted others, and there are presumably still more). The implication is that challenging certain of the ways in which space and place are currently conceptualized implies also, indeed necessitates, challenging the currently dominant form of gender definitions and gender relations.

The most abstract and perhaps the most complex version of the proposed view of 'the spatial' is presented in the final paper in this collection: 'Politics and space/time'.

Central to that paper is the argument that space must be conceptualized integrally with time; indeed that the aim should be to think always in terms of space–time. That argument emerged out of an earlier insistence on thinking of space, not as some absolute independent dimension, but as constructed out of social relations: that what is at issue is not social phenomena in space but both social phenomena and space as constituted out of social relations, that the spatial is social relations 'stretched out'. The fact is, however, that social relations are never still; they are inherently dynamic. Thus even to understand space as a simultaneity is, in these terms, not to evacuate it of all inherent dynamism. The initial impetus to insist on this came from an urge to counter those views of space which understood it as static, as the dimension precisely where nothing 'happened', and as a dimension devoid of effect or implications. But the argument was buttressed by debates in other disciplines. In biology, Mae-Wan Ho was arguing that 'form is dynamic through and through', a formulation which neatly undermines any idea of the temporal as process and the spatial as form-which-is-therefore-lacking-in-process. It is only in our experience, Ho goes on to argue, that things are held fast, if only for a second. 'There is no holding nature still.'[2] Physics, since the beginning of the century, had been advocating similar views. Thus Minkowski:

> The views of space and time which I wish to lay before you have sprung from the soil of experimental physics, and therein lies their strength. They are radical. Henceforth space by itself, and time by itself, are doomed to fade away into mere shadows, and only a kind of union of the two will preserve an independent reality.[3]

The view, then, is of space–time as a configuration of social relations within which the specifically spatial may be conceived of as an inherently dynamic simultaneity. Moreover, since social relations are inevitably and everywhere imbued with power and meaning and symbolism, this view of the spatial is as an ever-shifting social geometry of power and signification.

Such a way of conceptualizing the spatial, moreover, inherently implies the existence in the lived world of a simultaneous multiplicity of spaces: cross-cutting, intersecting, aligning with one another, or existing in relations of paradox or antagonism. Most evidently this is so because the social relations of space are experienced differently, and variously interpreted, by those holding different positions as part of it. But it may also be seen to be so by continuing the analogy with modern physics. For there too the observer is inevitably within the world (the space) being observed. And this in turn means that it partly constitutes the observer and the observer it, and the fact of the observer's constitution of it means that there is necessarily a multiplicity of different spaces, or takes on space. (Thus my arguments about the general nature of space in 'Politics and space/time' and in 'A global sense of place' do not imply that there is only one space/spatiality. They are arguments at the same level as, for instance, Ernesto Laclau's claims that existence is necessarily dislocated. They are of the same status as saying space is fractured, or paradoxical.) Moreover, this point applies specifically to the concept of simultaneity employed above. Thus, as Unwin argues: 'According to the special theory of relativity, simultaneity is relative, dependent on the choice of a frame of reference in motion'.[4] All 'observers' (participants in social life) move relative to one another, each thinking of themselves at rest, and each therefore 'slicing the space–time continuum at different angles'.[5] Indeed, as the quotation from Ho indicated, simultaneities themselves are our own constructions. It is consciousness which introduces a notion of 'now'.[6] Moreover, this in turn provides a further source of dislocation within space/space–time, for people are everywhere conceptualizing and acting on different spatialities ('A global sense of place').

The reasons for arguing all this, however, are not just intellectual, or in order to be consistent with physics; nor is there any commitment to this view of space as more eternally correct than any other. It is, however, a view of space that may have important characteristics which lend it an especial appropriateness for debates of the moment. Thus, from the argument so far it seems to me important to establish the inherent dynamism of the spatial, at least in the sense that the spatial is not simply opposed to the temporal as its absence, as a lack. The argument thus releases the spatial from the realm of the dead.[7] Further, such a view directly relates spatiality to the social and to power. Thinking in terms of stretched-out social relations confronts an important aspect of the spatiality of power itself.

Further yet, within this dynamic simultaneity which is space, phenomena may be placed in relationship to one another in such a way that new social effects are provoked. The spatial organization of society, in other words, is integral to the production of the social, and not merely its result. It is fully implicated in both history and politics.

'The spatial' then, it is argued here, can be seen as constructed out of the multiplicity of social relations across all spatial scales, from the global reach of finance and telecommunications, through the geography of the tentacles of national political power, to the social relations within the town, the settlement, the household and the workplace. It is a way of thinking in terms of the ever-shifting geometry of social/power relations, and it forces into view the real multiplicities of space–time. It is a view of space opposed to that which sees it as a flat, immobilized surface,[8] as stasis, even as no more than threatening chaos – the opposite of stasis – which is to see space as the opposite of History, and as the (consequently) de-politicized. The spatial is both open to, and a necessary element in, politics in the broadest sense of the word.

Moreover, thinking about space in this way can also challenge some influential conceptualizations of place. Since the late 1980s the world has seen the recrudescence of exclusivist claims to places – nationalist, regionalist and localist. All of them have been attempts to fix the meaning of particular spaces, to enclose them, endow them with fixed identities and to claim them for one's own. Within the academic literature as well as more widely there has been a continuation of the tendency to identify 'places' as necessarily sites of nostalgia, of the opting-out from Progress and History. There was within the discipline of geography a fiercely negative reaction, on the part of some Marxist geographers in particular, to the move to include within the compass of radical geography a focus on 'locality studies' (see part II).

Briefly, it seemed to me that such political and academic positions all rested on a particular view of place. It is a view of place as bounded, as in various ways a site of an authenticity, as singular, fixed and unproblematic in its identity. It is a conceptualization of place which rests in part on the view of space as stasis.

If, however, the spatial is thought of in the context of space–time and as formed out of social interrelations at all scales, then one view of a place is as a particular articulation of those relations, a particular moment in those networks of social relations and understandings (see 'A global sense of place' and 'A place called home?').[9] But the particular mix of social relations which are thus part of what defines the uniqueness of any place is by no means all included within that place itself.[10] Importantly, it includes relations which stretch beyond – the global as part of what constitutes the local, the outside as part of the inside. Such a view of place challenges any possibility of claims to internal histories or to timeless identities. The identities of place are always unfixed, contested and multiple. And the particularity of any place is, in these terms, constructed not by placing boundaries around it and defining its identity through counterposition to the other which lies beyond, but precisely (in part) through the specificity of the mix of links and interconnections *to* that 'beyond'. Places viewed this way are open and porous.[11]

All attempts to institute horizons, to establish boundaries, to secure the identity of places, can in this sense therefore be seen to be *attempts to stabilize the meaning of particular envelopes of space–time*. They are attempts to get to grips with the unutterable mobility and contingency of space–time. Moreover, however common, and however understandable, they may be it is important to recognize them as such. For such attempts at the stabilization of meaning are constantly the site of social contest, battles over the power to label space–time, to impose the meaning to be attributed to a space, for however long or short a span of time. And there are two levels at which such contests may be joined: the first, and the most usual, is simply over the label/identity/boundary to be assigned; the second, the one being pressed here, is the insistence on pointing out – and thereby challenging – the nature of that debate itself.

Anthony Giddens has argued that one of the consequences of modernity has been the separation of space from place:

In premodern societies, space and place largely coincided, since the spatial
dimensions of social life are, for most of the population . . . dominated by
'presence' – by localised activity . . . Modernity increasingly tears space away
from place by fostering relations between 'absent' others, locationally distant
from any given situation of face-to-face interaction. In conditions of modernity . . . locales are thoroughly penetrated by and shaped in terms of social
influences quite distant from them.[12]

The argument here is that we must not only recognize these changes in
the spatial organization of social relations but must also, in consequence,
*rethink the unity of space and place in different terms*, thereby concep-
tually confronting in a constructive way this changed state of the world.
Indeed, Edward Said, in his second Reith Lecture, delivered while I was
writing this introduction, argued that rejecting such notions of place-
identity must be a central task for intellectuals today:

With regard to the consensus on group or national identity, it is the
intellectual's task to show how the group is not a natural or god-given entity
but is a constructed, manufactured, even, in some cases, invented object,
with a history of struggle and conquest behind it, that it is sometimes
important to represent.[13]

However, these lines of debate over the conceptualization of space and
place are also tied up with gender, with the radical polarization into two
genders which is typically hegemonic in western societies today, and with
the bundles of characteristics typically assigned to each.

Thus the discussion of space in 'Politics and space/time' relates the
strategy of radically polarizing time and space, and of defining space by
the absence of temporality, to the broader western mode of dualistic
thinking which has been widely criticized by feminists and linked into the
same system of thought which so sharply distinguishes between masculine
and feminine, defining them through continuous series of mutual oppositions. Thus this pervasive and influential view of the relationship between
space and time sees them as dichotomous and as dichotomous in a
particular way. It is a formulation in which time is the privileged signifier
in a distinction of the type A/not-A. It is, moreover, time which is typically
coded masculine and space, being absence or lack, as feminine. Moreover,
the same gendering operates through the series of dualisms which are
linked to time and space. It is time which is aligned with history, progress,
civilization, politics and transcendence and coded masculine. And it is the
opposites of these things which have, in the traditions of western thought,
been coded feminine. The exercise of rescuing space from its position, in
this formulation, of stasis, passivity and depoliticization, therefore, con-

nects directly with a wider philosophical debate in which gendering and the construction of gender relations are central. However, the issue in which I am interested here is not so much the coding of space as feminine (although it raises an interesting question about the masculinism of geography),[14] but the radicalism of the dualistic distinction between space and time and the relationship of that not only generally to other dualistic formulations but also – and crucially – to the violent either/or distinction between polarized genders which is currently hegemonic in so much of western society. The argument is that it is the very form of such dichotomies which must be challenged.

The construction of gender relations is also strongly implicated in the debate over the conceptualization of place. The view of place advocated here, where localities can in a sense be present in one another, both inside and outside at the same time, is a view which stresses the construction of specificity through interrelations rather than through the imposition of boundaries and the counterposition of one identity *against* an other. But why is it that settlement or place *is* so frequently characterized as bounded, as enclosure, and as directly counterposed to spaces as flows?[15]

One way of reflecting on this draws on object-relations theory and a number of other, psychoanalytic, approaches to identity-formation ('A place called home?'). In brief, the argument is that the need for the security of boundaries, the requirement for such a defensive and counter-positional definition of identity, is culturally masculine. Moreover, many feminists have argued against such ways of thinking, such definitions of identity. The argument is that we need to have the courage to abandon such defensive – yet designed for dominance – means of definition. Many feminists have argued for 'thinking in terms of relations'. It is the strategy adopted here, in very general terms, for rethinking the concepts of space and place.

There are in this way many parallels between the current debate about personal identity and the construction of political subjects and the argument here about the identity of place ('The political place of locality studies'). Just as personal identities are argued to be multiple, shifting, possibly unbounded, so also, it is argued here, are the identities of place. Thus Chantal Mouffe has written that

> many communitarians seem to believe that we belong to only one community, defined empirically and even geographically, and that this community could be unified by a single idea of the common good. But we are in fact always multiple and contradictory subjects, inhabitants of a diversity of communities (as many, really, as the social relations in which we participate and the subject-positions they define), constructed by a variety of discourses

and precariously and temporarily sutured at the intersection of those positions.

Teresa de Lauretis, indeed, has argued that the construction of subjectivity in this way is a specifically feminist project.[16] The concept of place advanced here is very similar to that. It is a concept which depends crucially on the notion of articulation. It is a move, in terms of political subjects and of place, which is anti-essentialist, which can recognize difference, and which yet can simultaneously emphasize the bases for potential solidarities. Moreover, if places are conceptualized in this way, and if their definition is amplified to take account of the construction of the subjects within them, which are part and parcel of what it is to talk about place, then the identity of place is a double articulation.[17]

There are, however, also distinctions which can be drawn between the arguments around the identity of political subjects on the one hand (whether individuals or collectivities) and the identity of places on the other. Arguments for strategic or operational essentialism, put forward by Spivak for instance, whatever their validity in relation to political actors, seem to have less purchase in debates over place (nationalism, localism, and so on). As Fanon and Said have argued, even in the case of national liberation movements (perhaps the classic case of place-based struggles against oppression) it is still necessary to ask what one is fighting *for*. Or again, on a lighter note, Schiller in answer to his own question, 'what is national identity?' replies, 'There is no totally satisfying definition. It is much easier to recognise its absence. A Kentucky Fried Chicken franchise in Paris, for example, surely does not qualify as part of a French national identity. A McDonald's outlet in Kyoto hardly expresses the Japanese ethos'.[18] While this is in some sense true (at least in the sense that 'one knows what he means') it is also important to remember that the national identity of which Kentucky Fried Chicken is not part was itself formed over centuries by layer upon layer of interconnections with the world beyond what was to become France. Some of the elements which are now as obviously French as the Kentucky Fried Chicken is not must once have seemed just as 'alien', similarly imported from the global beyond.[19] Moreover, it is also important to note that such ideas of place-identity are also always constructed by reference to the past. Preservationists of place – those fighting perhaps to keep out the Kentucky Fried Chicken – are in this sense seeking to fix, to stabilize, the identity of a particular place, but around an identity which itself is most unlikely to be the product of an autochthonous history. This does not mean that there is no justification for any notion of conservation, but it does mean that the debate should focus on the terms and nature of both conservation and innovation. And that leads in turn into wider realms of social debate and politics (it may be racism, it may be a class issue – the case of the yuppie 'invasion' of Docklands is examined in the introduction to part II) rather than issues of the supposed authenticity of a particular locality. What is at issue is the understanding of – the politics of definition of – a particular envelope of space–time.

The question of the conceptualization of place also links in again to the issue of dualisms. For, as with space, so with place certain formulations of the concept are embedded in concatenations of linked and interplaying dichotomies which in turn are related, both in their general form and in their specific connotational content, to gender. In the pair space/place it is place which represents Being, and to it are attached a range of epithets and connotations: local, specific, concrete, descriptive. Each of these carries a different burden of meaning and each relates to different oppositions. The contrary to these classically designated characteristics of place are terms such as: general, universal, theoretical/abstract/conceptual. It was this kind of opposition, these sets of dualisms, which were in play when a number of Marxist geographers criticized so strongly the renewed interest in localities in the 1980s ('The political place of locality studies').

It is interesting in that context to ponder the gender connotations of these pairings. The universal, the theoretical, the conceptual are, in current western ways of thinking, coded masculine. They are the terms of a disembodied, free-floating, generalizing science. (Though they do not have to be; this is not in any way an argument against theory. It is merely to point to the gendered systems of meaning in which its current definition and characteristics are caught up.)[20] On the other side of the pairings, the term 'local' itself displays, on the one hand, a remarkable malleability of meaning and, on the other, a real consistency of gender association.

First there is the argument of an association between the feminine and the local because – it is said – women lead more local lives than do men; it is an argument which clearly relates to that about the public/private division. Like that argument, however, it should be treated with caution. Most evidently, the whole purpose of the argument here about place has been to problematize the distinction between the local and the global; if each is part of the construction of the other then it becomes more difficult to maintain such simple contrasts.[21] None the less, in terms of the usual meaning of the word 'local', the association with the feminine probably does have some symbolic force. It is, however, even at this level an association which is not generalizable beyond certain cultures at certain times. Writings on the diaspora and on slavery, for instance, indicate the lack of its purchase on the lives of women in cultures other than the white/ western ones of the last two centuries. And even within those specific cultures the actual relation between women and 'the local sphere' has by no means been absolute nor held good for many women who did not live in heterosexual couples, with children, in suburbs.[22]

And yet, in spite of all these reservations, some culturally specific symbolic association of women/Woman/local does persist. Thus, the term local is used in derogatory reference to feminist struggles and in relation to feminist concerns in intellectual work (it is *only* a local struggle, only a *local* concern). Neither, it is often argued, possesses the claim on universalism made by a concern with class (see 'Flexible sexism'). That bundle of terms local/place/locality is bound in to sets of dualisms, in which a key term is the dualism between masculine and feminine, and in which, on these readings, the local/place/feminine side of the dichotomy is deprioritized and denigrated.[23]

The association between place and a culturally constructed version of 'Woman' operates along other dimensions as well. Thus, two other connotations of place emerge strongly in the papers here. The first is an association between place and 'Home' and the second imbues place with inevitable characteristics of nostalgia ('A place called home?', 'The political place of locality studies'). In the first case place is longed for and romanticized, in the second – in the versions which are challenged here – a longing for place is interpreted as a form of nostalgia and aestheticism *and on those grounds criticized*. In both versions, and whether longed for or feared (or both), place is interpreted as being important in the search for identity in this supposedly troubled era of time–space compression.

Now, it is clear that the conceptualization of place which is advocated in this volume does not allow such readings, such recourse to place as a haven from the global world. But the versions of place which see it as an unproblematical 'home', as a site of indulgence in nostalgia, are relying on a very different concept and it is one which is very tied in with gender. Again, this is culturally specific (as well as in some ways, and maybe increasingly, gender-specific), but it is none the less strong – in the cultural circles under discussion – for all that. Woman stands as metaphor for Nature (in another characteristic dualism), for what has been lost (left behind), and that place called home is frequently personified by, and partakes of the same characteristics as those assigned to, Woman/Mother/lover. The literature on this is now becoming extensive, but in a particularly appropriate passage which brings together that anti-localism which would denigrate it as 'non-theoretical' and the version of place as nostalgic home-base, Genevieve Lloyd writes: 'Woman's task is to preserve the sphere of the intermingling of mind and body, to which the Man of Reason will repair for solace, warmth and relaxation. If he is to exercise the most exalted form of Reason, he must leave soft emotions and sensuousness behind; woman will keep them intact for him.'[24] This is a view of place which searches after a non-existent lost authenticity, which lends itself to reactionary politics, and which is utterly bound up with a particular cultural reading of something called Woman. And it is a view of place which is contested here.

In fact, of course, such a view of place does not encapsulate the lives of real women, even in the cultural milieu to which it refers. Many feminists are heartily suspicious of such notions ('A place called home?'); the fact is that the home may be as much a place of conflict (as well as of work) as of repose; it is on the basis of such arguments and the greater difficulty of escaping the norms of sexuality and gender formation – especially heterosexuality – that writers such as Sue Golding and Elizabeth Wilson have celebrated the possibilities (along with the attendant divisions and dangers) of life in the big city as opposed to that of the small 'community'.[25] Many women have had to *leave* home precisely in order to forge their own version of their identities, from Victorian Lady Travellers to Minnie Bruce Pratt.[26]

Moreover, in certain cultural quarters, the mobility of women does indeed seem to pose a threat to a settled patriarchal order. Whether it be the specific fact of *going out to* work in nineteenth-century England (see 'A woman's place?') or the more general difficulty which Wilson alludes to of keeping track of women in the city. The relation to identity is again apparent. The mobility of Cindy Sherman's identity is troubling to the patriarchal gaze; Owen's comment about 'the masculine desire to fix the woman in a stable and stabilizing identity' ('Flexible sexism') may be tied in with a desire to fix in space and place. One gender-disturbing message might be – in terms of both identity and space – keep moving! The challenge is to achieve this whilst at the same time recognizing one's necessary locatedness and embeddedness/embodiedness, and taking responsibility for it.

The papers in this collection develop these themes through analysis of a fairly coherent set of foci – the construction and understanding of geographical diversity, particularly diversity in terms of economic and social structure, in the UK in the period from the mid-1960s to today.

Many of the arguments develop from quite concrete, and very often immediately political, concerns. And one of the issues which raises its head at points throughout the collection is that of what it means to be an intellectual, and specifically a committed intellectual. Some of these papers were written for a directly political audience, some for an academic one. Many of them are searching after the most appropriate way to use such writing to participate in political debates. The style of writing therefore varies considerably and is itself an object of explicit concern. The aim has been, somehow, to keep a hold on both political engagement and specifically intellectual contribution.

The core of the book is the nature of and the relation between the concepts of space and place, and some aspects of their relation in turn to gender. The papers trace the development of an argument about the nature of each individually and about their interconnections. The three parts are gathered together under the three terms in sequence, and the introductions likewise concentrate in turn on one term of the three. But all the three concerns are present in each part: the gendered nature of regional geography features in part I and the very last paper in part III presents an argument about the concept of space. The separation of the parts is a question of emphasis, not of exclusion.

Whereas this general introduction has highlighted some conceptual issues, the introductions to parts I, II and III draw out more empirical connections between space, place and gender and their mutual structuring. These introductions also set the context for the debates in the papers which follow. In particular, the introductions to parts I and II try to set the papers in the context, both of the debate within geography, and of the social and political changes against which they were set and to which they were in no small measure a response. Inevitably, and perhaps particularly in the case of the former, the story of the debate is a partial one, and specifically one drawn from my own point of view; these are particular slices through what were complex, shifting, and by no means linear, discussions. The reason for including them in this way is that I want to present the context *as I saw it* in order to explain where the papers were coming from, why it was that I was trying to say *that, then*.

The introduction to part III, which focuses more centrally on gender, does not take this form, or does so to a lesser extent. There the attempt is rather to pull out from the papers some of the links between these debates, with a particular concern about space and place and empirical issues of the construction of gender.

This formulation is deliberate. The concern is not with the geography of women but with the construction of gender and gender relations. Moreover, intellectual work as a feminist involves not only working *on* gender but also, and I think in the end perhaps even more importantly, it involves confronting the gendered nature of our modes of theorizing and the concepts with which we work. Thus I want to argue that certain of the (always culturally specific) 'masculine' elements in the currently dominant constitution of the concepts of space and place have become problematical in these times. The issues around conceptual dualisms of the either/or variety, around concepts of place-identity which call upon exclusivity and boundedness, and the sentimentalized association of place with home are examples of such elements. All of these are currently not serving us well; they have run into blockages both intellectual and political. The aim, however, is not to substitute a 'feminine' view for a 'masculine' one (though it may be to substitute a particular variant of a femin*ist* one), but rather to problematize the whole business. The argument is that some currently widespread and significant ways of conceptualizing space and place are constructed in the same manner as, and both reflect and affect, the contemporarily dominant western modes of conceptualizing gender. And so it is that the papers in this collection move from an awareness of spatial differences in the construction of gendered persons, through to a questioning of the relationship between, on the one hand, the current, culturally specific, construction of these genders and, on the other hand, certain aspects of our conceptualization of space and place.

## Notes

1   It was Foucault in *Power/Knowledge* (Brighton, Harvester, 1980), p. 149, who referred to the way space is thought of as 'the dead, the fixed, the undialectical, the immobile', but many others have adopted that position (see 'Politics and space/time'). On the use of the term 'spatial' in debates over structuralism see the writings of Lévi-Strauss, Sartre, Ricœur and Braudel.
2   Mae-Wan Ho, 'Reanimating nature: the integration of science with human experience', *Beshara*, 1988, pp. 16–25; here p. 19.
3   He was speaking in 1908, the citation is from a book published in 1964: H. Minkowski, 'Space and time', in J.J.C. Smart (ed.), *Problems of Space and Time* (New York, Macmillan, 1964, pp. 297–312; the quotation is from p. 297), but I read it in 1993 in Tim Unwin's *The Place of Geography* (London, Longman, 1992), p. 199. In the last chapter of his book Unwin is putting a very similar case about time and space to the one I am arguing here.
4   Unwin, *The Place of Geography*, p. 201.
5   R. Flood and M. Lockwood (eds), *The Nature of Time* (Oxford, Basil Blackwell, 1986), p. 4; cited in Unwin, *The Place of Geography*, p. 201.
6   See R. Stannard, *Grounds for Reasonable Belief* (Edinburgh, Scottish Academic Press, 1989).
7   The argument in 'Politics and space/time' addresses Ernesto Laclau's *New Reflections on the Revolution of our Time* (London, Verso, 1990) on this matter, for he is one of the most recent and most influential proponents of this view. It seems to me that when Laclau refers to the spatial in this way as representation, as ideology, as closure – he may be confusing the realm of the spatial with the notion of a *map*. A map is of course by no means the same

thing as 'space itself' but it does have precisely those connotations of representation and of ideological fixing-in-place (the attempt to impose an order on the world, to get one's bearings) which he is seeking to capture.

8   In 'Politics and space/time', it is argued that we should try to escape from 'a notion of society as a kind of 3-D . . . slice which moves through time'. Once again there is a parallel with arguments in physics, provided by Unwin. Thus he cites Schlick as writing, 'One may not, for example, say . . . that the three-dimensional section which represents the momentary state of the actual present, wanders along the time-axis through the four-dimensional world. For a wandering of this kind would have to take place in time; and time is already represented within the model and cannot be introduced from outside.' See M. Schlick, 'The four-dimensional world', in J.J.C. Smart (ed.), *Problems of Space and Time* (New York, Macmillan, 1964), pp. 292–6; this quotation is from p. 293 and cited in Unwin, *The Place of Geography*, p. 200.

9   I say 'one view' because there has been some very interesting writing recently on the double-sided nature of place, as articulated relations but also as absolute location (e.g. Andrew Merrifield, 'Place and space: a Lefebvrian reconciliation', *Transactions of the Institute of British Geographers, 1993*, vol. 18, no. 4, pp. 516–31). It is an argument which also draws on physics, in particular the quantum mechanics view of dual existence as wave and particle. It is also very interestingly related to Marx's work on fetishism. In that regard, and in the context of the kinds of views of place which it is my aim to challenge, or at least to disturb, I would see it as most important at the moment to press the concept of place as interrelations. Marx did speak of the commodity as being both thing and relations, but it was the former view which he labelled as fetishism and which, by bringing to the fore its relational nature, he was seeking to unsettle.

10   These are not the only sources of uniqueness; see 'A global sense of place'.

11   The original statement of this approach to places and their uniqueness, as the complex result of the combination of their succession of roles within a series of wider, national and international, spatial divisions of labour, can be found in my 'Industrial restructuring as class restructuring: production decentralisation as local uniqueness', *Regional Studies*, 1983, 17(2), pp. 73–89, an expanded version of which forms ch. 5 of *Spatial Divisions of Labour* (Basingstoke, Macmillan, 1984; 2nd edn forthcoming in 1994).

12   Anthony Giddens, *The Consequences of Modernity* (Cambridge, Polity, 1990), p. 18. Although I agree with the general point Giddens is making, his distinction between 'presence' and 'absence' seems too absolute and susceptible to the general critique of a metaphysics of presence (see 'A place called home?', and Sayla Benhabib, 'Epistemologies of postmodernism: a rejoinder to Jean-François Lyotard', *New German Critique*, no. 33, 1984, pp. 103–26; and Iris Marion Young, 'The idea of community and the politics of difference', *Social Theory and Practice*, vol. 12, no. 1, spring 1986, pp. 1–26). Such a metaphysics is itself linked in to particular logics of identity, and the instituting of borders, which underlie the type of place-identity being criticized here (see also below).

13  Edward Said, 'Holding nations and traditions at bay', the second Reith Lecture in his series 'Representations of the Intellectual', 1993. An edited text of this lecture was printed in the *Independent*, 1 July 1993, p. 14.

14  This point has also been raised by Liz Bondi in her 'Feminism, postmodernism and geography: a space for women?', *Antipode*, vol. 22, 1990, pp. 156–67. Without here entering into the complexities of the argument, it would seem that this could be one of the ways in which geography's social scientific masculinism is complicated by a valorization of – in very general terms – aesthetics (a valorization which itself takes the form of a masculinism). In this way, as Gillian Rose argues in *Feminism and Geography* (Cambridge, Polity, 1993), 'Geographical discourse is ... extremely mobile: it shifts focus, and remains explicitly concerned with both sides of its constitutive opposition. It is a field fascinated by the other as well as hostile to it' (p. 77).

15  See K. Robins, 'Prisoners of the city: whatever could a postmodern city be?', *New Formations*, 15, 1991, pp. 1–22; and P. Emberley, 'Places and stories: the challenge of technology', *Social Research*, 56(3), 1989, pp. 741–85.

16  Chantal Mouffe, 'Radical democracy: modern or postmodern?', in Andrew Ross (ed.), *Universal Abandon? The Politics of Postmodernism* (Minneapolis, University of Minnesota Press, 1988), pp. 31–45. The quotation is from p. 44. See also Anna Yeatman, 'A feminist theory of social differentiation', in Linda J. Nicholson (ed.), *Feminism/Postmodernism* (London, Routledge, 1990), pp. 281–99. Teresa de Lauretis, 'Feminist studies/critical studies: issues, terms and contexts', in T. de Lauretis (ed.), *Feminist Studies/Critical Studies* (Basingstoke, Macmillan, 1986), pp. 1–19. It is worth noting that this view of identity, when applied to place, problematizes still further any assumptions of coincidence between community and locality.

17  See also Doreen Massey, 'Double articulation: a place in the world', in Angelika Bammer (ed.), *Displacements* (Indiana University Press, forthcoming).

18  Herbert I. Schiller, 'Fastfood, fast cars, fast political rhetoric', *Intermedia*, vol. 20, nos. 4–5, August–September 1992, pp. 21–2. The quotation is from p. 21.

19  Thus, ' "the local" is not to be considered as an indigenous source of cultural identity, which remains "authentic" only in so far as it is unsullied by contact with the global. Rather the "local" is itself often produced by means of the "indigenization" of global resources and inputs' (David Morley, 'Where the global meets the local: notes from the sitting room', *Screen*, vol. 32, no. 1, spring 1991, pp. 1–15; here pp. 9–10).

20  See, for instance, Genevieve Lloyd, *The Man of Reason: 'Male' and 'Female' in Western Philosophy* (London, Methuen, 1984).

21  This also relates to the frequent conflation of the 'local' with 'everyday life' about which I also have serious reservations, see Doreen Massey, 'Localities in regional geography', in La Societat Catalana de Geografia (ed.), *Regio i geografia regional* (in Catalan – mimeo in English available from author). Michael Peter Smith also challenges the local–global dualism, and its practical expression in what he sees as the simplistic exhortation to 'think globally and act locally'. Drawing on studies of the politics of transnational migrants he

outlines cases of 'thinking locally while acting globally' and of 'living and acting multilocally' ('Can you imagine? transnational migration and the globalisation of grassroots politics', paper presented to the Conference, 'World Cities in a World System', Sterling, Virginia, April 1993, mimeo).

22  See Toni Morrison's *Beloved* (London, Pan, 1987), or bell hooks on discussions of 'home', and the concern with bridges and frontiers in C. Moraga and G. Anzaldúa (eds), *This Bridge Called My Back: Writings by Radical Women of Color* (Watertown, Persephone, 1981). The problematical nature of the public/private distinction in the geographies of certain lesbian cultures is well brought out by Gill Valentine in her article 'Negotiating and managing multiple sexual identities: lesbian time–space strategies', *Transactions of the IBG*, vol. 18, no. 2, 1993, pp. 237–48.

23  See, for instance, Elspeth Probyn, 'Travels in the postmodern: making sense of the local', in Nicholson (ed.), *Feminism/Postmodernism*.

24  Lloyd, *The Man of Reason*, p. 50. Gillian Rose's, *Feminism and Geography* takes up this issue in detail.

25  Sue Golding, 'Reclaiming the "impossible" urban as site specific for a radical democracy', paper presented to the Institute of British Geographers Annual Conference, Swansea, January 1992. Elizabeth Wilson, *The Sphinx in the City: Urban Life, the Control of Disorder, and Women* (London, Virago, 1991). Gill Valentine, 'Out and about: a geography of a lesbian landscape', *International Journal of Urban and Regional Research* (forthcoming 1994), likewise documents the movement of lesbians from rural to urban areas.

26  On this, see also Patty Chalita, 'Voices from across the hall: mapping spatial metaphor and the politics of difference', paper presented to the American Association of Geographers, 1992.

# PART I

*Space and Social Relations*

# Introduction

The main burden of the papers in this part is a theoretical one. It concerns the conceptualization of the spatial, and it moves from a critique of a certain kind of spatial fetishism to an attempt to think the spatial in terms of social relations. At this level it is an extremely abstract argument; and it concerns a debate which still continues.

The origins of this debate, however, at least within the discipline of geography in the United Kingdom were to a large extent grounded in arguments about very concrete issues. This is important to recognize for two reasons. First, the particular nature of the issues within which the broader conceptual arguments took shape moulded the development of those arguments. The issues concerned primarily questions of the economy and of class structure, rather than, for instance, politics or cultural identity. But second, it is important to recognize this grounding in concrete questions because it brings home quite clearly that these philosophical debates matter. The questions which were at issue when these papers were written concerned the industrial geography and the changing social structure of the country. And these questions were fundamentally political. In the late 1970s 'the inner-city problem' had risen to prominence on the political agenda. The combination of dramatic economic decline, crushing poverty and incipient social unrest kept them in the public eye. As had been the case with 'the regions' before them the easy response of the politicians was to look within the areas themselves for the cause of their malaise. A geographical version of the well-established strategy of blaming the victim for their own misfortune was widely adopted. It therefore became urgent to argue that events in the cities could not be so explained, that the cities really were in some sense victims, but victims of wider circumstances; that the fortunes of individual places cannot be explained by looking only within them; that the loss of jobs in urban areas was due to the particular form being taken by a wider and even more fundamental problem: the lack of international competitiveness of much of British manufacturing industry. It was an industry which had largely slept through the expansive 1950s, padded by Commonwealth Preference, the Korean War, and cost-plus contracts with the state. In such a context, while ethnic minorities, single-parent families, 'the unemployable', and local authority planners were all in various ways being blamed for the misery in the cities, it was important – or so it seemed to me – to demonstrate (and to demonstrate through detailed empirical work) that the situation was exactly the contrary. It was not the cities (nor, indeed, the regions) which had failed industry, but British industry which had failed the cities.

There were similar, immediately political, issues at the regional level about, for instance, the degree of success of regional policy. The questions here revolved around the degree to which changes in the geography of industry could be attributed to regional policy, and the degree to which an equalization of unemployment rates between regions could anyway be seen as an unmitigated success. Again the arguments involved setting individual spaces (in this case the regions) within the larger spaces of capitalism – in what sense were these *regional* problems? But they also involved introducing the notion of power relations between regions (through spatial structures, or spatial divisions of labour).[1] Different levels of unemployment, it had to be argued, are not the only component of, nor even necessarily the best way of thinking about, uneven development.

There were debates, too, which emerged directly from the labour movement. There was the divisiveness introduced by industrial transfer – in particular at this period, workers in the cities blaming regional policy for what looked like the loss of their jobs to the regions. It was issues such as these which provoked the first forays into what was to prove to be the ever-expanding debate over the nature of social space.

The papers in this part cover, in their content, the period from Wilsonism to Thatcherism, from a modernizing social democracy supposedly run by experts to a neo-liberal free market (though heavily subsidized in its most symbolically important bits) supposedly run by entrepreneurs. The contrast between the two is sharp; from the Wilsonian emphasis on government intervention and on the need for scale, to the Thatcherite era of casualization and the rhetoric of small firms. Yet throughout this whole very varied period geographical inequality (more broadly, the spatial organization of society) was of crucial importance, either as an explicit political issue or as a less-recognized but fundamentally significant component of the changes under way in economy and society. Indeed, it could be argued that regional inequality was one of the rocks on which Thatcherism foundered (having been one of the bases on which initially it was built). Looking back now, from the grotesque inequalities of the 1990s, it is important to be reminded of the problems entailed in Wilsonian social democracy. The emphasis on modernization (of a particular sort), on size, and above all on technocratic expertise, were what lay at the basis of the newly emerging form of geographical inequality of the late 1960s. It was this new form of uneven development (crudely caricatured as the spatial separation of conception from execution) which gave birth to the concepts of spatial structure and spatial division of labour. What was clear, as one watched that combination of the financial concentration of capital with its geographical (and differential) dispersal which so characterized the UK in the sixties and seventies, was that what we were watching and experiencing was the reorganization of the relations of production over space.

But if there are contrasts between the periods there are also things which unite them; most particularly the seemingly endless search for a way out of British economic decline and the continuing debate about the nature of the changes going on in social structure. This latter was a particularly crucial issue within the left, for the conclusion one drew related closely to the political line one took on strategy. To what extent was 'the old working class' a thing of the past, and along with it the trade union movement? To what extent had the old-time labour movement (sometimes known as the men's movement) been such a great success even in its heyday? Here too spatial thinking could be integral to political debate, for the highly varied geography of the changing social structure, from the fragmenting working-class communities to the new and increasingly important bases of middle-class power, forbade any simple national-level conclusions to be drawn. Here again was a practical political issue where a geographer's voice could contribute.

What emerged from these attempts to investigate such issues from a geographical point of view was a theoretical/conceptual message about the nature of the spatial, in particular the nature of economic space and the space of class structure. It involved a process in which the spatial had first to be demoted in importance before its significance could be reunderstood in completely different terms. The first task was to blow apart the notion of a spatial world which was internally self-explanatory – where spatial change was explained by spatial factors (the movement of industry explained by regional policy), where the fortunes of areas were explained by their characteristics (blaming the cities). Thus it is that the main message of 'Industrial restructuring versus the cities' (written with Richard Meegan), the earliest paper in this collection, is devoted to *countering* a spatial explanation. So, too, is the argument about regional policy in 'In what sense a regional problem?' Spatial form, it is being argued in both these cases, is to be explained not by 'spatial' factors but by, for instance, what is going on in the economy. The spatial is, in that very material sense, socially constructed; and an understanding of the spatial must entail an analysis of the economy and society more generally. In that sense there is no hermetically sealed discipline of geography.

Yet the very form of the spatial reorganization taking place over these decades raised further issues. Within the economy what was under way was a reorganization of the spatial shape of production in its widest sense. The proliferation of branch plants of various types, the separation-off of headquarters, the burgeoning of separate locations for research and development and a host of production-related professional services, all of these pointed to a notion of the spatial organization of economic functions and thus of the spatial stretching-out of the social relations which connected them. Economic space could be conceived of as constituted by the geographical organization of the relations of production.[2] Similarly with class structure. If the emerging geography of social structure ('The shape of things to come') could be analysed, and if classes were conceived as mutually constituted through their interrelationships ('Uneven development') then class relations too could be understood as having a spatial form. The geography of social structure is a geography of class *relations*, not just a map of social classes; just as the geography of the economy should be a map of *economic relations stretched over space*, and not just, for instance, a map of different types of jobs. Most generally, 'the spatial' is constituted by the interlocking of 'stretched-out' social relations.[3]

Moreover, since it is those relations which constitute the social phenomena themselves (jobs, economic functions, social classes), the nature and the development of the phenomena and their spatial form are necessarily intimately related. And since social relations are bearers of power what is at issue is a geography of power relations in which spatial form is an important element in the constitution of power itself.

Seeing things this way gives a very different meaning to the term uneven development from that which is implied by looking only at, for instance, the differential distribution of employment/unemployment.[4] It points to its intractability, locates its sources in class power rather than in the immediacy of, say, a lack of jobs; and it points to the fact that the nature, and not merely the degree, of uneven development can change over time.

The concepts of spatial structure and of spatial division of labour were a means of getting to grips, in the economic sphere, with this notion of social relations stretched over space. Moreover, they also raised another issue for they were concerned with the way in which capital made active use of the forms of geographical variation and inequality which were presented to it. This was a very different formulation from that of industry responding to location factors. And its implication was that spatial form was implicated in the development of the economic (and by extension in the social more generally). This theme, which was to flower into the claim that 'geography matters', and which was explored in an earlier critique of industrial location theory,[5] is gradually developed in a number of directions in the papers here. At first it is the active use by individual companies of spatial variation and spatial movement that is stressed (see especially 'Industrial restructuring' and 'In what sense a regional problem?'). In 'The shape of things to come' and 'Uneven development' the more general case is made for the importance of geographical strategies in the reorganization of British capital and in, for instance, its often vain attempts to preserve UK Fordism through spatial decentralization. 'The shape of things to come' pulls out the importance of geographical change in the reconstitution of, and the problems facing, the trade union movement, and argues strongly for the significance of geographical variation within the processes of class restructuring and the importance of spatial specificity in the construction of political interpretations and responses and in the maintenance, and fragmentation, of political traditions. 'Uneven development' completes the circle by arguing that spatial form and geographical location are themselves significant in forming the character of particular social strata. Thus the very fact of social relations being 'stretched out over space' (or not), and taking particular spatial forms, influences the nature of the social relations themselves, the divisions of labour and the functions within them ('Uneven development'). Social change and spatial change are integral to each other.

## Notes

1   There was some evolution in the definition of these terms. In my book *Spatial Divisions of Labour: Social Structures and the Geography of Production* (Basingstoke, Macmillan, 1984), where the main statement takes place, and in most other papers, a spatial structure refers to a particular geographical organization of the relations of production, most often within individual firms and possibly typifying individual sectors or parts of sectors. A spatial division of labour is a broader concept referring to the form of uneven development which results from the combining of a range of concurrent spatial structures. In

'In what sense a regional problem?', where the terms were first used, spatial division of labour had rather more of the former sense.

2   For the full argument on this see Massey, *Spatial Divisions of Labour*.

3   It is interesting to note that these ideas have a lot in common with Giddens's ideas of time–space distanciation. (See Anthony Giddens, *The Constitution of Society* [Cambridge, Polity, 1984].)

4   It also differentiates it very clearly from that view of uneven development as a kind of alternately tipping balance, sometimes expressed in the terminology of a 'see-saw'.

5   See Doreen Massey, 'Towards a critique of industrial location theory' in R. Peet (ed.) *Radical Geography* (Chicago, Maaroufa, 1977 and London, Methuen, 1978), originally published in *Antipode*, vol. 5, no. 3, 1973, pp. 33–9. This analysed in detail the disruptive impact of introducing the spatial dimension into the formal models and neo-classical frameworks of the then dominant line of industrial location theory.

# 1

# Industrial Restructuring versus the Cities

## Introduction and methodology

### The industrial location project

The decline of manufacturing in the cities has been the subject of much recent research. One unfortunate side effect of this concern, however, has been the tendency for the problem to be defined in spatial terms, and, consequently, for the causes of the problem to be sought within the same spatial area. This tendency to study the workings of the city in economic and spatial isolation from the rest of the national economy has often seen emphasis being placed, for example, on assessment of the influence of such factors as the built-environment of the inner-city areas (congestion, dereliction, site availability, etc.) or the personal characteristics of their residents (relating unemployment, say, to age, race or skill). The outcome of such research is often to blur and confuse the issue of causality.

The present decline in manufacturing in the cities is occurring at a time when fundamental structural changes are taking place at the level of the economy as a whole (Chisholm, 1976; Treasury, 1976). It is part of the wider phenomenon of contraction and change in the manufacturing base of the UK economy. The argument of this paper is that it is only in this wider context that the specific problems of manufacturing in city areas can be properly understood. The aim is therefore to demonstrate the link between locational change and developments at the level of the national and international economy.

The paper draws on research the broad purpose of which was to examine the locational implications of financial restructuring in British manufacturing since the mid-1960s (Massey and Meegan, 1979). This interest was focused down in the research project into a study of the spatial repercussions of the intervention of the Industrial Reorganisation Corporation into the electrical, electronics and aerospace equipment sectors. The Industrial Reorganisation Corporation (IRC) was established by the Labour government in 1966 '. . . for the purpose of promoting industrial efficiency and profitability and assisting the economy of the United Kingdom or any part of the United Kingdom' (HMSO, 1966). Its intervention, before it was abolished in 1971, took the form of encouraging mergers, intra-sectoral reorganization, and investment.[1] It should be stressed, however, that the fundamental concern of the research was with the processes of restructuring themselves rather than with their specific attribution to intervention by the IRC. The purpose of this paper is to draw out the implications of the results of this research for the major cities which were significantly represented in the survey.

The form of explanation adopted reflected the theoretical concerns and comprised four discrete stages. The first step involved an examination of the major characteristics of the overall economic situation within which restructuring was operating. These characteristics were analysed as being firstly the declining profitability and secondly the worsening international competitive position of British manufacturing industry. The second stage of the research was concerned with the precise ways in which these general economic forces operated at the level of specific cases, and, therefore, the ways in which they presented pressures towards financial restructuring. As a result of this analysis it was possible to develop a broad classification of the cases of financial restructuring which was directly related to macro-economic conditions. The next step was to assess the implications for production reorganization of each such category of restructuring. The question to be answered at this stage was therefore: what were the changes in the organization of production and use of labour allowed by the financial restructuring? The identification of the locational implications of these changes formed the fourth and final step in the research. With the completion of this stage it was thus possible to relate the spatial incidence of employment changes identified in the empirical research back through the production reorganization to the forms of restructuring themselves and their specific relation to changes in the national economy.

The survey examined the interests of twenty-five firms in the following Minimum List Headings of the 1968 Standard Industrial Classification:

*Order VIII: Instrument engineering*
MLH 354: Scientific and industrial instruments and systems

*Order IX: Electrical engineering*
MLH 361: Electrical machinery
MLH 362: Insulated wires and cables
MLH 363: Telegraph and telephone apparatus and equipment
MLH 364: Radio and electronic components
MLH 365: Broadcast receiving and sound reproducing equipment
MLH 366: Electronic computers
MLH 367: Radio, radar and electronic capital goods
MLH 368: Electrical appliances primarily for domestic use
MLH 369: Other electrical goods

*Order XI: Vehicles*
MLH 383: Aerospace equipment manufacturing and repairing

The sector produces both consumer goods and capital goods, includes major suppliers to the public sector and encompasses some of the country's major exporters. The sector is important not just for the stage that it has reached in its own technological development (with, for example, the transition from electrical to electronic components) but also for its potential contribution to technological changes in other manufacturing sectors. Although still predominantly based in the south-east, some of its industries, especially in electronics, are exhibiting an increased degree of mobility and are accordingly important in terms of regional policy. In 1966, there were 1,911,000 people employed in the sector, representing about 14 per cent of the total workforce in all manufacturing industries (Department of Employment, 1975). According to the Census of Production, the sector accounted in 1968 for 10 per cent of the net output of all manufacturing industries. At the time of IRC intervention, the survey firms employed 226,000 people in the sector, approximately 19 per cent of total employment in these industries.[2]

The restructuring processes which were analysed resulted in an overall net employment loss, in the survey firms, of 36,016 jobs: a decline of 16 per cent.[3] In terms of its geographical distribution, this overall change was dominated by three regions (the south-east, the north-west and the west midlands) which experienced major declines in employment in both absolute and percentage terms (Massey and Meegan, 1979). Together they accounted for 94 per cent of the net overall loss (34,016 out of 36,016). Further disaggregation of the data, however, showed that 89 per cent of the losses suffered by these regions could be explained by the significant declines which occurred in the four major cities located within them, namely Greater London, Liverpool, Manchester and Birmingham.[4] These four cities together lost 30,315 jobs in the sector, or 84 per cent of the overall net decline in the survey firms' employment. The seriousness of this decline for the cities was emphasized by the fact that at the beginning of the period they had only accounted for some 32 per cent of survey employment in the sector.

The problem addressed by this paper is therefore that of the explanation of this net loss of 30,315 jobs by direct reference to the economy-level pressures that were operating on the sector at the time. The approach will therefore be to suggest ways in which these various pressures moulded the form taken by inter- and intra-sectoral restructuring and helped to shape its differential spatial impact – and hence its specific consequences for the cities. Before this, however, it is necessary to describe briefly the classification of employment change that will be used in the analysis.

## A typology of employment changes

The employment changes can be divided into four categories: absolute loss, locational loss, absolute gain and locational gain. An *absolute* change is one which occurs at the level of the economy as a whole, where new jobs were created, or where they disappeared altogether. A *locational* change is one resulting from the locational transfer of production, the loss or gain thus being specific to a particular geographical area within the nation. The point of this categorization is to enable a distinction between those employment changes due to intra-national mobility of jobs and those due to differential growth and decline. This distinction is of obvious importance in any consideration of the potential effects of spatial policies.

Locational change needs to be more precisely defined, however. At any given level of spatial disaggregation, the total number of jobs lost through locational shift will equal the number gained. Such figures refer to jobs which were neither gained nor lost to the economy as a whole, but which changed location. Locational shifts, however, are rarely symmetrical. The figures given here under 'locational shift' represent the employment which actually arrived at the recipient location. This number is far smaller than the loss recorded at the original factories. Job movement, in other words, has frequently been either part of a process of overall cutbacks or has been the occasion for cutbacks. In the first case, overall cuts in capacity often entail concentrating the work of smaller factories on a reduced number of larger ones. Such moves are frequently announced as transfers, and indeed some production may well be moved. They do not, however, represent a transfer of all jobs at the previous location. In the second case, locational shift may be the occasion for major changes in production technology, again leading to a reduced workforce in the recipient region. The locational shift may be brought about because the nature of the technological change demands either new fixed capital or a new work-force. In the first case it may be necessary, in the second prudent, to move, thus reducing conflict with the trade unions. The figures for the number of jobs lost in the origin region, but never recreated in the recipient region, are included under the category of 'absolute loss'. Such jobs were lost to the economy as a whole. They are separately accounted for in the tables, however, by a disaggregation of absolute loss into *in situ* and *in transit* losses. *In situ* losses are straightforward losses in which no locational transfer of employment or production was involved. *In transit* losses are just as absolute, but they took place in the context of a locational change. The classification of *in transit* losses as part of absolute losses is important since, while a particular area may appear to be losing considerable numbers of jobs through locational shifts, only a small proportion of this employment loss may subsequently benefit another locality.

## The forms of restructuring and their employment implications for the cities

*Introduction*

Three different groups of stimuli for the financial restructuring were identified:[5]

Group 1: restructuring in the face of over-capacity and high costs;
Group 2: restructuring to achieve scale advantages; and,
Group 3: restructuring for reasons of market standing.

The inclusion of major multi-divisional firms made the analysis more complex, however, in that it necessitated a differentiation between those divisions which acted as stimuli to the subsequent reorganization and those which did not. The fact that certain divisions were not important stimuli for restructuring, however, does not mean that they can be assumed to be unaffected by it. The merger of multi-divisional firms including both stimulant and non-stimulant sectors alters the situation of the latter, which can be affected both by the indirect impact of the reorganization of the stimulant sectors (with, say, a shifting of emphasis within the newly merged firm) and by their own independent organizational integration. Moreover, such sectors are also subject to economy-level pressures (albeit not requiring financial restructuring). Non-stimulant sectors can therefore be regarded as responding to the *fact* of the merger rather than, as in the case of the stimulant sectors, to the reasons for it. To accommodate them in the analysis a separate 'secondary' classification was therefore required. Such cases are dealt with, in this paper, under the broad heading of 'non-stimulant sectors'.

The detailed impacts of the three forms of restructuring on stimulant sectors are best examined by taking each group in turn.

## Group 1: Restructuring in the face of over-capacity and high costs

This group included product groups within the following industries: heavy electrical machinery, particularly turbine-generators, switchgear and transformers (part MLH 361); supertension cables (part MLH 362); aerospace equipment (part MLH 383).

The circumstances of the individual product groups were different; but they all shared the same problems of excess capacity and the need to cut costs, and were all suffering from a pronounced deterioration in their competitive position. The power-engineering industry, in its domestic market, had to contend with a major downward revision of demand from its main customer (the Central Electricity Generating Board).[6] The potential for raising exports to counteract this shift was heavily constrained by increasing competition in overseas markets, particularly as a result of the end of Commonwealth Preference. The industry had therefore lost hitherto secure markets at home and abroad and faced increasingly severe competition in those that remained. For supertension cables, again the basic problem was a decline in domestic demand for which exports were unable to compensate. Exports to non-Commonwealth Third World countries did increase but margins were low and competition, especially from Japan, was particularly severe. The problem of over-capacity was made even more acute by the industry's high degree of capital intensity. The aerospace equipment industry was also suffering from increasingly severe competition from abroad (especially from the USA) as a result of the ending of the Korean War, defence cancellations at home (TSR2, 1154 and 681), and the eventual collapse of the sellers' market which had followed the Second World War. The failure of Rolls Royce served to intensify the industry's problems.

There were thus two particularly dominant pressures for financial restructuring at work in Group 1: (1) there was a problem of over-capacity; and (2) there was a need to cut production costs in the context of increasing international competition and a general slackening of the rate of growth of markets. Financial restructuring was needed in this situation to enable co-ordinated capacity cutting and to facilitate the reallocation of capital into other more profitable areas of production. The financial restructuring itself allowed a number of responses in terms of actual production reorganization. The reaction to the problem of excess capacity involved straight cutbacks in production, characterized by factory closures and major redundancies. The need to cut production costs and increase relative profitability resulted in an attempt by the firms concerned to increase individual labour productivity and to reduce aggregate labour costs. This was attempted in a number of ways:

1 the selection for closure of the most labour-intensive plants;
2 intensification – the reduction of the labour-force in any given production process (without any change in output or production techniques);
3 partial standardization (which in turn allowed some automated methods in production, and cuts in labour costs with the ensuing requirement overall for less-skilled labour);
4 the introduction of numerically controlled machine tools in production processes where full automation was not possible (usually small-batch processes). This allowed an overall reduction in the labour required and a dichotomization of skills of the remaining labour-force;
5 finally, in some cases a shift to mass-production techniques was possible, enabling large reductions in the workforce and a change in the type of labour from craft to semi-skilled.

These measures all featured in the reorganization of production in the industries in Group 1. How did they make themselves felt in the cities? Table 1.1 shows the overall employment changes in Group 1 in the four conurbations. It is clear from the table that the restructuring in Group 1 had a particularly severe impact on the four cities. Together they lost some 21,084 jobs as a result of the processes at work in this group. This amounted to 70 per cent of the cities' total net loss of survey employment during the period under study.

The 'typology' of this overall employment change is particularly revealing. Nearly three-quarters of the jobs lost to the cities in this group were not linked in any way to the transfer elsewhere of either capital equipment or jobs (15,528 *in situ* absolute loss). This is not surprising however, for, as argued above, the pressures for capacity-cutting and cost reduction, and the nature of technological change in this group of industries, meant that employment change was dominated by absolute cutbacks in employment – losses both to individual locations and to the economy as a whole.

**Table 1.1** *Employment change in Group 1: the four cities*

| Category of employment change | No. |
| --- | --- |
| Absolute loss | |
| in situ | (15,528) |
| in transit* | (4,980) |
| Locational loss** | (606) |
| Total loss | (21,114) |
| Employment gain | |
| Absolute gain | 0 |
| Locational gain** | 30 |
| Total gain | 30 |
| Net gain/(loss) | (21,084) |

*Figure includes 1,750 jobs which were linked to transfers of production within or between cities.
**Figure excludes 330 jobs which were transferred within or between cities.

Furthermore, of those jobs actually linked to some locational transfer, the vast majority (89 per cent) disappeared *in transit*.[7] Even in such cases of transfer, then, the loss to the cities was not matched by corresponding gains elsewhere, potential job mobility being constrained by the overriding need for absolute cutbacks in both capacity and employment. Thirdly, the cities themselves did not experience any significant gains from the locational shifts of jobs that were occurring in the country as a whole. In return for their locational loss of some 606 jobs, the cities received 30. Finally, there were no new jobs created in the cities as a result of the restructuring in Group 1 (absolute gains were zero). The consequences for the cities of restructuring in the Group 1 industries were therefore especially traumatic. There are three major threads in the explanation for this:

1 *The Group 1 industries were heavily represented in the cities*   At the time of IRC intervention, the survey plants located in the cities accounted for approximately 44 per cent of employment in the dominant Group 1 industries (MLHs 361, 369 and 383)[8] yet their share of

total employment in the survey only amounted to 32 per cent. Therefore, even had the impact of the production reorganization in Group
1 been in proportion to employment, the cities could be expected to
have been significantly affected.

2   *The plants in Group 1 industries located in the cities were particularly
    susceptible to the processes of restructuring*   In fact, however, the cities
    experienced higher than proportionate employment losses as a result
    of the restructuring in Group 1 – approximately 88 per cent of the
    total net national employment loss in Group 1 occurred there (21,084
    out of a total net national decline in Group 1 of 24,013). This was
    largely explained by the fact that the choice of plants for closure (the
    first of the five measures listed above) was based primarily on con-
    siderations of labour productivity. The overriding pressure in the
    production reorganization in Group 1 was the need to cut labour costs.
    The plants chosen for closure therefore had to be those which were
    relatively labour-intensive and these factories were predominantly
    located in the older industrial areas of the cities.

3   *The cities did not gain from the locational shifts of production that
    occurred in the restructuring in Group 1*   The cities were the origin
    of the bulk of the jobs which actually shifted location in the restructur-
    ing in Group 1. Nationally, there was a locational shift of some 966
    jobs in Group 1 and, of these, 936 had their origins in the conurba-
    tions. 330 of these 936 jobs were transferred either within or between
    individual cities whilst the remaining 606 jobs shifted to locations
    outside them. At first sight, this locational shift appears relatively small
    but it must be remembered that it in fact represents only one (and the
    smaller) component of the process of job movement. In forms of
    restructuring in which retrenchment is the dominant feature, job
    relocation is inevitably linked to high *in transit* absolute loss. In Group
    1 locational loss and *in transit* absolute loss accounted for approxi-
    mately 26 per cent of total employment decline in the cities (5,586 out
    of 21,114).

Even in those cases where the cities retained some employment in the
geographical reorganization of production, employment losses far out-
weighed any gain. Part of the restructuring in Group 1, for example,
involved the redistribution of 150 jobs previously carried on in London,
between factories in Birmingham, Manchester and Newcastle. The gain to
these locations, however, has to be balanced against the disappearance of
1,850 jobs at the original sites in London. The same phenomenon also
occurred at an intra-city level. Economies of scale were frequently
achieved by the closure of small and outlying factories with the 'drawing-

in' on major locations thus allowing savings primarily on service-labour costs.

The cities were also affected by the concentration of production at a number of major plants in such medium-sized towns as Bradford, Lincoln, Stafford and Rugby. The first three locations, for example, gained 376 jobs as a result of the restructuring of the Group 1 industries in the four cities, whilst the last site was the only major factory to experience an absolute gain of employment in Group 1. The process of restructuring in Group 1 thus involved the (albeit limited) strengthening of the position of certain favoured locations, and few of these were in the cities.

Locational transfer was also linked to the changes in production techniques. One important case of production transfer in this group followed the introduction of product standardization which allowed the use of mass production methods (involving an *in transit* absolute loss of 300 jobs and a locational transfer of 100 jobs). This change not only meant that new plant and equipment were needed but also, and perhaps more importantly, that the production process in question was effectively freed from its existing ties to the cities as a result of the changed skill requirements of the labour-force. The location which benefited from this particular transfer was in a Development Area – a site which now combined the attraction of government assistance with a newly suitable and readily available labour-force (predominantly unskilled workers). Such developments clearly have serious portents for the inner cities.

## Group 2: Restructuring to achieve scale advantages

The cases in Group 2 were primarily in the following sectors: industrial systems, process control, etc. (MLH 354); electronic computers (MLH 366); radio, radar and electronic capital goods (MLH 367).

Pressures for restructuring in this group operated at two distinct levels: at the level of the economy as a whole, and at the level of the individual firms involved. In the first case, government intervention was designed to facilitate the increased *application* of the products of these capital goods industries to improve the productivity of *other* manufacturing sectors. There was, therefore, general pressure at the level of the economy for both an increase in, and a cheapening of, the output of the Group 2 industries. At the same time there was growing pressure at the level of the individual electronics firms for increased scale of resources to keep up with the rapid rate of technological innovation which was, for them, the dominant aspect of international competition. An integral feature of the financial restructuring in Group 2 was thus the need to increase the absolute amount of financial resources at the disposal of individual firms. This was necessary to enable a reduction in the proportion of funds devoted to research and development, the financing of high absolute costs of development of new products and the self-financing of large investment programmes (to overcome the problem of raising capital for long-term, high-risk projects).

The pressures for restructuring in Group 2 were therefore: (1) to increase the output of these industries; (2) to cheapen the production of that output; and (3) to keep up with the rapid rate of technological innovation. The subsequent reorganization of production responded to these pressures in a number of ways:

1 The need to cheapen output led to increased efforts to reduce the labour content of the products with the introduction, where possible, of numerically controlled machine tools and mass-production techniques. This is a long-term process and not one produced just as a result of restructuring.[9] Moreover, the potential for the introduction of automated techniques varies between and within industries and product groups. Mass production, for example, is not feasible in the manufacture of industrial and scientific instruments, which is still heavily dependent on small-batch production processes. In those cases where automated techniques were introduced, however, there was a significant reduction in the overall size of the labour-force.

2 This enabled a reduction in the level of skill required of the production workforce, and produced a growing dichotomization of skills in the labour-force between production (predominantly semi-skilled assembly work) on the one hand and R & D control functions on the other.

3 The need for increased output meant that major new capital investment was required.

4 The consolidation of research and development facilities into a smaller number of larger groupings was generally necessary if the rate of technological innovation was to be maintained.

How did the reorganization in Group 2 affect the cities? Table 1.2 shows the overall employment changes that occurred in this group. Together the cities lost some 1,466 jobs as a result of the restructuring in this group – 5 per cent of the cities' total net loss of employment during the period. This small proportion nevertheless represented 42 per cent of the total national employment decline in Group 2. The significance of this loss is emphasized even more by the fact that, at the time of IRC intervention,

**Table 1.2** *Employment change in Group 2: the four cities*

| Category of employment change | No. |
| --- | --- |
| Absolute loss | |
|    *in situ* | (1,350) |
|    *in transit*\* | (136) |
| Locational loss\*\* | 0 |
| Total loss | (1,486) |
| Employment gain | |
|    Absolute gain | 0 |
|    Locational gain | 20 |
| Total gain | 20 |
| Net gain/(loss) | (1,466) |

\*Figure includes 130 jobs which were linked to a transfer of production between two cities.
\*\*Figure does not include a transfer of production between cities of 13 jobs.

the cities only accounted for 18 per cent of total national employment in MLHs 354, 364, 366 and 367 in the survey.

The explanation for this performance, as in Group 1, is to be found in the economic pressures which created the need for restructuring. The overall process of output cheapening including the impact of long-term technological change was particularly important for the cities. The 1,486 absolute loss of jobs in Group 2 occurred in MLH 366 and the factories affected were relatively labour-intensive, mainly producing electro-mechanical equipment. The increasing pressure for savings in labour costs within the industry and the concomitant move towards more automated production techniques rendered such plants obsolete. This orientation meant that the plants were particularly susceptible to the increasing pressure for labour cuts in the production workforce.

This is only part of the explanation for the effects of Group 2 restructuring on the cities, however. Nationally, Group 2 was responsible for 90 per cent of the absolute gains in the survey (1,750 out of 1,970). The cities did not benefit from any of these developments. This is partly explained, of course, by the fact that the initial distribution of employment in the Group

2 industries was biased against the cities. As already stated, the cities only accounted for about 18 per cent of this employment. Any 'incremental growth' (i.e., additions to existing facilities on site) in these industries was unlikely therefore significantly to benefit the cities. Yet even where major new developments occurred they were not sited in the conurbations. In the cases examined in the survey, these new investments took the form of 'greenfield developments' in locations outside the cities, and particularly in the Development Areas.

## Group 3: Restructuring for reasons of market standing

This Group can be quickly dealt with. The mergers which it covered came from a range of product groupings, as follows: military manpacks and nucleonics (part MLH 354); medium-sized electrical machines (part MLH 361); computer software (part MLH 366).

The financial restructuring in this group was aimed essentially at increasing the market standing of the firms involved through sheer size, and, for example, market share. The achievement of this did not require any major reorganization of production and there were therefore no major effects on the spatial distribution of employment. Some changes in production did occur, however, usually as a result of organizational integration after the mergers (with, say, the elimination of duplicated research facilities). Moves of this type accounted for a net loss of 200 jobs from the cities.

## 'Non-stimulant' sectors

In mergers involving multi-divisional firms, the framework for analysis of stimulant sectors was extended to non-stimulant sectors. The effects of the reorganization of these latter sectors were particularly significant for the cities, accounting for about 25 per cent of their total net loss of employment (7,565 jobs). These losses occurred in three industries (MLHs 354, 363 and 367) and although the reasons behind them differed in individual cases, the *forms* that they took had much in common with those displayed by Groups 1 and 2. All involved closures of old, labour-intensive plants in inner-city locations; and in the telecommunications case in particular provided a further example of the way in which technological changes within an industry can influence the spatial distribution of its activities (Massey and Meegan, 1979).

## Employment change in the cities

This section will attempt to draw together the employment implications of the forms of restructuring discussed above to show how they shaped the overall performance of the cities in the survey. This perspective is best provided by a breakdown of the overall employment change into its different components.

The complete breakdown of *employment loss* in the four cities is given by the figures quoted in table 1.3. It is immediately clear from this table that the majority of jobs lost to the inner cities (58 per cent) resulted from either closures or capacity cuts *in which no locational change was involved*. This is an important finding, for it contradicts the widely held view that the inner cities are losing employment predominantly because of job relocation – usually, so the argument proceeds, to the Assisted Areas, and as a result of the various government incentives.

The great majority of the employment lost in the inner cities in our survey (89 per cent) comprised jobs lost to the economy as a whole, and such losses are in no sense locationally divertible by regional policy measures. Locational losses (in other words, that employment which was actually lost to the inner cities and gained by another location)[10] formed a relatively insignificant component of decline in the cities. Excluding those jobs which were transferred either within or between the four cities in the survey, this category comprised only 3,252 jobs or 11 per cent of total job loss.

It is nevertheless the case that of the jobs which did shift location, 62 per cent (2,012) went to the Development Areas. The argument is not

**Table 1.3** *Employment losses in the four cities*

| Job loss | No. | % |
|---|---|---|
| Absolute loss | 27,113 | 89 |
| *in situ* | 17,478 | 58 |
| *in transit* | 9,635 | 31 |
| Locational loss* | 3,252 | 11 |
| Total | 30,365 | 100 |

*Excluding 373 jobs transferred within or between cities.

therefore that the cities do not lose employment to locations in Assisted Areas but rather that the numerical significance of this loss can be much exaggerated. Moreover the policy significance even of the employment which was relocated to Assisted Areas is further reduced by the fact that only 3 per cent (60) of these gains to such areas were in city locations. In other words, it is entirely possible that restructuring could have led to a city/non-city move even in the absence of regional policy. The argument is further strengthened when Liverpool's performance in the survey is examined. As table 1.4 demonstrates, that city's status as a Development Area certainly did not accord it any immunity. The processes examined in this paper would have resulted in serious employment losses in the inner cities with or without the existence elsewhere of Development Areas.[11]

The *employment gains* to the cities as a result of locational shifts of production were negligible. In the survey as a whole, there were 4,495 jobs identified as locational transfers. Of these, 3,625 had their origins in plants in the four conurbations whilst the remainder (870) were initially located in other parts of the country. The cities only retained 373 of the former and only received 30 of the latter. Moreover, there were *no new jobs* created in the cities as a direct result of the processes examined in this paper (absolute gains were zero). The lack of employment gains (both locational and absolute) could, of course, again be argued to be a result of the diversionary impact of regional policy. But, once again, it should be pointed out not only that Liverpool (which is in a Development Area) performed in the same manner as the cities in the non-assisted parts of the country, but also that, conversely, of the mobile employment identified in the survey only 10 per cent (433/4,495)[12] went to cities at all.

Table 1.5 illustrates the impact of the employment changes on the four cities. The proportionate change, expressed as a percentage of initial employment, was significantly greater for the cities than it was for the aggregate national total in every component of employment loss. The gains were negligible.

The discussion of the employment changes has so far been conducted solely in terms of the numbers of jobs gained or lost. The restructuring, however, also had profound implications for the *type of labour* demanded, both in the sector as a whole and in the cities in particular.

The first point to be noted is that, in absolute terms, the bulk of the losses in the cities was of relatively skilled jobs. The broad occupational distribution of employees within the sector is given in table 1.6.[13] May 1970 is the earliest date for such a disaggregation using the 1968 SIC. The table therefore already reflects some of the changes brought about by the processes discussed in this paper.[14] It is none the less indicative.

It is clear from table 1.6 that the reorganization of production in the

**Table 1.4** Net change in employment: the four cities

| City | Total employment at time of IRC intervention | Absolute loss | Locational loss | Locational gain | Absolute gain | Result | Difference | % Change |
|---|---|---|---|---|---|---|---|---|
| Birmingham | 11,950 | − 3,020 | – 0 | +40 | +0 | = 8,970 | (2,980) | (25) |
| Greater London | 26,473 | 10,228 | 2,563[a] | 20[a] | 0 | 13,702 | (12,771) | (48) |
| Liverpool | 11,350 | 4,910 | 250 | 0 | 0 | 6,190 | (5,160) | (45) |
| Manchester | 22,740 | 8,955 | 542[b] | 93[b] | 0 | 13,336 | (9,404) | (41) |
| Total | 72,513 | −27,113 | −3,252[c] | +50[c] | +0 | =42,198 | (30,315) | (42) |

[a]Excludes 30 jobs transferred within London but includes 103 jobs transferred to other cities.
[b]Excludes 240 jobs transferred within Manchester.
[c]Total column does not add as it excludes all jobs transferred within and between cities.

**Table 1.5** *The components of employment change*

| Components of employment change | All survey firms | | Cities | |
|---|---|---|---|---|
| | No. | No. as % initial employment | No. | No. as % initial employment |
| Absolute loss | (37,986) | 17 | (27,113) | 37 |
| in situ | (26,741) | 12 | (17,478) | 24 |
| in transit | (11,245) | 5 | (9,635) | 13 |
| Locational loss | – | – | (3,252) | 4 |
| Absolute gain | (1,970) | 1 | 0 | 0 |
| Locational gain | – | – | 50 | 0 |
| Net change | (36,016) | 16 | (30,315) | 42 |

Group 1 industries was bound to have a particularly significant impact on male, skilled labour. MLHs 361 and 383 have the highest percentage of skilled workers and the lowest share of female employees. For MLH 362, the official statistics give a different picture with 61 per cent of the total workforce being unskilled or semi-skilled.

**Table 1.6** *Percentage distribution of employees (male and female)\* by broad occupational category and industry at May 1970*

| MLH | Administrative, technical and clerical | Skilled operatives | Semi-skilled | Other | Total |
|---|---|---|---|---|---|
| 354 | 36.6 (31.4) | 24.6 (6.4) | 26.7 (58.0) | 12.1 (38.4) | 100 (33.2) |
| 361 | 34.9 (26.7) | 26.9 (2.7) | 24.5 (50.3) | 13.8 (22.9) | 100 (26.0) |
| 362 | 30.9 (32.4) | 8.5 (3.1) | 42.6 (36.8) | 18.0 (14.7) | 100 (30.6) |
| 363 | 29.7 (28.6) | 12.4 (3.0) | 51.0 (66.2) | 6.9 (8.8) | 100 (44.3) |
| 364 | 32.1 (29.8) | 11.9 (5.3) | 47.0 (77.4) | 9.0 (28.6) | 100 (50.8) |
| 365 | 25.7 (37.7) | 10.5 (15.3) | 53.8 (79.9) | 10.1 (20.9) | 100 (57.0) |
| 366 | 64.2 (22.3) | 14.0 (5.1) | 15.8 (68.3) | 6.0 (25.5) | 100 (27.6) |
| 367 | 57.9 (24.1) | 18.6 (6.2) | 15.4 (75.0) | 8.1 (41.3) | 100 (29.4) |
| 368 | 31.2 (38.6) | 11.3 (2.1) | 37.5 (56.0) | 20.0 (23.3) | 100 (28.1) |
| 369 | 27.4 (35.6) | 15.3 (2.9) | 43.8 (71.4) | 13.5 (27.2) | 100 (46.1) |
| 383 | 44.6 (20.2) | 33.8 (0.5) | 11.0 (19.4) | 10.6 (20.1) | 100 (13.6) |

\*Figures in brackets refer to percentage of category accounted for by females only.
*Source*: derived from *British Labour Statistics*, 1970, table 100.

This initial assessment must be qualified, however. The survey results for MLH 362 related to the rationalization of the supertension cable industry only. In a detailed interview with the company involved in the major closure in this sector, the problems of skill classification became fully apparent. Thus, hourly paid workers in the industry are divisible into two categories: process workers (primarily semi-skilled, working the machines) and skilled workers (mechanical and electrical maintenance workers). The second category (skilled) is small in relation to the semi-skilled category. But the semi-skilled category is itself divided into eight grades, with workers in the top two grades having a very high degree of specialized skill and training. The skill, however, is one acquired on the job and, most importantly, is one entirely specific to the supertension cable industry. On the general job market which they now face, these workers are effectively unskilled or semi-skilled. Since basic pay was negotiated nationally in line with these eight grades (with individual companies having their own incentive schemes), the loss of the top jobs in the grades, even when new employment is found, is likely to mean both a decline in the degree of skill used and a fall in income. The workers occupying these jobs were mostly male.

The employment losses occurring in the conurbations as a result of the restructuring in Group 2 also had implications for the skill levels of the workforce involved. The losses in this Group took place in the older electro-mechanical factories which employed more traditional engineering craft skills. Moreover, the restructuring was itself part of an overall trend towards a further dichotomization of skills within the Group 2 industries and this too has its implications for the cities. The workforce in these industries is increasingly coming to be divided between highly qualified scientific and technical staff and semi-skilled (predominantly female) assembly workers. This dichotomization of skill within the labour-force has some tendency to be reflected within the spatial pattern of the industry. On the one hand there is a growing concentration of skilled and qualified workers predominantly in the outer south-east; on the other hand semi-skilled production increasingly favours non-urban locations within the Development Areas.

The general conclusion must therefore be that, as far as the processes we are studying are concerned, the bulk of the losses are of relatively skilled jobs. Moreover, most of these losses are absolute (see table 1.3).

This conclusion is interesting in that the factor of labour skill is one frequently mentioned in the context of industrial migration from the cities. None of the evidence that we have unearthed, however, suggests that firms have moved out of the cities in search of a *more* skilled manual labour force.

## Conclusions

A major aim of this paper has been to reformulate the 'problem of the city' in such a way that it can be related to an analysis of the changing structure of the national economy.[15] It is clear that the repercussions of the processes of restructuring outlined in this paper have had considerable implications for the cities, and, further, that it is only at this level of analysis that the employment changes identified could have been adequately accounted for. It is also clear that such a form of analysis may lead to rather distinctive policy conclusions.

First, while the focus of *interest* in the present paper remained at the level of the city, the nature of the definition of the problem meant that its causes did not also have to be located within the same confines. One result of this is that, to a considerable extent, such an approach shifts the locus of 'blame' away from local authorities. This is not to deny that the processes of planning and of development control have any negative impact at all; it is rather to stress that that impact operates within the context of circumstances determined at, for instance, the level of the economy as a whole.

In another way, too, the results of this research lead us to argue that it is incorrect to interpret the present problems of the cities as in some way the 'fault' of state policies. In this case we refer to regional policy. It is a common proposition that the existence of regional policies has been significantly responsible for the decline of manufacturing employment in major cities. The major consideration is of course that a large part of the decline identified consisted of *absolute* loss. Such job losses are in no way divertible by spatial policies, nor are the reasons for the cutbacks likely to be influenced by such policies. These reasons were discussed above; it should be noted here, however, that the losses did *not* result from company failure, a possibility which might, in turn, be attributable at least in part to detrimental locational conditions. On the contrary, it must be stressed that the closures, the redundancies, and the cutbacks which occurred indicate not failure but the only possibility for 'success'. Such action was necessary in order to increase the firms' profitability and international competitiveness.

The remaining loss (11 per cent gross) did, however, as recorded above, occur through, or as part of, a locational change. Two questions arise here: the first is whether regional policies form part of the stimulus to, or critically enable, the processes involved in the locational change; the second is, given that some locational change may occur, whether the existence of regional policies influences the 'destination' of these changes.

Falk and Martinos (1975), who discuss the importance of factors such as those considered here, argue that the system of regional incentives has not merely influenced subsequent locational choices, but has made possible the processes themselves: regional assistance 'has made mergers and the subsequent rationalisation of plants easier, and has encouraged concentration and the substitution of capital for labour' (p. 14). One of the implications of this argument is that regional policy is, at least to some extent, part and parcel of overall national economic policy. It is part, in other words, of the same strategy as the IRC. This is an important point, and one for which there is considerable evidence. However, if regional policy is not simply regional policy, but is part of the attempt to increase the productivity of industry, and if it is thereby reinforcing employment problems in inner cities, that does not mean that one can simply abandon regional policy. Alternative and at least equally effective means have to be found, which increase competitiveness without producing such problematical spatial repercussions.

The relationship between inner-city problems and regional policies is anyway more complex than that. In the first place, mergers, rationalizations, and the concentration and reorganization of capacity rarely demand investment in brand-new plant. This will usually only be necessary when other changes (for instance in production techniques) are implemented at the same time. In most cases, therefore, regional incentives on capital investment will be (mainly) inoperative, and, on the other hand, IDCs will be unnecessary since existing capacity will be used.[16] Thus much of the locational loss of employment to the cities resulting from the processes studied here may have produced relative gains elsewhere, but has done so within existing plant, and within the medium-sized towns of the non-assisted areas of England (see on this, for example, Eversley, 1975). A few cases were found, indeed, where closures occurred in an inner city (Liverpool) in a Development Area, with transfer of part of the production and job opportunities to non-assisted areas. These aspects of mergers and subsequent rationalization, then, are not themselves frequently influenced by incentives (or disincentives) available as part of regional policy.

As the analysis above showed, however, this does leave 62 per cent of the net locational loss to the cities, which was involved in locational moves to the Assisted Areas. The nature of these moves should therefore be examined in more detail. In the first place, and at a simple numerical level, it should be pointed out that it was the locational losses in this category which were responsible for the greater part of absolute losses *in transit*. The number of new jobs directly created in the recipient Development Areas was less than one-third of the number lost in the cities.[17] The figures in table 1.7 are for the plants, by Development Area, receiving production from the largest of the inner-city closures.

**Table 1.7** *The effect of a major move from an inner city on development areas*

| Development Area | At time of merger | | One year after merger | |
|---|---|---|---|---|
| Wales | 480 | | 603 | |
| North: Plant 1 | 1,500 | | 1,802 | |
| Plant 2 | 5,400 | 7,340 | 4,450 | 6,577 |
| Plant 3 | 440 | | 325 | |
| Scotland: Plant 1 | 1,140 | 2,100 | 923 | 2,063 |
| Plant 2 | 960 | | 1,140 | |
| Total | 9,920 | | 9,243 | |

These employment figures of course cover all the employment in the receiving plants, and not just that transferred, and, moreover, other changes and reorganizations in the sector were going on at the same time. The numbers indicate, none the less, that a massive loss to the cities, and an apparent transfer of work, did not mean a corresponding gain to the Assisted Areas. Moreover, since the second date, and as a result both of increasing efficiency (increasing the capital : labour ratio) and of reduced orders, employment at all of the plants has been further reduced, and one of them has been closed. The conclusion must be that if the *processes* involved are going to continue even (if they could do so) without a change in location, they will anyway involve considerable losses of employment in the inner cities.

Part of the argument is, however, that the processes themselves are enabled or encouraged by regional policy, and particularly by the incentives available. While not disagreeing with this position, it is also necessary to ask whether the locational attractions may be characteristics of Development Areas *other than* the availability there of regional policy incentives. In other words, to what extent is movement to a depressed area an integral part of the economic process? One such frequently quoted attraction is space availability, including both absolute availability and price. There was one 'location factor' for which we did find some evidence on this score. This was that of labour. It should be stressed again that in terms of actual location shifts we refer here to only a small number of cases, but we can for the purposes of this argument also use evidence from the absolute gains in employment which benefited the Assisted Areas. The main result of the analysis is that the jobs created in the Development Areas were almost entirely semi-skilled. That is: they demanded less skill than the employment lost in the cities in these industries over the same period and, in the cases where an actual spatial shift was involved, this took place in a context of technological change and, consequently, both an absolute reduction in the total number of jobs and a downward change in the nature of skills required. Four conclusions emerge. First, and most conclusive; none of the evidence that we have suggests that in this situation firms will move out of industrial cities in search of a *more* skilled labour-force. Second, even had it been possible for the restructuring processes to have occurred *without* locational change, there would none the less have been a considerable downward shift in the balance of labour skills demanded in the major industrial cities studied. Third, given the direction of change in production-skill requirements indicated by our study, it may be that the balance of location factors is changing to release such industries from their previous requirement for highly skilled labour. This, in turn, may loosen their existing spatial ties to the major, established industrial cities. This, of course, while indicating a shift away from metropolitan areas, does not necessarily imply growth in assisted regions. The fourth, and very tentative, indication of our results was that, given this changing demand for labour, more emphasis may now be placed in the location decision on locationally differentiated characteristics of *less*-skilled labour. There are, of course, reserves of unemployed unskilled and semi-skilled labour in the cities. The indications were, however, that such labour was regarded as probably more expensive, and potentially more militant. In contrast, that of small towns in Development Areas was cheaper and, because of its pressing need for employment, less demanding.[18]

Although this paper considers only one major sector of industry, Harris and Taylor (1976) argue that the restructuring of the labour-force is an economy-level phenomenon. Under such circumstances it would seem that the problem of the cities can not be approached by setting them up as yet more areas with incentives of the regional policy type. The question is one of national-level planning, not one of increasing the number of competing incentives for any given piece of new capital investment. Moreover, regional policy incentives as they stand at present would be inoperative at the level of detail required to attack the problems of the inner cities. In order adequately to counter the present population/ employment imbalance within these areas, it would be necessary for a policy to be able to specify/influence the kind of industries attracted and, further, to operate at a fairly precise spatial level. That is to say, it would be necessary to be able to distinguish between location policies for the inner city and location policies for outer regional areas. General incentive policies are rarely able to achieve such precision.

The major concern of this paper has been to relate the employment changes at present going on in the cities to economic processes at national and international levels. Although any individual case was the result of a complex of causes, the dominant processes affecting the four cities under study were clearly responses to problems of over-capacity and relative technological shifts in favour of cheaper (in all our cases less labour-intensive) production processes. Frequently the major companies involved were seeking to change the balance of their home production away from the heavy electrical part of the sector. Cuts in capacity thus added to the viability of the firm as a whole in international competition in its other products. These specific processes were found to be important partly *because* the study was of the IRC, whose activity was focused on such cases, but it should be noted that their effect was proportionately more important on the cities than on the nation as a whole. We should argue that, as a general form, such restructuring and reorganization of major sectors and of particular product groups is a necessary process in the development of the UK economy. It is not therefore possible to consider policy options which rule out the operation of the economic processes themselves. If there is a contradiction at the heart of this process of decline, our research would indicate that it is not between inner cities and policy-aided Development Areas, but between the cities and the demands of profitability and international competitiveness.

London
published in 1978

# Notes

1  These various forms of intervention will be referred to collectively under the general heading of 'financial restructuring'.
2  The total figure does not relate to a single point in time since the individual cases of intervention took place over a period of four years. The percentage is therefore a 'rule of thumb' measure derived by comparing the survey total with total national employment in the sector at the beginning of the period (1966).
3  Between 1966 and 1972. Although the IRC was most active in the sector in 1968 and 1969 and was abolished early in 1971, evidence was found of post-merger rationalization, following its intervention, as late as 1972. Indeed there was one case identified which involved the opening of a new plant in 1976 as a direct result of the production reorganization following an IRC-sponsored merger six years before.
4  The geographical areas used were as follows: Birmingham: Birmingham CB; Liverpool: Liverpool CB (inc. Netherton); London: Greater London Council

Area; Manchester: Manchester CB. Newcastle was the only other city for which survey observations were recorded. Unlike the other cities, however, these observations were confined to one plant and one specific product group. Because of the limited nature of the results for Newcastle, this paper will concentrate on the changes experienced by the four cities already mentioned.

5 The group titles relate specifically to the forms of restructuring identified in the survey and do not constitute absolute types which can be expected to occur in every instance of restructuring. Thus 'restructuring in the face of over-capacity and high costs' will not always produce the particular forms discussed in this paper.

6 This was not an *ad hoc* phenomenon. It occurred in the context of a general decline in the rate of growth of demand for electrical energy, a situation exacerbated by the onset of recession in industrial activity.

7 That is, *in transit* absolute loss expressed as a percentage of total *in transit* and locational loss (4980 out of 5586).

8 These industries do not correspond exactly to Group 1. Indeed it is important to stress again that the Group classification was based on examination of national economic pressures for restructuring. These did not follow any precise sectoral break-down. In particular, parts of MLH 361 fall into Group 3, and parts of MLH 354 could be included here under Group 1. It was not possible to tabulate the initial distribution of the survey firms' employment by group.

9 With each new generation of computer, for example, it is estimated that the direct labour content is reduced by one-tenth (interview with survey firm).

10 We are only concerned here with numbers of jobs – the type of employment may also change *in transit* – see later.

11 Of course, it could be argued that the processes themselves were enabled by the very existence of regional policy. This point will be returned to later.

12 Figure includes results for Newcastle.

13 For the sector as a whole and not just the survey firms.

14 If anything, this means that it will underestimate the levels of skill at MLH level.

15 It should be emphasized that this is a study of only one branch (though a major one) of that economy. In particular, we have not considered the possibility of employment growth in the service industries.

16 Industrial Development Certificate.

17 It should be pointed out that it was this category of changes which was most dominated by a few large moves, and the figures should be treated accordingly. On the other hand, evidence available from other sources (e.g. Keeble, 1971, and Firn, 1975) indicates that one would *expect* this category to be the one most dominated by a few large moves by a few large firms.

18 The Development Areas were not the only parts of the country apparently to be benefiting from such changes in labour requirements. Tourist areas where 'new' labour could be brought into the labour-force were also increasingly feasible (see Massey, 1977).

# References

Chisholm, M. (1976). Regional policies in an era of slow population growth and higher unemployment. *Regional Studies*, vol. 10: 201–13.

Department of Employment (1975). New estimates of employment on a continuous basis: United Kingdom, *Department of Employment Gazette*, 1037–9.

Eversley, D. (1975). *Employment in the Inner City: An Introduction*. EIC WP. 1.

Falk, N. and Martinos, H. (1975). *Inner City*. Fabian Research Series 320.

Firn, J. (1975). External control and regional policy. In *Red Paper on Scotland*. Edinburgh: EUSPB.

Harris, D.F. and Taylor, F.J. (1976). *The Service Sector: Its Changing Role as a Source of Employment*. Department of Environment, Leeds Regional Office.

HMSO (1966). *The Industrial Reorganisation Corporation Act*. London: HMSO.

Keeble, D. (1971). Employment mobility in Britain. In M. Chisholm and G. Manners (eds) *Spatial Problems of the British Economy*. Cambridge: Cambridge University Press.

Massey, D. (1977). A review of D. Keeble, *Industrial Location and Planning in the United Kingdom* (Methuen, London, 1976), *Town Planning Review*, 48, 454–6.

Massey, D. and Meegan, R.A. (1979). The geography of industrial reorganisation: the spatial effects of the restructuring of the electrical engineering sector under the Industrial Reorganisation Corporation. *Progress in Planning* (Oxford: Pergamon), vol. 10, pt. 3.

Treasury (1976). Economic Progress Report (February).

# 2

# *In What Sense a Regional Problem?*

## Introduction

The aim of this paper is to raise some questions about common conceptions of 'regional problems' within capitalist societies. Some of the points to be made are well known, others are raised less frequently; some challenge explicit positions in the established theory, others implicit assumptions in methodology. The hope is that, by collecting these points together, and indicating some of their interrelationships, the implications of each one may be taken more seriously.

## Regional differentiation and the concept of the spatial division of labour

This section of the paper presents a framework for the analysis of regional differentiation. Such a framework will, of necessity, be rather abstract at this stage, but later sections will attempt to put more flesh on the bones.

One thing should be made clear from the start, and that is that there always has been spatial (or regional) inequality. This is a historical statement, and the kind of general framework to be introduced here is a framework for the analysis of real historical processes. It is only in formal models that one starts with the featureless equality of a clean sheet.

A second point, however, is what one means in such a context by 'inequality'. The word tends to get used indiscriminately in the literature in two rather different ways. First, there is inequality in the degree of attractiveness of a particular area to the dominant form of economic activity; second, there is inequality in terms of various indicators of social well-being (rate of unemployment, per capita income, degree of external control of production, for example). The two are evidently not necessarily the same. In a crude sense, one is a cause and the other an effect. It is the first with which this paper is concerned at this point – that is: regional inequality in the degree of attractiveness to, and suitability for, economic activity. At any point in time, in other words, there is a given uneven geographical distribution of the conditions necessary for profitable, and competitive, production.

A third point is that such geographical inequality is a historically relative phenomenon. It is historically relative (in other words, it will change) as a result of two processes. On the other hand, it will respond to changes in the geographical distribution of the requirements of production – which are frequently called changes in the spatial, or locational, surface – such things as actual changes in the distribution of the population or of resources, or changes in relative distances caused by developments in transport and communication. On the other hand, the pattern of spatial inequality may change as a result of changes in the requirements of the production process itself, in other words because of changes in the locational demands of profitable economic activity. In turn, such changes in the requirements of production are themselves a result, not of neutral technical advance, but of the imperatives of the overall process of accumulation.

However, in any particular period, new investment in economic activity will be geographically distributed in response to such a given pattern of spatial differentiation. A fourth question then arises, however, as to what 'in response to' means, and it is here that I want to introduce the term *'spatial division of labour'*. The term is introduced in order to make a point. The normal assumption is that any economic activity will respond to geographical inequality in the conditions of production, in such a way as to maximize profits. While this is correct, it is also trivial. What it ignores is the variation in the way in which different forms of economic activity incorporate or use the fact of spatial inequality *in order to* maximize profits. This manner of response to geographical unevenness will vary both between sectors and, for any given sector, with changing conditions of production. It may also vary with, for instance, the structure of ownership of capital (depending on, for example, the size and range of production under single ownership). The determination of this manner of response will itself be a product of the interaction between, on the one hand, the existing characteristics of spatial differentiation and, on the other hand, the requirements at that time of the particular process of production. Moreover, if it is the case that different industries will use spatial variation in different ways, it is also true that these different modes of use will subsequently produce/contribute to different forms of geographical inequality. Different modes of response by industry, implying different spatial divisions of labour within its overall process of production, may thus generate different forms of 'regional problem'.

One schematic way of approaching this as a historical process is to conceive of it as a series of 'rounds' of new investment, in each of which a new form of spatial division of labour is evolved. In fact, of course, the process of change is much more diversified and incremental (though certainly there are periods of radical redirection). Moreover, at any given historical moment a whole number of different spatial divisions of labour may be being evolved, by different branches of industry. In any empirical work, therefore, it is necessary both to analyse this complexity and to isolate and identify those particular divisions which are dominant in reshaping the spatial structure. The geographical distribution of economic activity which results from the evolution of a new form of division of labour will be overlaid on, and combined with, the pattern produced in previous periods by different forms of division of labour. This combination of successive layers will produce effects which themselves vary over space, thus giving rise to a new form and spatial distribution of inequality in the conditions of production, as a basis for the next 'round' of investment. 'The economy' of any given local area will thus be a complex result of the combination of its succession of roles within the series of wider, national and international, spatial divisions of labour.

## Different forms of the spatial division of labour in the United Kingdom

As a way of illustrating some of the points already made, and as a basis for discussion in later sections, it is worth at this point running briefly through two forms of spatial division of labour which have been, or are, significant components of the 'regional problem' in the United Kingdom.

The first of these examples is so well known as to warrant only brief attention. It is that form of the spatial division of labour which structured the spatial organization of the UK during much of the nineteenth century (McCrone, 1969, p. 16), and which took the form of sectoral spatial specialization. It was the UK's early dominance of the growth of modern industry, its consequent commitment both to retaining that dominance through free trade and to its own specialization in manufacturing within the international division of labour, which enabled the burgeoning growth up to the First World War of major exporting industries based on coal, shipbuilding, iron and steel, and textiles. In establishing their spatial pattern of production *within* the UK these industries were not faced with an undifferentiated geographical surface. The aspects of differentiation which were significant to these industries at that stage of development were such things as access to ports for export, and for import of raw materials (e.g. cotton), a supply of skilled labour, and, to some extent still, access to coal. The form of spatial division of labour to which this conjunction of production requirements and geographical differentiation gave rise was, as already stated, that of sectoral spatial specialization. The different sectors simply concentrated all their capacity in the areas most propitious in terms of their requirements for production. Moreover, because these were among the dominant industries in terms of new investment and growth in output and employment, they were the structuring elements in the new emerging pattern of regional differentiation. 'Thus Clydeside meant ships and heavy engineering, the North East meant export coal, iron and steel, ships and heavy engineering, Lancashire meant cotton and some engineering; the West Riding meant coal and woollens; South Wales meant export coal and iron and steel' (Hall, 1974, p. 84). From the point of view of the individual localities involved, this led to a situation in which 'several of the major industrial regions had based their prosperity on a very limited economic base' (ibid., p. 83).

The subsequent effects of this particular form of the spatial division of labour are well known, but it is important to emphasize a number of points. First, in itself such a pattern of industrial distribution was not necessarily problematical, in the sense of producing geographical inequality. On the contrary, second, the resulting regional *problem* was precipitated by changes in the relation of the UK economy as a whole, and of these particular industries, to the international division of labour.

> It is really to the collapse of this policy (of international specialisation based on industrial dominance and free trade) that the regional problem, at any rate in the industrial areas, owes its origin. The over-valuation of the pound in the 1920s, the emergence of economic blocs in the 'thirties, changes in technology and competition from lower-wage countries, all combined to produce a secular decline in the traditional export industries. (McCrone, 1969, p. 16)

The 'regional problem' which emerged was thus produced by the effects on the spatial division of labour within these industries of the change in imperial relationships and the decline of the United Kingdom as a dominant world capitalist economy. Third, this process produced a specific form of regional problem. Sectoral decline brought with it specifically *regional* decline, and the indices on which the consequent regional inequality were measured were the well-known ones of rate of unemployment, amount of manufacturing employment, per capita earnings, and out-migration.

It has been this form of spatial division of labour which has frequently been analysed as being the root-cause of the 'regional problem' (at least the industrial region problem) of the UK. Thus the UK background paper for its submission to the European Regional Development Fund announces:

> The United Kingdom's regional problem is primarily one of decline in employment in the traditional industries – coal, steel, shipbuilding, textiles and agriculture, the reasons for the decline varying from industry to industry. Most of these industries are concentrated in a small number of areas and these are, therefore, disproportionately hard hit by their contraction. (Trade and Industry, 1977, p. 358)

Much present thinking and a number of continuing policy preoccupations (in particular, for instance, a general commitment to sectoral diversification as a basis for stability) reflect the experience of this early period. Indeed, there are intimations in a number of writings that the demise of this form of spatial division may herald the end (or at least the beginning of the end) of regional problems: 'Yet as time goes on, the structure of the problem regions is gradually becoming more favourable; the declining industries cannot decline for ever, and new industries are playing a larger part in the regional economies. As this process continues the problem should get easier' (McCrone, 1969, p. 166). And clearly there have been signs of change. On the one hand, many studies indicate a generally declining degree of sectoral specialization (see, for instance, Chisholm and Oeppen, 1973; Dixon and Thirlwall, 1975). On the other hand, there have been changes in the comparative rating of the regions on the indices relevant to this form of regional problem. Thus in a recent article, Keeble (1977) writes, 'the period since about 1965, and in fact particularly since 1970, has witnessed striking convergence of nearly all these different indices of regional economic performance towards the national average' (p. 4). The indices referred to are share of manufacturing employment, unemployment rate, earnings, and net migration.

Yet even as this 'convergence' (though admittedly around lower national norms) is being registered, other indices are being pointed to which imply, not the end of spatial differentiation, but its existence in a different form, in terms both of the nature of spatial inequality and of its geographical base. The new indices refer, for instance, to the degree of external ownership, to the effects of hierarchies of control, and to differentiation in employment type. Westaway (1974) points to a developing spatial hierarchy of ownership and control, and to its consequences for employment type, with the increasing dominance of multi-plant companies; and the work of North and Leigh (1976) and of Massey (1976) indicates the effects of hierarchization produced in recent years by the increasing degree of industrial concentration (see also Massey and Meegan, 1979). Firn (1975) examines evidence on the degree and type of external ownership and control of Scottish manufacturing; the work of McDermott (1976) is in the same vein. In terms of the changing *geographical* basis of 'spatial problems', it is of course the combination of regional 'convergence' with the new prominence of inner-city areas which is the dominant aspect of change.

In a paper of this length there can obviously be no pretence of producing a complete analysis of this spatial restructuring, but it is appropriate briefly to describe one emerging form of spatial division of labour which appears to be at least a contributory component.[1] While based in certain aspects (though not all) on the impact of the division already described, this form of spatial division of labour is completely different from that of sectoral spatial specialization. In particular, and perhaps ominously, the 'inequalities' inherent in this division do not appear only on its demise – they are integral to the form of spatial organization itself. Nor are the evolution and effects of this form dependent only on the ups and downs of whole sectors of the economy; they result also from changes in the form of organization of production *within* sectors.

Following the framework outlined in the last section, it is first necessary to specify the characteristics and requirements of production which, in combination with particular spatial conditions, form the basis of the development of a new division of labour. Such characteristics and requirements include the increasing size of individual firms, and of individual plants (see, for example, Dunford, 1977), the separation and hierarchization of technical, control, and management functions (see Westaway, 1974), and the division, even within production, into separately functioning stages (see Massey, 1976; Lipietz, 1977). Within the production process itself, there have also been considerable changes. On the one hand, the growing intensity of competition in recent years has led to increased pressure to cut labour costs and increase productivity, and this in turn has produced an apparent acceleration of the processes of standardization of the commodities produced (thus reducing both the number of workers for any given level of output, and the levels of skill required of them), of automation (with effects similar to standardization), and of the introduction of systems such as numerical-control machine tools (again reducing, in general, the number and skill requirements of the direct labour-force, but also needing a small number of more qualified technicians). In terms of the bulk of workers, then, a de-skilling process of some significance seems to have been in operation (see, for instance, Massey and Meegan, 1979). At the other end of the scale, both the changing balance between sectors of the economy, and the nature of competition (particularly the reliance on fast rates of technological change) in the newly dominant sectors, such as electronics, have increased the relative importance within the national employment structure of research and development.

Where such developments are occurring in countries in which there is already some degree of spatial differentiation in levels of skill (both within the production workforce, and between them and technical and scientific workers), in the wage levels of the relevant (i.e., increasingly only semi-skilled) sections of production workers, in the degree of organization and militancy of the labour movement, and in the level of presence of, for instance, the banking, commercial and business-service sectors, a new form of spatial division of labour has, in the last decade or so, begun to take root. Such is the case in most countries of Western Europe, and in the USA.

And it is precisely the changing conditions of production which are enabling industry to take advantage of spatial differentiation in this manner. For one typical 'use' by industry of this particular form of spatial differentiation is increasingly based on the geographical separation of control and R & D functions from those processes of direct production still requiring skilled labourers, and of these in turn from the increasingly important element of mass-production and assembly work for which only semi-skilled workers are needed. The expanding size of individual companies is central to this process. On the other hand, it is necessary in order to finance the huge costs of research and development (see Massey, 1976; NEDO, 1972; NEDO, 1973) and on the other hand it increases the number of products within a firm which are produced at a scale sufficient to warrant some degree of automation, and therefore in turn to enable reductions in aggregate labour costs and increases in individual labour productivity. Finally, of course, it is the greater size of individual units which increases the feasibility of separate locations for the different stages in the overall process of production, and consequently enables the establishment of locational hierarchies taking advantage of spatial inequality.

Taking the 'bottom' end of the hierarchy first, the mass-production and assembly stages of production are located increasingly in areas where semi-skilled workers are not only available, but where wages are low, and where there is little tradition amongst these workers of organization and militancy. Very frequently this will mean location in areas where there are workers with little previous experience of waged work. These may be areas suffering from the collapse of a previously dominant industrial sector, such as the former coal-mining areas of Northumberland, or the coal- or shale-mining areas of Scotland. In such cases, the labour drawn upon will not mainly be that previously employed in the former specialization, but more typically the women of the area. Other areas favoured for this stage of production include those where workers (again mainly women) do not become totally dependent upon (nor organized around) waged work. Seaside resorts with seasonal or part-time self-employment in tourism are typical of this second type of area. Although the introduction of this new investment in production facilities into such (frequently depressed) areas is new, and often hailed as beneficial, its positive effects may well be small. Wages and skills remain low, and it is not even necessarily the case that much new employment will result – one of the major characteristics of such factories is that they have few local links and stimulate little locally in terms of associated production (see, for instance, McDermott, 1976; Lipietz, 1977; Dunford, 1977; and hints in McCrone, 1975). Firn (1975), after documenting the extent and form of occurrence of external control in the Scottish economy, draws some preliminary conclusions about its likely effects. These closely parallel those implied by the argument above. Thus, Firn hypothesizes, it is likely that existing disparities in the type of labour available will be exacerbated. Such investment will not expand the local technical, research or managerial strata. Moreover, the lack of an R & D component will also, given the presently dominant nature of formation of new companies, reduce the likelihood of the internal generation of new firms. Again the division of labour exacerbates existing inequalities, in this case further reducing the degree of local control in such regions. Firn's hypotheses also accord with our own evidence (Massey and Meegan, 1979) on the effects on the direct workforce and on per capita income. Thus he writes:

> The nature of new jobs provided by external plants has been principally orientated towards female, semi-skilled assembly operations in, for example, electronics plants, whereas the jobs lost have been mainly of male, highly paid, skilled craftsmen. Therefore there seems to have been a net wage reduction per new job provided, as well as an element of deskilling, although this assertion remains to be proved. (p. 411)

Finally, in these regions, this form of spatial division of labour 'will express itself in terms of a very open regional economy, with a high degree of integration with other economic systems' (Firn, 1975, p. 411). Dunford

(1977) and Lipietz (1977) give similar evidence on this from Italy and from France.

The 'second stage' of production (that is, those processes not yet automated, reduced to assembly work, or producing standardized products) is still typically located in the old centres of skilled labour – primarily nineteenth-century industrial towns and cities. The critical characteristic of this stage, however, is its decreasing quantitative importance. More and more, the de-skilling processes already referred to are enabling industry to be locationally freed from its old ties to skilled labour (and consequently, one might add, from well-unionized workers). The effect of the relationship between such changes in the production process and the possibilities open to industry *as a result of* the spatial differentiation of labour, is one component of the present industrial decline of the inner cities (see Community Development Project, 1977; Massey and Meegan, 1978).

Finally, at the 'top' of the hierarchy, the central metropoles (which still include European cities such as London and Paris) are typified by the presence of control functions (including the allocation of production to other regions), research, design and development, and by the significant presence of managerial and technical strata (it is this presence, rather than the absence of manual work, which is distinctive).

In order to clarify the content of the term 'spatial division of labour' it is worth elaborating in what ways this is a different form of use by capital of spatial differentiation from the form described as sectoral spatial specialization. First, and most obviously, it is not a sectoral geographical division. It is an intra-sectoral division of labour within the overall process of production of an individual capital. Second, as already mentioned, regional inequality is inherent in its very nature, and not merely a consequence of its demise, as was the case with sectoral spatial specialization.

Third, and most importantly, its effects are different. Thus, although some of the 'indices of inequality' to which we have become accustomed may still be relevant, not all of them will be, and it may be necessary to devise others to capture the effects of this new form of differentiation. The important aspects of disparities in skill, control and wage levels have already been referred to. Perhaps the effect most commonly cited, however, is that, as a result of the high degree of external control at the 'bottom' end of the locational hierarchy, such regions have extremely 'open' economies. There are a number of implications of this openness. The first is that the regional economy is at the mercy of external economic changes. This is often argued to be a new effect, but in fact, as the 1930s showed, internally controlled sectoral specialization has similar implications. But in two other ways, the effects of openness in this spatial division of labour *are* very different from those in the case of sectoral spatial specialization. Moreover, both are related to the fact that openness is here a result of external control. The first is the likelihood of a very low local employment multiplier effect. The second is the probability of remissions of interest, profits and dividends to a parent plant outside the region of production.

The fourth way in which this form of spatial division differs from the first is that it implies a rather different geographical configuration of 'problem-areas' – as has been mentioned, it is a component of the present collapse of inner cities, both within and outside the assisted areas.

Fifth, and finally, a similarity: the development of this new spatial division of labour is once again a product of changes in production which are themselves a response to wider economic forces. The present crises of profitability and of markets have considerably reinforced both the pressure to increase the size of individual companies (with the implications already mentioned) and the pressure to reduce the costs of labour (see Massey, 1976; Massey and Meegan, 1979).

## Some implications

It is quite possible that what has been discussed so far seems unexceptionable. However, if such an approach is taken seriously, it would appear to have substantial implications for certain assumptions commonly made at the moment about the nature and causes of 'regional problems'.

Perhaps the major point to be made is that questions of regional problems and policy are normally analysed as problems solely of geographical distribution. The previous framework and examples, however, emphasized their basis in the form and level of the process of *production*, and its relation to the existing pattern of geographical inequality. The normal emphasis simply on geographical distributional outcome goes along with a predisposition for analysis to concentrate only on space, on spatial differentiation, and on changes in the spatial surface. In fact, while spatial changes are most certainly important, the foregoing discussion has indicated that one should not assume that the rest of the relevant world remains constant over time. The requirements of production also change – in response to the pressures of the international and national economic system – and, therefore, so does the relevance to production of any given form of spatial differentiation.

An example is in order, so as to avoid any impression that only straw people are being attacked here. We shall concentrate on the issue of 'convergence' already referred to (and documented in Keeble, 1976; 1977). As has already been said, such convergence refers only to certain indicators, and by no means foreshadows the end of the regional problem, but clearly some changes are underway. Why?

In fact, most studies which cover this period (the mid-1960s to the early 1970s) are absolutely clear on the matter – the convergence was due to regional policy. Now, while I do *not* wish to argue that policy did not have an effect, it is interesting to examine a bit more closely how this conclusion is frequently reached. A common procedure is to project through time some notion of 'what would have happened', and then to analyse deviations from this putative behaviour pattern. The variable which is projected in this way is normally industrial location behaviour – or some effect of it, such as the inter-regional distribution of manufacturing employment – with appropriate proxy adjustments, for instance for cyclical variations in pressure of demand. The question asked is: did this effect of locational behaviour show any significant change around the mid-1960s – in other words at the period when regional policy was strengthened?

The method of inquiry, therefore, is couched entirely in terms of an explanation of changes in the locational behaviour of industry which relies on changes, not in industry itself, but only in the environment within which the locational decision takes place (the locational surface). In so far as production is considered, it is dealt with by trend projections. Such a method does not allow for account to be taken of any structural shifts within the economy. Neither does quantitative trend projection yield any information on the mechanisms underlying those trends. But it is precisely those mechanisms which may imply significant changes in the locational requirements of industry.[2] In contrast, the application of regional policy is seen as having increased in intensity relatively suddenly in the mid-1960s.

Now regional policy *was* certainly increased in intensity in the mid-1960s, and it certainly did alter the locational surface – for instance by changing the distribution of costs. But it is also true that over this period enormous changes have taken place within industry itself. Moreover, some of these changes increased in importance in the mid-1960s – precisely the period from which the phases both of intensive regional policy and of convergence also date. There have been structural changes both in the world economy and in the UK's relation to it. Competition has become more severe. There has been a collapse of profitability and a decline of markets. There is at the present moment in the UK the most serious economic crisis since the 1930s. It can hardly be expected that these events would fail to have an effect on production. The relevant point here is that these developments have increased the relative importance of changes within the production processes of a number of sectors of industry. Moreover, our own research indicates clearly that these changes in production have in turn changed the locational requirements of the sectors concerned, and changed them in a manner which would indicate some tendency, quite independent of regional policy, towards convergence (see, for a detailed report on this, Massey and Meegan, 1979; and Massey, 1976). The 'labour factor' is a case in point. Thus, as already indicated in the consideration of spatial divisions of labour, recent changes in production in some sectors have tended to reduce the general level of skill requirements, and thus to free industry from former locational constraints. Relatively, availability and low cost of labour are increasing in importance for many direct-production processes, in comparison with skill and adaptability. And it is in availability and low cost that peripheral regions have an advantage (see the review of evidence presented in Keeble, 1976, ch. 4). In other words, as well as the spatial surface changing, the response of certain industries to a *given* form of regional inequality – the nature of their spatial division of labour – may be being redefined. Given that some of the sectors affected in this way are quantitatively significant in the present evolution of spatial employment patterns, such changes could well be important components of the process of convergence which has been registered on certain indices of employment and unemployment.

The changes in regional distribution of employment, therefore, could be being contributed to, not only by regional policy, but also by the effects of the present crisis on industry's requirements. But many approaches to regional policy evaluation do not even include this as a possibility. Regional policy – i.e., the spatial surface – emerges as the only explanation because it is the only explanatory factor which is allowed to vary over time. The demands of industry are held constant. In fact, from the evidence I have examined, I should argue that it is likely that the *combination* of changes, in industry and in policy has been mutually reinforcing.[3] But the point which really emerges out of this illustrative example is that, commonly, the regional distribution of employment (and consequently the 'regional problem') is not just seen as a spatial *phenomenon*, it is also (if only implicitly) interpreted as being the result of purely spatial *processes*.

Something of an aside is necessary here. It should not be thought that the above discussion is intended to present an alternative analysis of changing regional patterns. It merely indicates an important component not considered by most current approaches. The changing use of space by a number of important sectors, and the emergence of new forms of spatial division of labour, have not on their own produced the considerable changes in spatial pattern at present under way. It has been combined with other effects of the economic crisis. In particular, it has been increased in relative importance – and consequently in its impact – by the slackening of the rate of growth of a number of sectors of manufacturing output. In such a situation, while new investment in capacity embodying new technology may continue, in response to competitive pressures to reduce costs, it will now – more than in a period of fast growth – be 'compensated for' by the scrapping of the least profitable capacity. (In a period of fast growth, in contrast, such new investment could simply add to capacity.) There is thus a double spatial effect. The new technology embodied in the new investment may enable, and require, a changed location, while employment is lost at the original point of production. Empirical investigation of such behaviour, and a detailed formal framework for its analysis is at present being elaborated in work by the present author and Richard Meegan at CES.[4] The points to note in relation to the present argument are the following. First, *even if* the new investment is located in Development Areas entirely as a result of regional policy (which the previous argument about production technology would at least throw open to question) it is not this alone which would account for convergence. If the original location is in a Development Area there will of course not necessarily *be* convergence. And if the original location is in a non-assisted part of the country, it is not the location of the new investment alone, but its combination with a loss of jobs in the non-assisted area, which produces convergence. Second, it is necessary, if such phenomena are occurring, to be careful about the claims made for the effect of regional policy (or, in other words, purely spatial changes). While it will be true, on these assumptions, that the Development Areas will have more jobs than otherwise, this is not the same as regional policy accounting for convergence. Still less does it mean that regional policy has been a success. The regional problem continues. But third, and most important, is that such developments are crucially a result of changes, not in spatial configuration within the UK, but in the relation of the UK to the world economy as a whole.

In summary, I am not at all arguing that regional policy has had no effect (and certainly not that it should be discontinued). It is, however, important that assessments of this effect do not fail to take account of the changes going on in industry itself. Too many current interpretations of changing regional patterns ignore this relation to production and to the overall economic system. Too frequently spatial distribution is given its own autonomous existence. The fact that each form of distribution is the result of specific forms of production is lost. This, in turn, enables problems which are in fact direct results of the productive system to be treated as matters entirely of spatial arrangement. The second thread of what is being argued is that, in any case, the convergence of regions on certain indices does not *in any way* imply an end to regional inequality. It is not merely that this is a convergence in a context of overall decline, but that, with the emergence of new forms of use of spatial unevenness by industry, the very *form* of regional inequality may to some degree be changing.

In what sense, then, are 'regional' problems *regional* problems? Clearly such inequalities do not result from a simple absolute deficiency. They are, rather, the outcome of the changing relationship between the require-ments of private production for profit and the spatial surface. Again, while such a statement may appear as the essence of the obvious, its implications are frequently ignored. How many times has the 'inner-city problem' been 'explained' in terms of characteristics totally internal to those areas? – to a supposed lack of skilled labour (the bulk of the evidence being to the contrary – see, for instance, Massey and Meegan, 1978), to the actions of planners (hardly likely, anyway, to be a dominant cause), or, worst of all, to the psychological propensities and sociological characteristics of their inhabitants? In fact, the reasons have changed over time, but the recent dramatic decline has resulted from pressures similar to those already mentioned – pressures for rationalization and restructuring which derive from the crisis of the economy as a whole (see also Falk and Martinos, 1975). Again, how often are the problems of peripheral regions laid at the door of 'a lack of native entrepreneurship', a 'deficiency of atmosphere of growth'? But these are effects, not causes (and indeed if they are causes the policy implications are hard to imagine); Firn (1975) gives some hints of the mechanisms involved.

By this means, regional problems are conceptualized, not as problems *experienced by* regions, but as problems for which, somehow, those regions are to blame. Moreover, this subtle substitution of geographical distribution alone for its combination with the changing requirements of production has a political effect. As with all purely 'distributional strug-gles', it is divisive: it sets one region against another, the inner cities against the peripheral regions, when the real problem lies at the aggregate level, in an overall deficiency of jobs, for instance, or an overall problem of de-skilling.

For what is at issue is the changing form of creation, and of use, by industry of specific types of spatial differentiation. Regional inequality is not a frictional or abnormal outcome of capitalist production. As the first example of a spatial division of labour indicated, the process of capital investment has historically normally been one of the opening up of some areas, and the desertion of others. The inner cities, at this moment, are being deserted. They are, moreover, being deserted for reasons relating directly to the requirements of internationally competitive and profitable production. The Community Development Project (1977) put it well:

> It is clear that there are similarities between the way in which the urban problem is being discovered, defined and tackled now and the way the regional problem was taken up during and after the depression. Both are ways of defining particular problems of capital as problems of certain spatial areas, due to the characteristics of those areas. The importance of this technique is that it diverts attention from the way in which the problems that appear in particular places are really particular manifestations of general problems – problems of the way the economic system operates.
>
> Such an approach also puts across the problems of these areas, regions, inner cities and so on, so that they seem *marginal* – not in the sense of unimportant, but certainly peculiar to these areas; while things in general, of course, are fundamentally alright and 'normal'. All that remains to be done is to equalise indices of deprivation, achieve a 'balanced' population, and so on. (p. 55)

I would suggest, however, that the problem goes deeper than that. For it is also the case that spatial inequity may be positively *useful* for unplanned private production for profit. It may be the fact of spatial separation which enables the preservation for a longer period than otherwise of certain favourable conditions of production – low wages and lack of militancy may be easier to ensure in isolated areas, dependent maybe on only one or two sources of employment. The ability of a firm to move, say from an area in which labour is well organized to an area in which it is not, may well make easier – for the firm – the introduction of new production methods which involve a change of workforce. The analysis by Secchi of the Italian 'regional problem' reports on work which argues that

> the existence and growth of regional inequalities made the Italian economic system more flexible in terms of labour supply than it would have been in a better balanced regional situation, given an equal rate of employment in the various sectors of the economy; or, in other words, that it gave the Italian economic system the possibility of a higher rate of technical progress for a given investment rate, than would have occurred in a well-balanced regional situation. (1977, p. 36)

Finally, some comments on policy. While clearly the analysis so far indicates that the problem is not simply soluble, neither does that mean one can do nothing. First, at the simplest level of all, it is important to recognize that the problem will change – in nature and in geography. My contention is that something of that order is happening now. But it will only be possible to get to grips with analysing what is happening now if an effort is made to go beyond essentially statistical techniques and distributional outcomes to understand theoretically the mechanisms behind the numbers. Second, if the 'regional problem' is not a problem produced by regions, but by the organization of production itself, neither is its solution simply a technical question. If production for profit may actually both imply and require such inequality, the issue of policy must be 'who pays?' There is a need to make explicit, political choices. Finally, the implication of this analysis is that intervention in spatial distribution cannot be divorced from issues of intervention at the level of production. To see regional policy and regional problems as simply questions of spatial distribution is completely inadequate.

London
published in 1979

# Notes

1 It must be emphasized that this spatial division of labour *only characterizes certain sectors*, but sectors which appear to be important in the present establishment of new aggregate geographical patterns of economic activity.
2 This criticism applies also to the normal method of assessing the effect on regional employment distribution of the absolute decline in manufacturing employment. This decline is normally considered simply as a quantitative constraint (for instance on the availability of mobile manufacturing employment). In fact it is itself only a reflection, but a reflection of important underlying changes – of increasingly critical conditions facing manufacturing industry, and of its response in terms both of declining rate of growth of output and of relatively increasing growth of labour productivity – with all the attendant implications for production and locational requirements.
3 By 'mutually reinforcing' is meant more than simply the operation of industry and policy changes as additive factors. In particular, changes in production may have been one of the pre-conditions for advantage to be taken of regional policy. It is also possible, of course, as a number of authors argue, that the combination worked also the other way around – that regional policy (through the grants available at a period of restricted company liquidity) in turn encouraged or even enabled some of the investment in new processes of production.
4 The Centre for Environmental Studies.

# References

Chisholm, M. and Oeppen J. (1973) *The Changing Pattern of Employment: Regional Specialisation and Industrial Localisation in Britain*. Croom Helm, London.
Community Development Project (1977) *The Costs of Industrial Change*.

Dixon, R.J. and Thirwall, A.P. (1975) *Regional Growth and Unemployment in the United Kingdom*. Macmillan, London.

Dunford, M.F. (1977) 'Regional policy and the restructuring of capital', Sussex University: Urban and Regional Studies, Working Paper 4.

Falk, N. and Martinos, H. (1975) *'Inner City'*, Fabian Research Series 320, May.

Firn, J. (1975) 'External control and regional development: the case of Scotland', *Envir. Plann., A* 7: 393–414.

Hall, P. (1974) *Urban and Regional Planning*. Penguin Books, Geography and Environmental Studies, Harmondsworth, Middlesex.

Keeble, D. (1976) *Industrial Location and Planning in the United Kingdom*. Methuen, London.

—— (1977) 'Spatial policy in Britain: regional or urban?' *Area*, 9: 3–8.

Lipietz, A. (1977) *Le Capital et son espace*, Maspéro. Economie et Socialisme.

Massey, D.B. (1976) 'Restructuring and regionalism: some spatial effects of the crisis'. Paper presented to American Regional Science Association. Centre for Environmental Studies, Working Note 449.

Massey, D.B. and Meegan, R.A. (1978) 'Restructuring vs the cities', *Urban Studies*, 15; this vol. ch. 1.

—— (1979) 'The geography of industrial reorganisation: the spatial effects of the restructuring of the electrical engineering sector under the Industrial Reorganisation Corporation', *Progress in Planning*, vol. 10, pt. 3. Pergamon, Oxford.

McCrone, G. (1969) *Regional Policy in Britain*, Unwin, University of Glasgow: Social and Economic Studies, 15.

—— (1975) 'The determinants of regional growth rates' in *Economic Sovereignty and Regional Policy* (Vaizey, J. ed.), pp. 63–79. Gill & Macmillan, Dublin.

McDermott, P.J. (1976) 'Ownership, organisation and regional dependence in the Scottish electronics industry', *Reg. Studies*, 10: 319–35.

NEDO Electronics EDC (1972) Annual Statistical Survey of the Electronics Industry, HMSO, London.

—— Industrial Review to 1977: Electronics, HMSO, London.

North, D. and Leigh, R. (1976) 'Reflections on the micro-behavioural approach to regional analysis'. Paper presented to the ninth annual conference of the Regional Science Association, mimeo.

Secchi, B. (1977) Central and peripheral regions in a process of economic development: The Italian case, in *Alternative Frameworks for Analysis* (Massey, D.B. and Batey, P.W.J. eds). London Papers in Regional Science, vol. 7. Pion, London.

Trade and Industry (1977) Regional Development Programme for the United Kingdom, *Trade and Industry*, 11 February, pp. 358–62.

Westaway, J. (1974) 'The spatial hierarchy of business organisations and its implications for the British urban system', *Reg. Studies*, 8: 145–55.

# 3

# *The Shape of Things to Come*

## The changing composition of the workforce

The British labour-force is not what it was twenty years ago. The immediate disaster of Thatcherism has thrown into high relief major changes in its composition. Employment in manufacturing has collapsed since the 1979 election. Skilled manual jobs are being cut back drastically. There has even been a drop in the total workforce. It has felt like devastation, and it has been. But the intensity of the effect of Tory policies should not blind us to the fact that underlying them are longer-run processes of change. The working class, and the labour-force more generally, are undergoing structural changes in composition.

They are profound changes, profound enough to mean that some of the old ways of thinking and working are no longer adequate or appropriate. The labour movement too, if it is to keep ahead of events, must restructure itself, recognize the shifts, address new questions.

But it is not only the social composition of the labour-force that is changing. Its geography is also being transformed. The urban and regional structure of the Britain of tomorrow (even after, that is, some recovery from Thatcher) will be different from what we have come to know, and to know how to work within. Regional divisions are being broken down. To be sure, the old north/south divide is being reinforced in terms of voting patterns, but it is not the same old north/south divide of the 1930s. Further, the pattern in which most working-class jobs, particularly in manufacturing, were gathered in the towns and cities is crumbling. 'Rural areas' are no longer places without major non-agricultural employment.

This changing geography compounds the challenge facing the labour movement. The changing location of industry breaks down established relations between workplaces, and between workplaces and communities. And the new locations are different. The factory or office is situated in a different context, to which previous forms of organization may be inappropriate. Geographical change can, in other words, alter the wider social context of the politics of the workplace at the same time as the social composition of the workforce itself is changing. And, indeed, the two processes are related. The geographical reorganization of British capital has been fundamental to all its attempts over the last twenty years or so to become more competitive, hold down wages, restructure itself out of crisis. Geographical restructuring has already been important to capital, and it should be important to labour.

## The national level

At the national level there have been significant changes in balance between different elements of the workforce. Figure 3.1 shows one of the divisions which has long been central to labour movement organization – that between manual and non-manual workers. Manual workers, from having made up over 60 per cent of the working population in 1961 are now down to only about 50 per cent.[1] This change in the shape of the labour-force has been going on throughout the post-war period – manual workers having declined by about 5 per cent as a proportion of the total workforce in each post-war decade. To some extent what these figures reflect is the loss of jobs in manufacturing. This too is now a well-established phenomenon. The number of jobs in manufacturing in 1961

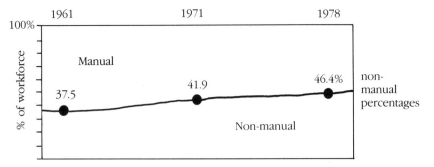

*Source*: calculated from Warwick University Manpower Research Group

**Figure 3.1** *The changing balance between manual and non-manual workers.*

**Table 3.1** *Occupational changes 1961–1978* (% of workforce)

|  | 1961 | 1971 | 1978 |
|---|---|---|---|
| Administrators, managers | 6.6 | 7.8 | 8.7 |
| Professionals | 6.6 | 8.1 | 9.8 |
| Engineers and technicians | 3.5 | 4.2 | 4.7 |
| Clerical workers | 14.0 | 15.0 | 15.9 |
| Craft workers | 19.7 | 17.6 | 15.9 |
| Skilled operatives | 3.2 | 3.1 | 2.7 |
| Other operatives | 22.9 | 20.4 | 18.5 |
| Personal services | 8.9 | 10.5 | 11.2 |
| Other | 14.6 | 13.4 | 12.5 |
|  | 100 | 100 | 100 |

*Source*: Warwick Manpower Research Group

was 8.2m. Since then it has fallen by a quarter and, from 36 per cent in 1961, manufacturing now makes up only 28 per cent of jobs in the economy.

These major shifts are mirrored in the changing occupational structure of the workforce. Within the generally expanding non-manual groups, it has been the higher-status jobs which have been growing fastest as a proportion of the total workforce. And this growth has been accompanied by shifts in the internal composition of each group. The particularly rapid rise in importance of professionals, for example, has been due especially to public sector expansion (we are talking here of the last twenty years!) in health and education. Similarly that wide spectrum of occupations referred to in table 3.1 as 'engineers and technicians' has seen engineering-based professionals, draftspeople, and so forth, dwindling in importance, while the computer whiz-kid and the research scientist increase in both numbers and status. The managers and administrators have expanded in all parts of the economy: public sector and private, manufacturing and services. In contrast, the increase in the number of clerical workers is not so marked – each clerical worker is evidently now supporting more professionals. The declining groups reflect the obverse of these processes. And here, too, there are significant shifts in the internal composition of each category – the generally declining 'other operatives' group, for instance, includes a growing army of assembly workers.

## Participation of women

Perhaps best known and most important is the increased participation of women in the paid workforce. Figure 3.2 gives some details. The rise in the number of women in the labour-force has not in fact been steady (the figure for 1982 is actually below that for 1964). But the increase in the proportion of the workforce which is female has been far more consistent. This obviously reflects what is happening to male employment – the recent dramatic collapse of jobs for men resulting in a rise in the importance of women in the workforce even though their own numbers were shrinking too.

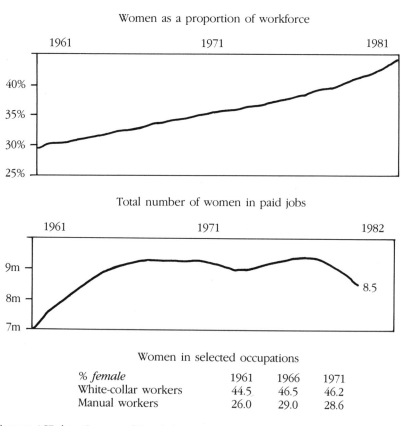

Women as a proportion of workforce

Total number of women in paid jobs

Women in selected occupations

| % female | 1961 | 1966 | 1971 |
|---|---|---|---|
| White-collar workers | 44.5 | 46.5 | 46.2 |
| Manual workers | 26.0 | 29.0 | 28.6 |

*Sources*: ACE data; *Censuses of Population*

**Figure 3.2**   *Women in the workforce*

But these are all national changes. They are substantial enough as they stand, but they also hide a lot else which has been going on. For these national changes are highly differentiated from one part of the country to another and very different kinds of class changes and shifts in social composition are under way in different regions. A new geography is in the making.

Behind this new geography lie a number of interlocking processes. Each of them is related to long-term shifts in the economy as a whole and to the changing place of Britain in the international system. They can, roughly, be divided into two groups: elements of the geography of decline on the one hand and the emergence of new patterns on the other.

## The geography of decline

The pattern of employment decline in Britain today is actually the result of *two* different patterns, the one superimposed upon the other. On the one hand, there is the long-term decline of a range of 'old basic' sectors; on the other hand, there is the newer, though by now also well-established, loss of employment in manufacturing. These two waves of decline hail originally from different periods, each reflecting the previous dominance of different international divisions of labour, and different structures of the British economy. Each, too, has its own particular geography.

### *The thirties revisited*

First, there is the long-term decline of jobs for men in the old basic industries of the Development Areas – south Wales, central Scotland, the north-east of England. The loss of jobs in industries such as coal mining and shipbuilding, which once formed the economic core of these areas, has been going on for much of this century. It was the collapse of these pillars of empire which lay behind the regional concentrations of unemployment and the appalling poverty in these areas in the thirties. (Unemployment rates in the south-east were relatively low.) And it was the sudden and rapid loss of jobs in these industries (particularly shipbuilding) which heralded for British industry the end of the long post-war boom and, with that, the re-emergence of 'the regional problem'. Since then the loss of jobs has varied in pace and been modulated by economic climate and political strategy. The contraction of this central element of the working class, then, is long term, and it has had and continues to have a very definite geographical pattern. It is the decline of employment in these industries which is at the heart of the 'traditional' form of the British regional problem.

But that well-known pattern is now being overlaid by another, equally dramatic, pattern of decline.

## Deindustrialization

Deindustrialization – reflected in the loss of jobs in manufacturing – has hit the headlines under Margaret Thatcher. But it, too, is a longer-term phenomenon. The absolute *number* of jobs in manufacturing has been shrinking in the UK for nearly twenty-five years now – ever since the mid-1960s. And manufacturing's *share* of total employment has been declining for far longer.

Deindustrialization is certainly of a different order under this government. It has accelerated, and it has spread to virtually all manufacturing sectors. Moreover, it is not just employment, it is also output which is now falling. In the late sixties job loss in manufacturing took place in a context of rapidly rising productivity and technological change (it was the age of the white heat and productivity agreements). Today, far more of it is due simply to the closure of capacity. So there is no question but that what is happening now is of a different order. But the decline of jobs in manufacturing is not itself a new phenomenon.

Now, the geography of the decline of manufacturing is very different from that of the decline of the old basic sectors. For one thing, it is more general – it is not confined to two or three regions of the country. But it does have a definite geographical pattern. The first areas to be hit by deindustrialization were the cities. Greater London has seen the most spectacular falls. Every five years from 1961 to 1976 200,000 manufacturing jobs were lost from the city's economy. By the end of last year the number of manufacturing jobs in the GLC area was only two-fifths of what it had been in 1961.

A large proportion of the overall decline of jobs in urban areas has in fact been due simply to this decline of manufacturing industry. There has been a relative 'shift' of employment from bigger cities towards smaller towns and more rural areas. But the term 'shift' (the term most frequently used) can give the impression that the whole thing took place through actual geographical movement. It didn't. Much of it has been a process of differential growth and decline. A large part of the loss of manufacturing jobs in major urban areas has taken place through straightforward closure, with no new investment elsewhere – or certainly not in the UK.

## Decline of the cities

The loss of manufacturing jobs in the cities has not, for the most part, been because they had a high proportion of jobs in industries which were declining fastest nationally. It was not, in other words, a result of the cities' industrial structure – as it was the industrial structure of south Wales and the north-east which lay behind the collapse of their employment in the thirties. The cities suffered most because, *within* particular industries, they tended to have the oldest factories and the oldest production techniques. Most of all they had the lowest levels of labour productivity.

There were other reasons, too. In a number of cases we studied in the late 1960s, management argued that it was easier to close a plant in a large and complex labour market than in a smaller town – the job losses are absorbed, the unemployment diluted, and less 'blame' gets pinned on the individual company.[2] It was also the case that workers in the cities had often won higher wages and, in manufacturing industries, were better organized than those in more out-of-town locations. Whether explicitly motivated or not, the decline of manufacturing industry in the cities has certainly taken with it some of the old bastions of trade union strength.

But it is not *only* the cities which have been hit. As deindustrialization has accelerated, it has spread both to more and more industries and to more and more places. The regions which have been worst affected have been those with the greatest reliance on manufacturing. The economies of the engineering-based regions, in particular the west midlands and the north-west, have been shattered. Manufacturing employment in the north-west has been falling since the early sixties, gradually picking up speed to lose 20 per cent between 1966 and 1976. In the west midlands manufacturing jobs carried on increasing until the early seventies. But in the four years from 1978 to 1982 each of those two regions lost over 200,000 jobs, a further 20 per cent of the manufacturing workforce in each case.

## The changing map of unemployment

So two contrasting patterns of job loss, stemming initially from very different eras, have in recent years been superimposed upon each other. The result is that the map of unemployment is now very different from the one we have been used to since the thirties. Some elements have acquired an apparent permanence – the unemployment rate in Northern Ireland is now almost 20 per cent. But the rates in the north-west and the west midlands are now above that of Scotland. Only the south-east stands

**Table 3.2** *Unemployment 1983
(seasonally adjusted)*

| Region | % |
| --- | --- |
| Scotland | 14.6 |
| North | 16.7 |
| Northern Ireland | 19.6 |
| North-west | 15.4 |
| Wales | 16.2 |
| South-west | 11.4 |
| Yorkshire and Humberside | 13.8 |
| West midlands | 15.6 |
| East midlands | 11.8 |
| East Anglia | 11.1 |
| South-east | 9.4 |

*Source*: Department of Employment, February 1983

out as significantly better than the national average. And that itself conceals enormous differences. Within each region, the inner cities of the major conurbations have rates of unemployment far above the national average. In London most inner-area boroughs have more in common with inner cities elsewhere than with the outer-metropolitan area.

## The shape of the new: geographical restructuring

But it is not all decline. The employment which remains is also being restructured geographically. And the sectors which are growing (at least over the longer term) have very different geographical patterns from the ones they are replacing. The way industry makes use of the British space is being reorganized. This process has been particularly marked since the mid-1960s when pressures of increasing international competition and a shifting world order began to enforce a restructuring of British industry. That restructuring has changed a number of times in both its form and its pace in the years since then. But its net result has been to produce a major shift in the social geography of the workforce. The geography of each element of that workforce is being reorganized. And this is happening at the same time, remember, as the balance between these different elements is also shifting (table 3.1).

The changing balance of corporate structures in the economy is reflected most obviously in the changing geography of management. This is discussed next. Having established that framework, it is then easier to examine the internal reorganization of the rest of the workforce, concentrating here on the categories of production and clerical workers, and scientists and technicians.

## The geography of management

Look first, because it is the simplest, at the changing geography of management. At the heart of this change is the increasing size of individual companies and the growing dominance of the top few hundred firms. As firms have grown there has been a tendency for their head offices and upper echelons of administrative, marketing, financial and legal staff to be split off spatially from production, and increasingly the tendency is for them to be concentrated in London and the south-east of England. As table 3.1 showed, this stratum of managerial and associated groups has been expanding as a proportion of the national population, and it should be stressed that employment in this kind of white-collar work has been growing in all regions.

But as it has grown it has also become more highly differentiated, both functionally and socially; management hierarchies have lengthened. And hand in hand with this increasing social differentiation has gone increasing geographical differentiation. The lengthening managerial hierarchies, with their associated hierarchies of functions and social status, have been stretched out over space. And the geographical pattern has taken on a very definite form – the higher-level functions, the ultimate control over production, over the relations of economic ownership and possession, and the upper echelons of social strata with which such functions are associated – are increasingly concentrated in the bottom right-hand corner of the country. In 1977, 350 of the top 500 UK companies had their headquarters, and therefore all their top management, in London and the south-east. In contrast, the lower the level of management, the nearer to actual production it tends to be geographically. And while HQs concentrate in the south-east, the corollary is that other regions are increasingly becoming 'branch-plant' economies.

## Decentralization of production and clerical jobs

In contrast to what has happened to management, and contrary to a long and dearly held thesis on the left, the concentration and centralization of capital in ownership terms has *not* led to the geographical concentration of jobs in *production*. Indeed, at precisely the same time as the concentration (both spatial and a-spatial) of ownership and control has been going on, the location of production itself has become more decentralized, both within individual regions, outwards from cities, and from the south-east and midlands of England to the regions of the north and west.

Some of this relative shift has been associated with changes in the technology of production. In a whole range of industries the kind of technological change which has been going on over the last twenty years or so has been associated with a changing demand for labour. Industries such as telecommunications, parts of electrical engineering, and electronics, are the most obvious examples. In such industries, both changes in the product (e.g. in telecommunications from electro-mechanical to semi-electronic switching gear) and changes in the production process towards more highly mechanized techniques or techniques involving major assembly stages have gone along with a shift in the kind of labour employed. The archetypal shift is from male manual workers classified as skilled to female assemblers classified as unskilled or semi-skilled.

Such changes in the social composition of the labour-force are often accompanied by geographical recomposition. They have 'freed' industry from its traditional sources of labour in the old centres of manufacturing skills and have been part and parcel of a significant decentralization to pastures, and labour-forces, new. The existing workforce has been abandoned and new and different labour employed in areas with no tradition in the industry, or indeed any industry at all. The social recomposition of the labour-force, changes in the technology of production, and changes in location are in such cases integral to one another.

## The service sector

Technical change has been one significant force behind the decentralization of production, but it has not been the only one. There has also been a significant outward movement of manufacturing jobs, particularly jobs traditionally done by women, but where there has been little technological change in production. Here the driving force has been to find cheaper sources of labour. The clothing industry is a good example. In the sixties it was caught in a vice. It was under competition from low-cost imports. But its own usual supply of women workers in urban areas (particularly London) was threatened by the expansion of the service sector. Big firms in the industry solved the dilemma by changing location. New sources of labour, more vulnerable and with fewer alternative sources of employment, were sought out. The new source of labour was older, married women, the new locations were smaller towns, trading estates and sometimes quite isolated locations in the peripheral regions of the country – the rural areas such as the south-west and old heavy-industry areas such as the coalfields.

Nor has it just been manufacturing which has decentralized. Not many years later the service sector adopted the same strategy, and new geographical patterns of employment were developed there too. Both clerical wages and office rents decline once you get further than about sixty miles from London, and from the 1970s departments of the central state and large private sector firms began decentralizing the more routine elements of clerical work. Clerical workers are an increasingly important part of the labour-force (see table 3.1), and this decentralization is therefore a significant element of its changing geography. Longbenton in the north-east is a classic example – 6,000 clerical workers process you through the DHSS here. Driving licences are issued by nearly 4,000 similar workers in Swansea. In some areas, such as the north-east, this has represented an increase in jobs available to women where there had been precious little before. In other cases the service industry arrived to compete with others, in the east midlands, for example, chasing the shoe industry (with many of the same pressures on it as in clothing) even further north.

## Scientists and technicians

While these changes have been affecting workers directly involved in production, other things have been going on at the other end of the social spectrum. An increasing proportion of the workforce is engaged in research and development and related activities, either in the research establishments of major corporations in a wide variety of industries, or in independent 'business-services' of various sorts (software consultancies, for example), or in the newly-developing high-tech sectors. To some extent the growth of this element of the workforce is bound up with the same technological changes which produced the de-skilled and decentralized production jobs. They are the necessary counterpoint to that production labour-force in a long process of the separation of conception from execution.

And their geographical distribution, too, is very different. As with managerial hierarchies, so with the technical division of labour – the separation-out of a whole series of distinct functions, each related to a particular social status, has enabled also their geographical separation. The further you are from production in a functional sense the further you can be distanced geographically. The industrial technologists of a generation and more ago had a far more intimate relationship to the actual process of production than do, except in the prototype stage, the emerging technologists of today. And big companies have taken advantage of that fact, separating out geographically the different parts of the organization into hierarchical geographical structures.

## *The British sunbelt*

The upper echelons of these technocratic strata have increasingly concentrated in a new 'region' of the country – the British sunbelt as it is called, that swathe of tamed rurality which stretches between Bristol, Southampton and round and up to Cambridge. The outer-outer metropolitan area. In startling contrast to the tedious assembly and clerical jobs which have for years been the main new source of employment outside this belt, and particularly in the old coal and steel areas, these jobs are almost all for graduates, and almost all for men.

And it is not just big companies. It is in this stretch of country that the new – and still small – breed of entrepreneur/scientist is gathered. Indeed it is only in this part of the country that 'the small-firm sector' lives up to its image of entrepreneurship and dynamism. What are biotechnology and software consultancies here tend in other areas to be sweatshops and scrap-metal dealers.

But why this part of the country? Certainly there are some plausible economic reasons; but there are social reasons too, and it is arguable that they may be at least equally important. The attraction of the area originally was a combination of accessibility to London and nearness to defence establishments. The latter provided both jobs for technicians and contracts for the growing electronics industry. But since then the place has taken off in another way. The research scientists, the technologists, those working in business services, make up the stratum of the labour-force most able to choose where to live, and assume that jobs will follow. And they do. And jobs do follow. The region *itself* now has a status, a cachet, attached to it. The highly interlinked and individualistic nature of the labour market for these groups reinforces the tendency to clustering, making it difficult for other areas to compete. (And if they do try they have to do it by projecting the same image – semi-rurality, detached housing, 'good' schools.) A whole new style is being created in living, and working, outside the city.

*A new geography*

Were all these trends to continue, the social geography of the British workforce would be transformed.

Compare today and tomorrow with fifty years ago. The old regional specialisms (cotton, coal, cars) have gone. The main regional contrast, in this future, is between control and conception on the one hand and execution on the other, between the sunbelt and the rest.

Of course in fact the picture is more complicated than this. Much of the old geography remains. The west midlands, the north-west, the big cities and the heavy industrial areas of the north and west, still retain much of their old economic structure. The development of the new geography (as opposed to the accelerated decline of the old) has in fact slowed down over the late seventies, and has been interrupted by Thatcherism. The expansion of technicians and professionals, and their concentration into the sunbelt, was at its height in the late sixties and early seventies. So was the growth of jobs in out-of-town and smaller-town locations. Many jobs for women, in the new decentralized branch plants, have disappeared in the last few years. But the shift towards a new geography is a long-term one, and is likely to re-emerge.

## The importance of local diversity

The fact that the social recomposition of the workforce also involves geographical reorganization has a number of implications. Most importantly, it means that completely different kinds of social change can be going on in different localities. Not everywhere mirrors the national pattern – in all likelihood very few places do. The classic picture of the dwindling and disintegration of the heart of the traditional labour movement is found most clearly in the old heavy-industry and coalfield areas (for instance south Wales). In these areas, certainly, there is the fragmentation of a previous, relatively coherent, economic structure based around a few industries, and a few unions. Here too jobs for women are expanding fast and jobs for men contracting, there is a proliferation of industries and employers, often with little connection to each other, and an expansion of white-collar strata.

But it is not everywhere like this. In some more rural areas the numerical importance and the structural coherence of the working class is actually *increasing* over the medium term as a result of the geographical decentralization of industry. Cornwall is an example. Here, new employment has come into an area where the previous economic and social structure was based around self-employment and small-scale employment in agriculture and tourism. Straightforward wage labour has been a very much less important element here than in other regions. Today that picture is changing. The traditional petty bourgeoisie is declining fast, and while a stratum of managers and professionals is certainly expanding, so too is the working class.

So the directions of social recomposition can be quite different from one area to the next. 'National' changes can take highly variegated forms across the country. The decline of the old is not always happening in the same place as the rise of the new. And what that means is that different problems are being faced, different battles fought out, in different places.

## The process of change

And it is important to remember that recomposition is a *process*. What has to be recognized politically is not just some end-state looking very different from what we've been used to, but also a process of social change which may often be difficult and painful. The actual process of change is itself an important determinant of the social and political response.

And this process of change varies locally. Where an area is coming from can be just as important as where it is going to for understanding the political climate. What are apparently similar numerical changes can have very different implications depending on the regional setting. The impact of rising unemployment, for instance, can vary dramatically depending on the wider social context, and on the historical experience of those in the area.

People in the west midlands are newly coping with not being the boom centre of the land. To some extent epitomized by the car workers, it has gone from cocky aggressivity to agreeing to new work practices. There is a real shock of sudden vulnerability and eroding status and relative, as well as real, wages. This shock of the new is in total contrast to the weary and deeply resentful return, yet again, to high unemployment, the status of disaster area, you feel in south Wales, the north-east of England or even Merseyside. In London and the south-east, the lengthy decline of the East End is apparently more like that of the older regions, but here the context is so different. From Docklands you can see the City and if you venture into town you are faced, still, with well-heeled white-collar workers and the denizens of the stockbroker belt.

*The geography of gender relations*

Nor is it just changes in class relations which vary across the country. There is a geography of gender relations, too. Particularly over the last twenty years, women have been increasingly participating in the waged labour-force in all regions, but the increases have been biggest in the peripheral regions (south-west, Wales, Scotland and the north-east), both urban and rural, to which jobs have been decentralized. And once again, the numbers don't tell the whole story. The impact of an increase in women's participation in paid employment depends on the prevailing system of gender relations. And this varies a lot between one part of the country and another.

Possibly the extreme cases are the old heavy industry Development Areas, especially the coalfields. The 'decline' of these regions should be assessed not just from the point of view that they were heavily working-class areas, and highly unionized, but also from the point of view that they were extremely *male*. As far as paid employment is concerned, the opportunities for women have been extremely limited in these regions throughout the century. This has in part been related to the nature of employment for men, and the status attached to it. The demands put on (female) domestic labour by male work down the mine are enormous. Shiftwork, too, makes it more difficult for both partners to be employed outside the home. The ideology of a sexual divison of labour between breadwinner and home-keeper has probably been more firmly entrenched in these areas than anywhere else in the country.

And the associated attitudes spread beyond the domestic sphere. In clubs, in politics, in unions, women have been excluded from all but a very minor role, perhaps especially in post-war years. Attitudes existed which would be unthinkable in Lancashire, say, or London. The now-mourned homogeneity of the labour movement in these regions was based around a rigid sexual divison of labour. And the shift in the sexual balance of the paid labour-force has sorely disrupted this established set of practices and relations. So much so, indeed, that the late sixties and seventies saw calls, from male trade unionists, academics and politicians alike, for more jobs specifically for men and, in some cases, fewer jobs for women – a House of Commons memorandum pleaded that the established sexual balance of employment should not be too severely disrupted.

It is interesting to speculate on the degree to which this highly patriarchial past has been one of the conditions for the threat currently posed to it. Certainly, given the previous reliance on female domestic labour, the decline of male employment was an important condition for the formation of the women of these areas into a 'reserve of labour'. They were, moreover, a particularly attractive one, from industry's point of view. More than almost anywhere else in the country they lacked previous experience of employment in capitalist wage relations. They were real 'green labour'. And their previous exclusion from public life seemed to make them ideal. To the extent that it was complicit in the rigidity of the sexual divison of labour in these regions, and in the exclusion of women from so many social activities, the old traditional heart of the (male) labour movement may well itself have been party to the creation of the new super-cheap labour-forces industry was searching out in the sixties and seventies. Certainly, the geography of gender relations has been an important element in British industry's attempts to reorganize geographically; to restructure itself out of crisis.

## Local politics and national politics

In the sixties and seventies much of the importance of 'local politics' was seen to be in linking the local to the national, the particularities of a local area to the wider underlying mechanisms of a capitalist society. Failure to make that link was often seen as failure of the exercise as a whole. That job is still there, still needs to be done. But it did perhaps lead to a tendency to see *only* the 'wider capitalist system' at work in every local situation. The local particularities were seen as something to be cleared away to reveal what was *really* happening. But part of the importance of local politics is precisely in learning how that 'capitalist system' gets worked out in people's lives in the detailed specificity of a vast variety of local situations. 'What is really happening' *is* actually very varied. Unity between those situations isn't constructed only by proclaiming that each and every local change is underlain by capitalism: only, in other words, by asserting 'the general'. It also needs, for a solid foundation, a recognition and understanding of the reality and conditions of diversity, and of the actual processes which link the local particularities.

Geographical diversity matters politically in other ways, too. Above all it can be divisive. It is not just that 'national' changes are reflected in a geographically differentiated form, but that geographical diversity can be used as a weapon in a wider politics. The way this happens can vary, has varied, widely. In the sixties, that combination of technological change and locational change which was mentioned earlier often set workers in one area against those in another, in the context of an individual company. More recently, as that process has slowed down, and high unemployment has spread to more and more places, 'inter-area competition' has become a weapon in the hands of both individual companies and the state. The Nissan episode, with over 100 local authorities competing against each other, has been the most glaring example of the former.

More generally, areas compete with each other by advertising the non-militancy of their labour. Regions are blamed for their own decline. The reputation for militancy of Merseyside workers is the most obvious case. In 1978 there was an attempt to draw up a local social contract; in 1979, just after the election, Prior visited the area to announce that if there were no strikes there for two years, some investment might be forthcoming. Only recently, a report on East Kilbride assured would-be investors that the situation was nothing like as bad as they might have thought – an investigation had shown that the workers there were hardly militant at all! And so the vulnerabilities of particular areas are used in a wider battle between capital and labour.

## The politics of recomposition

The joint social and geographical restructuring of the labour-force is, then, producing very different conditions for political organization and representation from those we have come to know and love. It is easy to feel that all is lost. Indeed a quick survey of socialist thoughts upon the subject of the presently emerging geography of the working class would indicate a depressing assessment of its potential as a base for organization.

Certainly we have been witness to the erosion of well-established and familiar bases. To the long decline of the industrial unions of the old periphery has now been added the subduing of the strength of the west midlands. In many areas the accustomed social infrastructure of organization has been torn apart by industrial decline. At the intra-regional scale, New Towns are well known for the passivity, in general, of their labour-forces. The *process* of geographical recomposition is itself a problem. Much of the strength of the labour movement is constructed around local histories, and their dislocation can produce a sense of placelessness in the strong meaning of that word.

But on its own that negative assessment misses a lot. It is not just decline that is going on; it is recomposition. And there have been such recompositions before. The interwar years saw a massive social and spatial restructuring of employment. It was then that the basic industries plunged into decline; and the new sectors which grew up were completely different. They were at the other end of the country – in the Midlands and southeast. They demanded different skills, implied a different social structure.

And the unions which organized in them (TGWU, NUGMW) were different, too. This is *not* to imply that each and every change should be accepted, nor, certainly, that the present form of spatial recomposition is politically inevitable. It is merely to point out that what we have now was once itself new and untried; the organizational frameworks which are now so familiar themselves had once to be built.

Moreover, much of what is now thought of as new has not been absent before; it has simply been ignored. The past which it is commonly thought we are leaving has been inaccurately mythologized. Take this 'new' entry of women into manual jobs – women now represent about 30 per cent of all manual workers, which is about the same as in 1911! If anything it has been the intervening years which have been the exception. Again, manufacturing employment has *never* been numerically dominant in the economy. And some of the strongest points of the labour movement have always been outside manufacturing – coal mining is the most obvious example.

So there is a need to readjust our stylized image of the past. And, anyway, we should not just be seeking the restoration of the old and well-tried. After all, it wasn't a spectacular success. We cannot re-create the old labour movement of the coalfields, for instance, and it, too, had its share of disadvantages and its own vulnerabilities.

But there *have* been major changes. And they do require a response. Is the outlook, then, as grim as most assessments would have it? Is no response possible?

One counter to the bleakest scenarios of the future is that they are, curiously, very geographically determinist. It is argued, for instance, that the great cities, with their variety of enterprises and industries, and with their anonymity, provided ideal places for union organization, and that that is now gone. In one sense it is true. But that union organization had to be constructed, and the form which it took corresponded to, took advantage of, the setting. That was how that particular 'geography', the urban form, was used to advantage. But by no means all the old centres of trade union strength had those characteristics. Some of the strongest bases were in small, single-industry settlements – colliery villages for example.

There are now different situations, demanding different strategies and forms of organization. The 'new geography' may look pretty unprepossessing at first sight, but there are possibilities. The problems of organizing in multi-regional companies are clear, but such companies do open up new potential contact between areas. It is a difficult potential to grasp, but then it wasn't so simple to build unity on the coalfields either. The growth in numbers, unionization and militancy of public-sector workers offers opportunities at local level for linking employment with community issues, and possibilities at national level for co-ordinated action entailing a presence in every locality, which no other industry provides.

The problem is that the movement always seems to be on the receiving end of such processes: never to hold the initiative. The impetus for industrial restructuring has come in an immediate sense from capital. And much of it is a response to, and an attempt to break, established elements of labour-movement organization. Certainly this has been true spatially. The decline of the cities has had as one element a relative shift away from better organized workers. At the other end of the process the decentralization of production has certainly seen managements seeking out potentially vulnerable and difficult-to-organize workforces. But the fact that that was part of the rationale does not guarantee success. At each end of the process there is now a fight back. The cities are far from dead politically, however much they might be losing jobs. The fact of decline, together with their changing social structure, has been a basis for some of them to become the seedbeds of a new kind of politics, based around new coalitions, and attempting a restructuring more on labour's terms. And it is not just the big cities. The examples of Plessey-Bathgate, of Lee Jeans and Lovable, give notice that capital might just have been mistaken in its assumption that the women workers of 'the regions' would not get organized.[3]

So the situation is *not* all gloom and doom. There are already attempts to respond, to take back some of the initiative. But for that to be possible in a wider way does demand that we recognize the extent and the depth of the structural changes which are going on. It is certainly not that old bases, either socially or geographically, should be abandoned. But it is urgent to recognize both that they themselves are changing and that new bases must be constructed – both amongst the expanding elements of the workforce and in new parts of the country.

London
published in 1983

## Notes

1 Thanks to Nick Miles for help in getting together the data for these figures.
2 Doreen Massey and Richard Meegan, 'The geography of industrial reorganisation', *Progress in Planning* (Oxford, Pergamon), 10 (3), 1979.
3 These were all prominent industrial battles of the time, conducted by women in 'the regions'.

# 4

# *Uneven Development: Social Change and Spatial Divisions of Labour*

## Uneven development

The concept of uneven development, if it is to have any purchase on the structure and dynamics of economy and society more widely, must refer to more than the fact that there are more jobs in some places than others, or even that there are better jobs in some places than others. Such measures are interesting, and they are important, but they do not in themselves link that inequality to its causes in the deeper structures of the organization of society. In order to do this, uneven development must be conceptualized in terms of the basic building-blocks of (in this case, capitalist) society. In this paper those are taken to be classes, and the focus will be quite narrowly on the relations within the economy, as these are assumed to be the primary foundation of class structure.

The term 'relations' is important, and is actually much more appropriate than 'building-blocks'. For the classes are not structured as blocks which exist as discrete entities in society, but are precisely constituted *in relation to* each other. Capitalist is defined in relation to worker, and vice versa. Carling (1986) argues for 'the reinstatement of societies as sets of relationships among individuals (and things)' in order to undermine 'the deeply ingrained habit of seeing societies in terms of hierarchies, pyramids, diamonds, heaps, layer cakes, jellies, blancmanges and other party pieces of social stratification' (p. 30). Where I disagree with him is that the prime focus should be on relationships between *individuals*. Much more impor- tant – certainly from the point of view of the analysis here – are relation- ships between classes and class strata. Where I agree is that the focus should be on relationships.

Different classes in society are defined in relation to each other and, in economic terms, to the overall division of labour. It is the overall structure of those sets of relationships which defines the structure of the economic aspect of society. One important element which any concept of uneven development must relate to, therefore, is the spatial structuring of those relationships – the relations of production – which are unequal relation- ships and which imply positions of dominance and subordination. It is on this that the paper will focus.

The notion of groups/classes being mutually defined by the relation- ships between them goes beyond the obvious case of capitalist and worker. It is not possible to have work which is predominantly 'mental' or 'intellectual' (in spite of the frequently applied epithet of 'knowledge- based society') without manual work. Steve Bell's cartoon in which yup- pies float off into the sky calling 'we don't need dustbins' makes a powerful point. They are wrong. They do. And they need people to empty them.[1] Similarly, it is not possible to have supervisory work without there being activity to supervise. It is not possible to have assembly without the manufacture of components. Thus, the different functions in an economy are held together by mutual definition and mutual necessity.[2] They are the basis of the (economic) division of labour in society and of the unequal relations of wealth and power.

Those unequal class relations do not, as the saying goes, exist on the head of a pin. They are organized spatially. And it is contended here that this spatial organization must be an important element in any exploration of the nature of uneven development.

One way of approaching this is through the conceptualization of the spatial structuring of the organization of the relations of production. Some spatial structures of the relations of production involve the geographical separation, within one firm, of headquarters and branch plant. Although the precise form will vary (branch plants can, for instance, have varying degrees of autonomy), what is at issue here is the stretching out over space of the relations of economic ownership and of possession (the functions of control over investment, of administration and co-ordination, and of the hierarchy of supervisory control over labour). Such 'managerial hierar- chies' have become longer and more complex with the development of capitalist production, and indeed with its increasing geographical spread. Or, again, a spatial structure might involve the geographical separation of the work of strategic conception from that of execution. A classic example here would be the separation of research and development from direct production. Or a production plant may be one in a series within the technical division of labour within a firm, each plant performing only one part of the overall production process. Here the relations between the plants will be planned within the firm rather than determined by the external market. Market relations are also conducted over space – exchange relations between firms within or between sectors – and these too may involve systems of unequal power relations, and of domination. Relations between small and large firms come to mind, but unequal power may also exist by virtue of other characteristics which structure the apparently equal relations of market exchange. Highly contrasting degrees of oligopolization between retailing (highly concentrated) and the production of final consumption goods (often very fragmented between firms) in the UK has long meant the dominance by the former over the latter.

Now, the potential variety of actual spatial structures is in principle infinite. Indeed, later sections of this chapter indicate that one of the characteristics of the current structural changes in the economy may well be the spawning of new types. But the point, at least here, is not to categorize or to produce a typology. Still less is it to produce stereotypes. It is, rather, to stress the importance of analysing the spatial ordering of the relations of production. For these different dimensions (of internal corporate structures, of the relationships of economic ownership and possession, of the technical division of labour) are dimensions along which run relations of power and control, of dominance and subordination. They are also dimensions which develop in systematic ways with the evolution of capitalist society.

So, interregional or inter-area relations, as they are so often called, are actually these relations of production stretched out between areas (at any scale of analysis from the very local to the international). To different degrees they are the relations of class power and control. These relations exist between functions within the overall division of labour. Regions or local areas may be specialized in the performance of a small number of functions and these in turn may be those to which attach power, and strategic control over the operation of the economy, or they may be those which are relatively powerless, subordinated. Most often, there will be a mixture.

But, further, the performance of particular functions within society is part of what defines groups within the class structure. One of the bases of the definition of classes and social strata is their place within the overall relations of production. The location of headquarters in one region/

country/local area and of branch plants in another will be reflected in the social compositions of those places. So will the location of the functions of research and development as opposed to shop-floor manufacturing, or of financial functions as opposed to more direct production.

Perhaps more importantly, and to return to the opening theme, to say that one area has all the high-status, white-collar jobs and another all the less well-paid, manual work, while important, is only to capture one element of the full meaning of uneven development. For that distribution of distinct occupational (and social) groups is itself one reflection of a perhaps more fundamental structuring of inequality between those areas – that carried by the organization between them of the relations of production (Massey, 1984).

All this immediately has two further implications. First, if these divisions of labour which are stretched out over space (spatial structures) consist, as we have said they do, of mutually defining elements, then the functional (and social) characteristics of some areas define the functional (and social) characteristics of other areas. If one region has all the control functions, and only control functions (to give an extreme example), then other regions must have all the functions which are controlled, the subordinated functions. This clearly has political and policy implications. Second, it means that as far as the characteristics we are considering here are concerned, any local area (region/country) can only be understood when analysed in relation to the functions in the wider division of labour which are performed within it, and in the context of its place within the wider system of relations of production. These characteristics of 'a local area', in other words, must be conceptualized in terms of the evolution of the wider structures of capitalist economy.[3]

There are other reasons why it is useful to conceptualize uneven development in terms of spatial structures, the spatial organization of the relations of production. For distinct spatial structures are likely to have different implications for the dynamics of growth in their constituent areas. The geographical separation of control functions and production (headquarters and branch plant) is an example. It may result in the flow of profits for subsequent investment from branch-plant region to HQ. It may imply much higher local multipliers for business services in the latter region than the former, since many such services are related to the functions of control and strategy rather than to direct production. That in turn will lead to a greater coherence between parts of the economy in the control regions than in the areas of branch plants. There may also, of course, be different income multipliers because of the likely higher salaries in the former regions than the latter. Workers in the branch-plant economy will have to negotiate either with a management which is local but does not have strategic power, or with a management based outside the region. And so on.[4] In cases where the branch plant is also simply one part in the technical division of labour within a company (a part-process structure), the local effects may be even more dismal. Not only is the level of local multiplier effects to the business-services sector likely to be restricted, but so also is the whole range of technological multipliers. Components will be brought in from another plant within the company (and the output, likewise, might simply be shipped off to yet another). These really are 'cathedrals in the desert' and their propulsive effects on local economies are likely to be minimal. (A plant producing similar physical output but not as part of a wider corporate structure might have different local effects, and one which was embedded, say, in the quasi-market relations of subcontracting might have different ones again.)

So, different spatial structures imply distinct forms of geographical differentiation, both in terms of the patterns of social differentiation between areas and in terms of the structures of interregional relations. What this means is that uneven development does not vary only in degree, as some of the arguments about it, and measures of it, would imply; it varies also in its nature. There can be different *kinds* of 'regional problem'.

There are, then, certain internal necessities to a spatial structure. The distinct elements within it are held together in a mutually defining tension. There are also likely implications: different spatial structures are likely to have different impacts on local areas. But it is also important to note what is *not* necessarily implied by a spatial structure. First, the fact that a spatial structure of production implies a particular division into functions within the overall relations of production says nothing about which groups in society (defined outside of occupational categories) will actually perform those functions. That is determined by its own set of causal relations only contingently related (though, indeed, probably related) to the logic of the spatial structure. Second, a division into functions does not necessarily imply the social value which will be accorded to the performers of those functions, their precise social status or, for instance, their monetary reward. All this, again, is contingent although, also again, it is likely to be related to the definitions of the functions themselves and to the nature of the groups performing them. Third, and finally, a spatial structure in itself does not say anything necessarily about its actual geography, in the sense of the particular places in which its constituent parts will be located. Once again, however, and as we shall see in a later section, although there may not be necessity in the *form* of their interrelation, all the elements above may influence each other.

Finally, the overlapping and interweaving of all these spatial structures is the basis for a spatial division of labour. In the mid-1960s a new spatial division of labour became dominant in the United Kingdom, in which control functions were concentrated, even more than before, in London, scientific and technical functions were clustered in the south-east (with some outliers in other places) and direct production, while present throughout the country was a higher proportion of economic activity in the regions outside of the south and east. That new spatial division of labour was the outcome of a whole series of changes affecting different parts of the economy in different ways. It was contributed to by shifts in the balance between sectors and the reorganization of, and development of new, spatial structures. It was the combination of spatial structures which produced a new spatial division of labour over the country as a whole. One question which the rest of this chapter will address is how much that scenario has changed in subsequent years.

## New directions

That period of economic and spatial reorganization of which the full establishment of this new spatial division of labour was a part lasted from the mid-1960s to the mid-1970s. Its ending coincided with further shifts both in the economy as a whole (at national and international levels) and in the political climate (see Massey, 1984). It had been a period in which geographical reorganization, and national economic and regional policy, were dedicated to 'modernization'. Moreover, it was a form of modernization which in turn could be interpreted as an attempt to prolong the life in Britain of what has been called Fordist production, broadly defined, and the social relations which went with it.

The old, basic industries, such as coal and shipbuilding were 'rationalized', resulting in major job losses and the creation of additional labour reserves in the 'peripheral' regions. Older means-of-production industries in manufacturing saw capacity closure and technical change, resulting in employment declines, especially for male skilled and semi-skilled workers, in the conurbations and nineteenth-century industrial areas. New means-of-production industries, especially in electronics, expanded employment. There was growth of R & D and technical occupations, particularly in the south-east, and also of assembly jobs, mainly for women, in all parts of the country, including some decentralization to 'the north'. Consumer goods industries grew slowly but did expand, especially those owned by big capital, and continued their longer-established decentralization of employment, including in particular jobs for women, to peripheral regions. Among services it was the public sector which grew most. While employment in the central state exhibited the classic divide, with high-status jobs concentrated in the south-east (mainly London) and some decentralization of lower-status and less well-paid employment to the regions, local authority employment both professional and manual, and that in health and education, was geographically more evenly distributed in its growth. Finally, in private sector services, it was producer services which showed the fastest rate of employment growth overall. Once again, the higher-status professional and higher-technical jobs were concentrated in the south-east.

The decentralization of manufacturing branch plants to the regions was in some sectors associated with technical change, and with an increasingly sharp technical division of labour within production. In other sectors, such as clothing, the move north or west was much more simply a means of cutting labour costs in the face of growing competition in a reorganizing international division of labour. Services, too, began to decentralize, but again it was only the mass-production parts which left the south-east.

As an attempt to use spatial reorganization to enable survival in a world where rules were changing, it failed. In those manufacturing sectors where competition was increasingly coming from the Third World, a move to the UK regions was insufficient. And if the decentralization of certain public sector establishments can be interpreted in terms of trying to cheapen the costs of collective provision and thereby prolong the life of the current mode of regulation, it too failed. In public sector services, locational change is inherently unable to reduce costs to any great extent because most of those services, and precisely those which grew most quickly in the late 1960s, such as health, education and social services, are inevitably tied both to national wages and to the geography of the population which they serve.

The dominant dynamics reshaping UK economy and geography since the mid-1970s have been different. Not only has the wider economic context changed, so also has the political and ideological prism through which it has been viewed by the prevailing government. Many of the same processes have continued, but in a different tempo or in a different way, and the balance between the processes, and the way they have meshed together, has been distinct from in the earlier period.

At a descriptive level, a number of important changes can be picked out. There have been further cuts in the basic industries of the old Development Areas – coal, steel, shipbuilding – though in a different social and political context from that of the sixties. The decline in manufacturing employment, under way since 1966, sharpened dramatically during the recession of the early 1980s, though easing somewhat again thereafter. Geographically, the impact of this decline was highly differentiated, the bulk of the jobs being lost in the regions outside the south-east, south-west and East Anglia. The long-term growth of service-sector employment also continued, but again there were marked changes both in its importance and in its character. In part because of the faster decline of manufacturing, the shift from manufacturing to service employment speeded up. But the nature of the growth in service jobs changed too: since the 1970s it has been overwhelmingly private sector services which have dominated employment growth. Not only is the geography of services as a whole different from that of manufacturing, but the geography of the two parts of the service sector is also highly contrasting. Since the late 1970s service-sector employment growth has been overwhelmingly in London and the south-east. The most important sectoral elements of this private service growth have been in business services and banking, insurance and finance, as part and parcel of the emergence of London and its region as a world city.

One process which certainly came to an end in the mid-1970s was the decentralization of manufacturing employment. The combination of investment, modernization through cutting labour costs, and geographical shift was abandoned in the face of accelerated decline. Whatever the effect of regional policy in the 1960s and early 1970s, it declined thereafter as the supply of potentially mobile investment dried up. Much of the decentralized employment has itself been subsequently lost. In other sectors which had been important underpinnings of the new spatial division of labour, the pattern of employment changed. 'Electronics' as a sector failed to become a major employer – indeed its employment nationally went into decline. Its internal structure of employment also changed. While the job losses mainly occurred among direct production workers, the numbers of professional and scientific workers continued to grow. Given the contrasting geographical distributions of these groups of workers, with the latter being more concentrated into the south-east, once again the geographical impact of these sectoral changes was highly differentiated.

But if the process of decentralization from the south and east is no longer important, the regions of the north and west are still subject to the arrival of branch plants and to branch-plant status. Now, however, they arrive as part of a different process, more often coming directly from abroad. Most importantly of all, the medium of branch-plant status is shifting from manufacturing to service industries. Leyshon, Thrift and Twommey (1988) give evidence of this in parts of financial services, and Allen's (1988) discussion of the penetration of multinational corporations of hitherto protected domestic markets hints at the process for a wider range of services, including contract catering and cleaning, and leisure and entertainment. While services as a whole continued their centralization in the south-east and south-west (with an outlier of expansion in

Scotland), the different constituent sectors behaved very differently. There were losses all round in public administration and defence, a continued growth with a (relatively) even distribution across the country in miscellaneous services (which includes education and health), further concentration (again except for Scotland) in distribution (in marginal decline) and professional and scientific services (marginal growth), and evidence of at least some regional decentralization in insurance, banking, finance and business services.

Finally, the last years of the 1980s indicate some new changes on the horizon, in particular a pushing out of growth from its established bases to colonize new areas. There has been a rediscovery by certain service-sector industries, preceded by the property developers, of selected parts of the inner cities, and some reworking of the north–south divide as growth spreads into some of the more southern, and the more rural, areas of 'the north'.

## Spatial structures

What insight can be gained about these changing patterns by employing the concepts of spatial structure and spatial division of labour?

At the level of occupational structure in the UK as a whole, the changes in direction which took place around the late 1970s seem to have reinforced many of the broad shifts which were already under way. Managerial and professional strata have continued to expand as a proportion of the economically active population; skilled manual workers have continued to decline quite rapidly and semi-skilled and unskilled manual workers together declined more slowly. The long, slow growth of clerical and sales workers, however, virtually ceased. The geography of the social structure also continued to move broadly in the same direction as previously, although there are some incipient changes, hinted at in the end of the last section, such as the invasion of certain inner-city areas by higher-income groups. But, most obviously, managers, administrators, professionals and technicians continued to concentrate in the south and east of the country.

In very broad terms, then, the spatial division of labour looks very similar, indeed is being reinforced. However, the balance of spatial structures underlying that spatial division of labour has changed somewhat since the late 1970s. There are a number of ways in which this can be illustrated.

First, as far as manufacturing is concerned, the regions of 'the north' remain very largely dominated by branch-plant structures. Indeed that

subordinate status was reinforced during the eighties. But in some ways
the nature of the branch plants has changed: the spatial structure of which
they are part is different. A higher proportion of them are responsible to
ultimate headquarters outside the UK. In part, this is because of the
decline of British-owned manufacturing within the UK; in part it is because
of new inward investment by foreign companies, the Japanese multinationals being the best known. Further, although many of these branch
plants are clearly part of production, or part-process, hierarchies, dependent on inputs from other plants in the same firm but based elsewhere,
the way those hierarchies work may be changing. If it is true that just-in-
time systems, for instance, are being adopted by more companies, then
these branch plants are less likely to be the classic 'cathedrals in the desert'
of the 1960s. Increasingly, they may demand that components suppliers
locate in their vicinity (Crowther and Garrahan, 1987; Oberhauser, 1987;
Schoenberger, 1987).

In other words, the 'branch-plant status' of much northern manufacturing remains, yet there is some evidence of two ways in which it may be
being transformed – and transformed because of a change in the type of
spatial structure into which the branch plants are inserted. The plants are
more subject to ultimate control from outside the UK (which may be
conceived of as negative) yet they may have rather larger technological
multiplier effects locally (usually assumed to be positive). Such a scenario
accords with the writing on neo-Fordism which foresees a process of
spatially decentralized concentration setting in. It has to be said, however,
that this possibility must be treated highly tentatively. Almost all the –
anyway fragmentary – evidence comes from the car industry (as it also
did, of course, for Fordism).

There is a further way in which these spatial structures are being
reworked and their local impacts thereby changed. This is the move
towards increased subcontracting and casualization, both of which change
the form of the social relations of production, either directly with the
workers concerned or with other firms. Here the increased importance
of short-term market relations in comparison with either long-term contracts or planned relations within firms is leading to dichotomization of
working conditions in manufacturing companies.

Secondly, and equally still only on the horizon in the late 1980s, is the
related possibility that the vertically integrated corporations argued to
have been key to the period of Fordism may become rather less important,
while more vertically disintegrated, or quasi-integrated, structures may
become more important (for example Christopherson and Storper, 1986).
There is, again, little systematic evidence yet of this in the UK, but there
are two developments which could be seen in this light. The first is the

increase in an independent technical services sector, including both R & D and such activities as software production. The second is the rise of a similarly independent (independent, that is, from manufacturing) sector within financial and other business services. Both of these phenomena are concentrated into (parts of) the south-east of England.

What they are evidence of is, with the increasing complexity and growth of this part of the division of labour, the externalization of certain functions from manufacturing. Thus new parts of the social division of labour, new sectors, are formed out of what were once parts of the technical division of labour within manufacturing-based corporations. What were once planned relations within firms are replaced by market relations between them (even if operating partly in 'non-market' terms – quasi-integration).

If these things are happening, then some aspects of the spatial structures which underlie the spatial division of labour within the UK are changing. One element of this is a shift in balance towards a sectoral division between north and south, with financial, technical and professional service firms, as a separate sector within the social division of labour, concentrated in the south, and away from domination of north by south through the part-process hierarchies of the technical division of labour. It is a shift in balance which would also result from the changing relative importance of different sectors in the economy, in particular the continuingly increasing importance of services in relation to manufacturing, and the declining relative importance of electronics.

We shall see later that the picture is actually much more complex than this; but consider the implications of the argument so far. Such a re-emergence of an element of sectoral division between north and south would more than anything else be likely to fuel even further the self-feeding cycle of the growth in the south-east. That process was already present in the 1960s and 1970s. The presence of control functions in London and the south-east is an important reason for the concentration of business services in the same region. It is HQ which deals with those relations. Moreover, the presence of business services, once established, is a further condition for the establishment and growth of other firms, especially small ones where buying in such services is necessary. The presence of the City assures a greater availability of venture capital in the south-east than in other regions (Mason, 1987). Even the higher house prices (a product of the concentration of growth, and of the higher incomes of these groups) means it is easier to raise initial capital. Higher incomes generate further growth through generalized demand. The finance sector generates demand for electronics hardware and software, for services such as design, for property development and construction

(Leyshon, Thrift and Daniels, 1987). And so on. It was already a virtuous circle which was further strengthened as financial and business services became the key growth sectors of the economy. In electronics, the tendency to cluster already operated both through firms wanting to be 'in on the scene' in a technical sense and through their needing to have access to the main pool of highly qualified labour. With vertical disintegration or quasi-integration, however, there is evidence that the tendency for agglomeration of this upper-echelon type of activity may be increased precisely as a result of the increased importance of market relations and thus of the need to be 'in on' the important social networks (Christopherson and Storper, 1986, p. 317).

To the extent that this scenario is correct, it has a further effect, for it reinforces a picture of increasing separation between the economies of the north and the south of the country. North and south are locked in very different ways into *international* spatial structures and the international division of labour. On the one hand there is the metropolitan region of the south-east of England, with London as one of the three prime world cities at its heart. It has for centuries been true that the financial City of London looked more outward to the world economy than 'homeward' to the UK economy. But it is more true today, and increasingly true of the economy of much of the south-east region. Indeed, Leyshon, Thrift and Daniels (1987) believe that 'the City constitutes one of the pivots, or perhaps *the* pivot of the economy of the South East of England' (p. 80). The finance and service sectors which are based in the region, and which are a growing part of its economy, are increasingly internationalized. London and the south-east are the first and often only point of entry to the UK for the globalized business service sector (Daniels, 1988). There has been a massive influx of foreign companies into the financial sector in London to the extent that it is non-UK institutions which are in the lead in the increasing international centrality of the City. The economy of London and parts of the south-east is in many ways more in competition with and linked to other international metropolitan regions and world cities than it is with the rest of the UK.

In contrast, the factories of the north are linked into, and in competition with, similar factories in similar regions in Europe, and also to some extent the Third World. The foreign investment in the north links the region into the world network of branch plants of production, not global financial systems.

And it is not just in terms of spatial structures and systems of competition that north and south are differently linked into the changing international division of labour. The same is true of labour markets. The elite strata of the south and east are increasingly part of international labour markets – indeed 'a spell abroad' may be an expected part of the climb up the career ladder.

And yet, of course, north and south *are* linked. One of those links, however, is much the same as the way in which the economy of London is linked to other parts of the world. It is the location of *control*. If the south is spawning its own economy relatively unconnected to the north, much of the economy of the north is still subordinate to London. Moreover, there are also increasing signs of an expansion northwards of some of the newer and fast-growing service sectors in the south. Although some decentralization of business services did occur in the 1960s and 1970s it was very limited, and was more often from London to the region around it than from south to north. There is no *major* interregional decentralization now, in the late 1980s, but there is evidence of some. Within the whole range of financial services, for instance, some elements have remained highly centralized in London and the south-east while others have shown definite signs of spreading their spatial structures out to major regional cities. Investment banking, accountancy and the commercial property sector are examples of the latter (Leyshon, Thrift and Twommey, 1988). This tentative relative decentralization to the regions (or rather, to certain cities within them) can take a number of forms including, in a few sectors, indigenous growth. Important, however, has been the expansion into the regions of large firms based in the south-east, either through the establishment of branch plants or through the acquisition of local companies.

In that sense, what is happening now in some service sectors reproduces what happened in manufacturing in the 1960s and the first half of the 1970s. The north's economy continues to be structured around branch plants and subordinated to control functions located in London and the south-east, and increasingly also ultimately abroad. As the national employment structure is increasingly dominated by services, so services are reproducing the branch-plant relation between the south-east and the rest of the country.[5]

However, these are not the same spatial structures as in the manufacturing decentralization of the 1960s, and the nature and the impact of the branch plants within them are also therefore different. So, too, are the interregional relations of dominance and subordination which they imply.

Take the example of certain parts of the financial sector. If spatial structures are thought of as the organization of the social relations of production, in their broadest sense, over space, then the spatial structures produced by the financial sector's establishment of branch plants in regional cities are sometimes quite different from those typical of the manufacturing decentralization of previous decades. Firstly, very different kinds of functions are involved, and therefore relations between functions. While there will certainly be a geographically structured managerial hierarchy, with ultimate control – and top management – remaining in London or the south-east, the London and regional offices are likely to differ in the type of function they perform. One typical scenario is that the office in the world city will be the transactional centre, and regional offices will be responsible for business generation and sales outlets within their designated regions (Cooke, 1988). Second, and relatedly, in some parts of the finance sector the nature of the functions means that the *reason* for regionalized offices is to perform an agency function in relation to a particular geographical market. This would be the case, for instance, with investment banking, where some relative decentralization has occurred. The point of such a branch plant is precisely to 'relate' to the local area rather than only the central headquarters. Its function is to find local investment outlets. Finally, there is evidence that the branch plants of City firms tend to have more autonomy than do the branches of manufacturing companies. Moreover, this autonomy may be expected to increase as the regional branch office integrates itself further within the local market. These, then, may be branch plants of a different type from the range of types already recognized within manufacturing.

Their impact on the local region is likely to be correspondingly distinct. Leyshon, Thrift and Twommey (1988) have carried out an analysis of this. They point out how different the local impacts can be from those associated with branch plants in spatial structures more typical of manufacturing in the 1960s and 1970s. The clearest contrast is that these branches have 'agency impacts', that is, their provision of finance or producer services may help encourage other local economic growth. This is particularly true for that subsector which provides perhaps the sharpest contrast to the 'normal' imagery of a branch plant – investment banking. The establishment of branch plants (even through acquisition) might be important in upgrading provincial financial centres and in counteracting the regional bias, mentioned above, in the availability of certain forms of investment capital.

Second, the establishment of such branches was found to have direct multiplier effects, particularly in the property and land market and on the construction industry. For such establishments need property to assert their status and little suitable building was either available or in suitable condition on their arrival in provincial centres. This, then, is an element of the 'rediscovery' mentioned earlier of the inner areas of certain northern cities.

In principle, the fact that they are branch plants and therefore in subordinate positions within managerial hierarchies, is, ironically, likely to mean that the multiplier effects of these offices, through purchases within the local economy, might be low. In this they might be more like the classic manufacturing branch plant. This could be compounded by the recent process of conglomeratization and internalization of services within these sectors in recent years. Even here, however, the greater degree of branch-plant autonomy might have an effect, and indeed Leyshon, Thrift and Twommey do suggest that local direct multiplier effects are likely to include the purchase of ancillary services.

They also point out that the impact will be different from that of the classic manufacturing branch plant in terms of the type of employment generated, for a very high percentage of the jobs will be in the professional and managerial groups. And this, in turn, will mean that the income multipliers within the local economy from their salaries will also be greater.

There seems little doubt, then, that these spatial structures are very different from those of the sixties, and that they have correspondingly distinct local impacts. None the less, Leyshon, Thrift and Twommey (1988) are restrained in their assessment of the overall effect, which they summarize as 'ambiguous'. In spite of the effects enumerated above, it is also

> undoubtedly true that the growth of the offices of large multinational financial and producer service conglomerates within the provincial cities of the north have themselves [sic] contributed to the extension of corporate control over financial and producer service activity. In this sense, the growth in the office networks of these large firms ... can be seen as a way in which the influence of the City of London is being extended throughout the regional economies. (p. 46)

Moreover, it must be stressed that this is not a major phenomenon. In all the listings of world financial centres of different ranks, no city in the UK other than London ever makes an appearance. The gap between London and the rest remains a huge one. Furthermore, it is only some regional cities within the UK which are seeing the establishment of many such branch functions. In effect, as far as the financial system is concerned, a considerable reorganization of the urban hierarchy is under way.

Finally, that kind of spatial structure, where relations of dominance and subordination may be more muted and local effects more positive, is by no means typical of service industries, nor even of the financial sector. Allen (1988) points to the very different structure in other parts of banking and commercial services and to part-process structures within insurance. Each of these will have different effects on the economies of the branch-plant cities. Even more negative will be the impact of the expansion of catering and cleaning services where they are increasingly taken over by multinational conglomerates and in particular where this is taking place in a context of privatization and/or 'contracting out'. As in the case of manufacturing mentioned earlier, the impact here is the reduction of wages and the deterioration in working conditions to levels well below those of the large-firm branch plants of the 1960s. In these cases, the implications for the north of being a branch-plant economy of London and the south-east are worse in the service industries than in manufacturing.

So, it would seem that the new spatial division of labour which was established in the UK in the 1960s in very broad terms continues its dominance. Since the later 1970s, however, there have been some shifts in its constituent spatial structures. As ever, and as they were in the sixties, the spatial structures generating a spatial division of labour will be a mixture (Massey, 1984) but since the late seventies that mixture may have changed somewhat in its balance and in its components. Correspondingly some of the effects within local regions may also have changed. If it is possible simply to summarize the evidence examined here, it indicates that the effects in the late eighties are more likely to produce polarization within local labour markets. Finally, there are the effects on relations between regions: the economies of London and the south-east increasingly integrated into the international spatial structures of financial and commercial services, the economies of the north bound into the very different global structures of manufacturing corporations. The south-east embarked on its own process of cumulative growth, the north still tied in, though in ways which are perhaps increasingly complex, to structures of control based in London. It is the ability to grasp these wider relations, that tie local and regional economies in various and changing ways into the evolving structures of capitalist production – the ability to go beyond uneven development as a set of surface distributions – which is provided by an approach through the concept of spatial structures.

## The geography of social structures

The concept of spatial structures thus provides a way in to the analysis of the economic relations between regions, the geography of the social relations of production which underlie any particular form of uneven development in capitalist societies. It also provides a basis for examining the geography of social structure, the geography of class.

If class is understood to be importantly (though not solely) defined by place within the relations of production, then the geography of those relations and the places within them, which spatial structures illuminate, begins to define a geography of class. It is not a deterministic relation, as was pointed out in the opening section and will be illustrated below, but if class is in any way based in production, then this is a way in.

We shall explore just one set of examples here. The fastest growing occupational groups in the economically active population of the UK are those which fall under the headings managers, administrators, professionals and technicians. We shall concentrate here on the upper echelons of these groups. What they mainly represent, in descriptive social terms, is a relatively high-income, high-status and non-manual stratum within society. There is a continuing debate about its precise class definition and character, which cannot be addressed here. The question here is what light can be shed on these groups, and on their geography, through an analysis of spatial structures of production.[6]

The first thing to be said is that in fact this broad grouping contains within it a mixture of different groups, each of which has its basis in distinct parts of the division of labour. Managers are distinct from technicians and specialist professional workers (Massey, 1984), public-sector employees from those in the private sector. They belong in different parts of the division of labour.

For that reason they also occupy different positions in spatial structures of production. And indeed they have different geographies. All are clustered into the south and east of the country, but managers are more specifically concentrated in London itself, with a very clear hierarchical ordering, the top echelons being in the capital, lower orders forming a larger proportion in the regions. What evidence there is indicates that scientific and technical strata are less focused on the metropolis and more spread through the less urban parts of the south-east region as a whole and its surroundings (Massey, 1984). These, then, are distinct geographies of different types of strategic control over British economy and society.

Moreover, there have been changes in the balance between the different elements of this group and in their class character. The 1960s and the early 1970s were the era of 'big is beautiful', of public sector growth and of manufacturing. Lash and Urry (1987), indeed, argue that this was the period of *formation* of what they call the service class in the UK, and they stress the significance of its public sector base. It was, precisely, a product of Wilsonian modernization. Today, the emphasis is less on the construction of complex corporate managerial hierarchies, and more on 'flexibility' and the promotion of the small firm. This in no way means that real control over society has been dissipated, still less democratized, but none the less the slackening growth of the purely managerial may be a reflection of the change of emphasis. Similarly, the typical scientist of the 1960s worked in a big corporate R & D lab (Steward and Wield, 1984); the equivalent employee in the late 1980s would be more likely to work in a smaller firm, certainly a smaller unit, and to combine with their scientific and technical functions some elements of management and even of ownership. This marks a change in their class position.

A contrast between the Southampton region and Berkshire is instructive here. In their study of the electronics and electrical engineering industry in the Southampton city region, Witt, Mason and Pinch (1988) demonstrate the connection between the *timing* of the growth of the sector in the region, its *place within the spatial structures* of the industry, and its *social character*. The growth of the industry in this region was early, occurring mainly in the late 1950s and the 1960s. It was also mainly a product of the in-migration of already operating companies, either through the establishment of new production branch plants or research and product-development establishments, or through the relocation of independently owned companies. It was, in effect, a product of a very early wave of decentralization of electronics mainly from its initial base in London. Local entrepreneurship played only a minor role. Moreover, most of the scientific and technical workers (which form a high proportion of the total) work either in big R & D labs or on sites which also have manufacturing functions (p. 30).[7]

The proliferating studies of Berkshire present a rather different picture. Here too, growth began in the 1950s, and was based around branches of major, often multinational, companies (Morgan and Sayer, 1988a). Recently, though, 'local' entrepreneurship has become more significant: 'there has been an increase in small indigenous hi-tech firms, often set up by previous employees' (Barlow and Savage, 1986, p. 160). The class character of the scientific and technical strata appears to be changing, and with it the spatial structures of which they are part. No longer so often employees buried in corporate structures and, although undoubtedly an elite, with their work subject to 'proletarianization', they are now increasingly combining the power which comes from their monopoly over technical knowledge with some of that which derives from ownership and control. All of this is integral to their place in the emerging spatial structures of this region outlined in the last section.

The groups which have been growing fastest of all have been the wide range of private sector 'professionals' associated with business, and especially financial, services. Thrift, Leyshon and Daniels (1987) have documented the explosive growth of this group, its changing class character and increasingly international outlook. But what all these groups share, simply as a product of their position within the unequal division of labour within society, is participation in and possession of strategic levels of power and control over the economy as a whole.

None of this, however, says anything necessarily about which groups in society (defined outside of production) fill these different elite positions within the various spatial structures. That is contingent to the division of labour itself; it is not necessarily implied by it. However, to take just one characteristic, even the most cursory of glances at the statistics demonstrates that these positions are filled overwhelmingly by men. The reasons vary, but in no case do they follow simply from class relations or the demands of capital.[8] Cockburn (1985) has analysed the case of those who in this schema are called (scientists and) technicians. She argues that the design and development of the means of production has always been a peculiarly crucial and powerful function within class societies (p. 26) and she documents the mechanisms by which it has always also been a part of the production system that men, as opposed to simply 'capital', have fought to dominate. She looked at three industries, and reported 'the significance of the role we have found women playing in all three new technologies is simple: they are *operators*. They press the buttons or the keys ... What women cannot be seen doing in any of these three kinds of workplaces is managing technology, developing its use or maintaining and servicing it' (p. 142, emphasis in original).

Another characteristic of this group is the degree of autonomy which it has within the workplace, the degree of control over the labour process (Massey, 1984). But this too has implications. One of them is that people work extremely long hours. Cockburn adds to the already considerable evidence on this, and to its implications. Many of them 'worked very long and irregular hours. Family commitments must come second. Such work is clearly predicated on not having responsibility for childcare, indeed on having no one to look after, and ideally someone to look after you' (1985, p. 181). Leyshon, Thrift and Daniels (1987) document a similar lengthening of the working day among City workers (p. 60). It is not inherent in the class structure or the technical division of labour that it should not be women who become technologists and have men at home doing the housework. It is, however, in fact men who are the technologists and that fact itself has an impact on the nature of the functions performed, and on how they are performed (Murgatroyd, 1985). Argues Cockburn,

> holding on to the heights of technological advantage is more and more important to them as women chip away at the foundations of other male citadels. Men can ill afford to lose their historic position as the world's engineers just at the point when they can no longer feel themselves secure in the status of family breadwinner and head of household. (1985, p. 235)

In 1984 in the British electronics industry 95 per cent of scientists and technologists, 96 per cent of technicians and 98 per cent of craft-workers were men. And for good measure so were 97 per cent of managers (EITB quoted in Cockburn, 1985, p. 225).

But if one contingent characteristic of these spatial structures (i.e., which social groups actually fill the variety of positions within them) has not changed much in recent decades, other characteristics *have* been modified. In particular, the relative privilege of these groups within UK society has considerably increased, in both income and status terms. There are a number of bases for this. In relation to the finance sector, and the City in particular, Leyshon, Thrift and Daniels (1987) document the impact on London salaries of the internationalization of the labour market.[9] The fact that in this case wages were forced up, rather than wages elsewhere being forced down, reflects again in part the power of these strata in the labour market. Big Bang and internationalization together produced major skill shortages. Skill shortages, exacerbated by low levels of training in the UK, and by a seepage of qualified people to the even better-paid financial sector, have also pushed up wages among the technical strata. Finally, all these groups benefited hugely through the redistributive government policies, from poor to rich, during the 1980s.

So far, then, what has been established is a deepening of the technical division of labour in electronics in such a way that spatial proximity between research and production is not always necessary,[10] and in some 'high-tech' sectors and parts of finance and business services a deepening of the social division of labour through externalization from manufacturing such that the need for spatial proximity may be greater within and between those sectors, and between them and the headquarters of major companies, than it is, again, with direct production itself. Secondly, many of these positions are filled by men, a fact which adds to the status given by the division of labour itself. Thirdly, the income and status of these groups have been considerably increased by other means. What has emerged is a set of spatial structures in which the spatial clustering of these groups, and their distance from the rest of the economy, is a prime characteristic.

There is, however, a further contingency to be structured into the discussion. For the actual geography of a spatial structure in terms of where the different elements in the division of labour will actually be located, is not given by the spatial structure itself. It is contingent, that is, dependent on a whole set of other causal systems not necessarily implied by the spatial structure itself. The location in the outer south-east of such a high proportion of these elite, white-collar strata, however, provides a fascinating example of the interaction of all the characteristics summarized above, and one in which spatial form and social form interweave and affect each other. In fact there is a whole range of factors behind the growth of this area, including nearness to London as a centre of control and of international linkages, the presence of Heathrow and good communications generally, and initially for the electronics industry the concentration there of government defence and research establishments. There is also the fact, referred to above, that the structure of these activities at the moment means that, once established, an area is likely to grow through the tendency to clustering. But another element which consistently shows up in research as being important is that the area itself has status.

The question then is, why? The development of the division of labour provides the possibility for these groups to be located separately from direct production. The high status which they have both striven for and been awarded perhaps inclines them to operationalize this possibility, to assert their separateness from the shop-floor and to locate in an area with cachet. But that does not explain why certain areas and not others should be seen in this way, nor indeed why separation from production should be seen as a status asset. References to 'high amenity areas capable of attracting a highly-qualified, highly-paid, highly-mobile workforce' (Hall, 1988, quoting Berry, 1970) and to 'psychic income' merely assume what is to be explored, and assign cause by simple inference from effect. The area *must* be 'high amenity' because that is where these people who have choice ('highly-paid, highly-mobile') choose to go. In fact, of course, such preferences are not innate; they have to be constructed. This is demonstrated in a very simplistic way by the most recent development of all, the rediscovery by the young and rich of the central city. In London some part of this is due to the pressures of the combination of the long hours demanded on the dealing floors and the commuting times now required if home is to be really 'out of town' (Leyshon, Thrift and Daniels, 1987). But a glance at the literature indicates that these areas are now considered 'high amenity' and that another innate preference has been discovered – that for living by water in the form of rehabilitated canals and docks (renamed 'quays').

So what *is* the attraction of the outer south-east? There is much evidence to suggest that it is mainly about self-assertion and class. It has been argued, for instance, that location in such areas enables self-definition through association with the trappings of some vision of 'the gentry' (Thrift, 1988). It is a means of asserting social arrival. Second, however, all this raises the question of whether the 'urban–rural shift' was urban–rural at all. Rather, it seems to have been from industrial (meaning manufacturing) to non-industrial. The beginnings of what may be a rediscovery of the urban, the boom of world cities (London's population is growing again) are some evidence of this. Keeble's work (1976, 1980) used manufacturing, not urban population, as a variable; Fothergill and Gudgin's work is precisely about *industrial* cities (Fothergill, Gudgin, Kitson and Monk, 1988); and Lloyd and Reeve (1982), for instance, point out that there are many small towns in the north which are not getting service growth or middle-class in-migration. They give examples: Shaw 80.5 per cent employment in manufacturing, Littleborough 99.2 per cent. What really does seem to be at issue is distancing from manufacturing production and from the physical *and social* context that goes with it. The invasion of the Docklands by the private sector middle class is very different from the public sector gentrification of other parts of inner London in the 1960s and 1970s. It involves completely clearing the area or refashioning it. It was a bold thing to move in early and the brave pioneers were often offered special incentives. Once established as 'acceptable' places, of course, such areas, whether they be Docklands or the M4 corridor, embark on another element of the virtuous circle of growth, but this time based on class. Third, however, the particular groups examined here must be set in a wider context. The south-east is home also to a broad range of other groups, which form part of the basis for the social character of the region, and which in turn forms part of the attraction of the region to the groups being analysed. They range from employees of the central state to workers in the whole gamut of cultural industries. And in particular they are there because of London, the capital city.

Everything points to the importance of class dynamics in a social sense as a factor in the emerging locational pattern of the currently dominant sectors and strata in the UK economy. Lash and Urry (1987) make two points which go to the heart of this. First, they argue that the main causal power of these strata is 'to restructure capitalist societies so as to maximize the divorce between conception and execution' (p. 177). Second, they argue that 'British professions followed the gentry model of "status professionalism" rather than the bourgeois one of "occupational professionalism"', and they note 'the spatial significance of London in this process of status professionalization which affected not only the old professions but new ones as well, such as engineering' (pp. 184–5). The increasing importance of these strata and their changing composition, especially since the late 1970s, has demonstrated the significance of both these points.

But if spatial structures are geographical systems of mutually defining elements, as argued in the first section of this chapter, then this clustering of certain functions in the overall division of labour has other implications. Most obviously, the existence of clusters in particular functions necessitates the existence also of areas deprived of those functions – in this case, within the UK, the northern regions of the country. Indeed, the evidence is that the concentration of this group in the south-east, and their increased relative incomes, is a prime element in accounting for one of the more obvious descriptive indicators of the north–south divide – that of salaries. While the bottom 10 per cent of incomes in the different regions of the country do not vary much, the variation in the top 10 per cent of *male non-manual* earnings is considerable, with the income levels of this decile in the south-east being far higher than those in other regions (Massey, 1988). Further, the fact of this spatial clustering itself has social effects. Most obviously, it has resulted in labour shortages for these groups in the south-east, thereby increasing salary levels still further. Yet at the same time those (far smaller numbers) in regions in the north who have the same skills either remain on lower income levels, or cannot find work and/or cannot afford to move south either to find work or to increase their salaries. In this way, the cumulative dynamics of the initial spatial concentration are reinforcing the income advantages of the already privileged in the south, and even producing geographical inequalities within the group as separate northern and southern circuits develop, those in the former on lower incomes and unable to move in even should they want to, those in the latter in increasingly powerful positions in the labour market, moving increasingly rapidly from job to job, bargaining themselves up the income scale, and seeing their wealth grow still further as house prices continue to rise.

We have then, changing divisions of labour, both technical and social, with a particular social content and consequences, which have enabled – and apparently in some measure been the cause of – new spatial structures, the location of which in turn has further moulded the social character of the constituent groups.

An interesting issue arises here. Marshall (1987) in his account of the long historical rises and falls of British regions (long waves of regional development) argues that the upswing of each new long wave sees the rise of new social and political forces, and moreover that these have been regionally based, in the areas where the long wave has had greatest impetus. He points to the Manchester free-trade movement in the first half of the nineteenth century, and the social imperialists of the west midlands in the late nineteenth and early twentieth. There is no sense in which the pre-eminence of the outer south-east and its outliers constitutes the same kind of phenomenon at the end of the twentieth. Nor, it should be stressed, can such political characteristics in any way be directly derived from spatial structures, nor from the social structures with which they are associated. However, although there is in no sense a 'movement', this region is clearly one the imagery of which is used in political discourse. It is the heartland of Thatcherism. Other regions are urged to 'follow its example', and become more 'entrepreneurial' (Massey, 1988). Moreover its location around London gives it a special pre-eminence. This time, the long wave has its greatest impetus in the region around the capital city, and the combination of the forms of dominance provides an even wider basis for a form of regionally based 'supremacy'. It is certainly the constellation of class forces based in this region which is currently dominating the social form taken by what has been called 'the fifth Kondratieff' in the UK.

## Uneven redevelopment: reproduction over time

The structures of uneven development are constantly evolving. While the mid-sixties saw the establishment of a new spatial division of labour, the years since the late seventies have seen some changes in the underlying spatial structures. What seems to be clear, however, is that, although change is continuous, there are also periodic bouts of more thorough-going transformation. In other words, there is structural change in types of uneven development as well as in other aspects of the economy. Moreover, each is integral to the other. (Decentralization in the sixties was part of an attempt to save existing forms of industrialization and a particular place in the world economy; the rise of the outer south-east is part of the assertion of a newer dominant international role.) There is, in other words, a relationship between the periodization of an economy and its regionalization (in the most general sense) – its forms of uneven development. And it seems clear that the major shift towards a new spatial division of labour, which began in the mid-sixties, is continuing today. If it began as part of an attempt to install one technocratic, social-democratic view of modernization, it is being perpetuated, probably reinforced, by the economic and political changes since the late seventies.

What the changes we have been discussing produce is a shifting kaleidoscope of local and regional variation. Both geographical surface and the demands of industry are constantly changing. To give an example of the former, recent evidence would seem to indicate that some regions of the north and west are no longer seen as having reserves of mainly female labour, as they were in the 1960s and 1970s at the height of manufacturing location there. That characterization of the local labour reserves was a result of the women of those regions being seen as 'green' labour and hence potentially vulnerable. Now, however, decades of unemployment, and of desperation for jobs, and the existence of a new generation of males without trade union experience, indeed often without experience of paid work at all, have transformed the male labour markets of these regions from being heartlands of trade unionism to ones where it is possible to introduce completely new forms of labour relations. The male labour of those regions may now also be viewed by industry as a vulnerable reserve.

'Geographical surface' and 'the demands of industry' always interact. Morgan and Sayer (1988b) give an example of such mutual adjustment precisely from the sphere of management–worker relations. 'General processes' only ever exist in the form which they take in particular circumstances. The new spatial structures and their social forms discussed in the last two sections take shape in the context of previously laid down spatial structures and social forms. Each has an impact upon the other. The arrival of vastly increased numbers of white-collar, high-income employees into the outer south-east has transformed the prospects of an older working class already living there. Either they have been able, through employment or through housing, to benefit from the influx or they have been marginalized. Just as the concentration of upper-income groups has had some effect on the character of those strata (see last section) so also it has affected those on below-average incomes. The experience of living on a fixed (for example, state) income in London or the south-east is very different from that in the north. Apart from the fact that the inequality is more visible, and probably that there are fewer supportive organizations, prices are higher, and housing is very difficult to find at an affordable price; the money goes less far. The south-east is the richest region in average terms, but it is the most unequal.

The conjunction of wider processes within a particular area can also set off other dynamics. The price of land has a long history in London of contributing to the difficulties of the manufacturing sector in the capital city, but the current conjunction of forces is particularly acute. The combination of the heightened international competition which was afflicting, at a national level, many of the sectors which figured prominently in the London economy, with pressures both on its labour supply and on its costs through increasing land and property prices, imposed difficulties which were not present in other parts of the country. Indeed, there is evidence that that kind of local impact now occurs also beyond London; Barlow and Savage (1986) give evidence from Berkshire.

Both these last two points have concerned conflicts of interest, or at least different interests, within particular areas, and both have been well studied. Characterizations of local areas may well vary between groups, and may often be conflicting. However, one issue which seems not to have been researched is the labour market for graduate women in the outer south-east. The dichotomy between 'male professional workers' and 'local workers' is frequently commented upon (for example, Barlow and Savage, 1986). But what of female (would-be) professional workers, of whom given the social structure there are likely to be many? In their study of Bristol, Boddy, Lovering and Bassett (1986) note a growing presence of younger women in certain technical and professional posts, but their overall conclusions are not hopeful for the quality of employment opportunities for women. They also point out that most jobs for women (low-paid ones) are in sectors generated by the spending-power of highly paid men. In other words, the wider implications of high, local income multipliers, discussed in the last section, may be further to fuel the growing polarization within local labour markets, given the low pay and conditions in other service sectors. It may be that the combination, discussed in previous sections, of spatial structures of production and the social character of the groups within them, is producing within the outer south-east yet another form of 'patriarchal region' within the wider spatial division of labour.

'Spatial division of labour' is not an explanatory concept in the sense that it embodies an explanation of any particular form of uneven development. In this it is like any other concept of division of labour. A longer perspective on history indicates that the reasons for uneven development taking any particular form will change over time. It is certainly not the case that 'labour-force characteristics' are always the dominant consideration (as proposed by Warde, 1985). Indeed, patterns of industrial location are not to be explained simply by lists of 'factors'. There are broad parameters, the maintenance of capitalist accumulation chief among them. But the way in which that operates to produce a particular spatial division of labour will depend on a whole host of things. Of supreme importance in explaining the shifting character, over two centuries, of uneven development in the United Kingdom have been the changing relation of the economy to the international division of labour, the (related) changing sectoral structure of the economy, and the dominant modes of technological and industrial organization. It is the structuring together of all these which will influence the kinds of spatial structures developed, the balance between them, and their overall resultant in a broad spatial division of labour. Further, as we have seen, it is also more than this. As well as the maintenance of capital accumulation, the form of uneven development will also reflect battles over the maintenance of class power (which, though clearly related, is certainly not the same thing) and will be refracted also through a wider level of politics, including the political interpretation of what *are* the requirements of capitalist accumulation. Since the late seventies, for instance, the strategy has been to emphasize and enable a particular dual role for the UK within the international division of labour: a combination of banking centre and low-cost production location. It is this, and the ascendancy of particular class strata, which lies behind one of the most important dimensions of uneven development in the UK today.

Milton Keynes
published in 1988

# Notes

1 Given the stage of development we are currently at, and the direction of this development.
2 An assumption is clearly entailed here that all the work done in a society, all the functions performed, are included in the characterization of the overall division. This raises two important issues. The first is that the system under consideration must be conceptualized as in principle international. The divisions of labour in which the economies of the regions of the UK are involved are frequently global in reach. The second issue is that the overall division of labour in society includes much work which is unpaid and therefore lies outside that which is normally considered to be 'the economy'. Thus, the 'economic' position of 'family breadwinner' implies another position (performer of domestic labour) which will probably fall outside the paid sector. Thus, it is correct to call for the inclusion of the reproduction of labour in the approach (Warde, 1985, 1988), something which, unfortunately, this chapter does not attempt to do, but this cannot be achieved simply by adding on further 'aspects' of local areas.
3 Which is not the same as saying that this is the only conceptualization which must take place – see later.
4 There is a much fuller discussion of these potential implications, and of the contrasting impacts of different spatial structures, in Massey (1984), especially chapter 3.
5 The rather inadequate statistics imply that in some sectors (only) Scotland may be a partial exception.
6 These issues were subsequently taken up in Massey, Quintas and Wield (1992).
7 However, the study did not include the independent R & D sector.
8 In relation to recent debates (see McDowell, 1988) it therefore seems better, as Cockburn (1985) and Walby (1985) argue, to keep the dynamic of patriarchal relations, however defined, analytically separate from that of capitalist relations. It also means that it may not be enough to ask simply about 'the effects on women' of industrial restructuring. 'The effects on women' do not only derive from the actions of capital but also from the effects of men's struggle to maintain their supremacy.
9 This impact of geographical change on salary levels must be one of the few times when international comparisons have forced wages to *rise*. (It happened at the same time as workers in branch plants in 'the north' were seeing their wages and conditions undermined by international comparisons – another

example of the different ways in which north and south are locked into the international division of labour.)

10 Though it may be: see Boddy, Lovering and Bassett (1986). And indeed we argue in Massey, Quintas and Wield (1992) that spatial separation may have negative effects.

# References

Allen, J. (1988) 'The geographies of service', in D. Massey and J. Allen (eds), pp. 124–41.

Barlow, J. and Savage, M. (1986) 'The politics of growth: cleavage and conflict in a Tory heartland', *Capital and Class*, no. 30, pp. 156–82.

Berry, B.J.L. (1970) 'The geography of the United States in the year 2000', *Transactions, Institute of British Geographers*, vol. 51, pp. 21–53.

Boddy, M., Lovering, J. and Bassett, K. (1986) *Sunbelt City?: A Study of Economic Change in Britain's M4 Growth Corridor*, Oxford, Clarendon Press.

Carling, A. (1986) 'Rational choice Marxism', *New Left Review*, no. 160, pp. 24–62.

Christopherson, S. and Storper, M. (1986) 'The city as studio; the world as back lot: the impact of vertical disintegration on the location of the motion picture industry', *Environment and Planning D: Society and Space*, vol. 4, pp. 305–20.

Cockburn, C. (1985) *Machinery of Dominance: Women, Men and Technical Know-how*, London, Pluto Press.

Cooke, P. (1988) 'Spatial development processes: organized or disorganized?', in D. Massey and J. Allen (eds), pp. 232–49.

Crowther, S. and Garrahan, P. (1987) 'Invitation to Sunderland: corporate power and the local economy', paper presented to the Conference on the Japanisation of British Industry, UWIST, Cardiff (mimeo).

Daniels, P. (1988) 'Producer services and the post-industrial space-economy', in D. Massey and J. Allen (eds), pp. 107–23.

Fothergill, S., Gudgin, G., Kitson, M. and Monk, S. (1988) 'The deindustrialization of the city', in D. Massey and J. Allen (eds), pp. 68–86.

Hall, P. (1988) 'The geography of the fifth Kondratieff', in D. Massey and J. Allen (eds), pp. 51–67.

Hamnett, C., McDowell, L. and Sarre, P. (eds) (1988) *Changing Social Structure* (Restructuring Britain, Open Text 2), London, Sage/the Open University.

Keeble, D. (1976) *Industrial Location and Planning in the United Kingdom*, London, Methuen.

—— (1980) 'Industrial decline, regional policy and the urban–rural manufacturing shift in the United Kingdom', *Environment and Planning A*, vol. XII, pp. 945–62.

Lash, S. and Urry, J. (1987) *The End of Organized Capitalism*, Cambridge, Polity Press.

Leyshon, A., Thrift, N. and Daniels, P. (1987) 'The urban and regional consequences of the restructuring of world financial markets: the case of the City of London', Working Papers on Producer Services, no. 4, Department of Geography, University of Liverpool.

Leyshon, A., Thrift, N. and Twommey, C. (1988) 'South goes North? The rise of the British provincial financial centre', paper presented at the Annual Conference of the Institute of British Geography (mimeo).

Lloyd, P. and Reeve, D. (1982) 'North West England 1971–1977: a study in industrial decline and economic restructuring', *Regional Studies*, vol. 16, no. 5, pp. 345–60.

Marshall, M. (1987) *Long Waves of Regional Development*, Basingstoke, Macmillan.

Mason, C. (1987) 'Venture capital in the United Kingdom: a geographical perspective', *National Westminster Bank Quarterly Review*, May, pp. 47–59.

Massey, D. (1984) *Spatial Divisions of Labour: Social Structures and the Geography of Production*, Basingstoke, Macmillan.

—— (1988) 'A new class of geography', *Marxism Today*, May, pp. 12–17.

Massey, D. and Allen, J. (eds) (1988) *Uneven Re-Development: Cities and Regions in Transition*, London, Hodder & Stoughton.

Massey, D., Quintas, P. and Wield, D. (1992) *High-Tech Fantasies: Science Parks in Society, Science and Space*, London, Routledge.

McDowell, L. (1988) 'Gender divisions', in C. Hamnett, L. McDowell and P. Sarre, (eds), ch. 5.

Morgan, K. and Sayer, A. (1988a) *Microcircuits of Capital: The Electronics Industry and Uneven Development*, Cambridge, Polity Press.

—— (1988b) 'A "modern" industry in a "mature" region: the re-making of management labour relations', in D. Massey and J. Allen (eds), pp. 167–87.

Murgatroyd, L. (1985) 'Occupational stratification and gender', in The Lancaster Regionalism Group, *Localities, Class and Gender*, London, Pion.

Oberhauser, A. (1987) 'Labour, production and the state: decentralization of the French automobile industry', *Regional Studies*, vol. 21, no. 5, pp. 445–58.

Schoenberger, E. (1987) 'Technological and organizational change in automobile production: spatial implications', *Regional Studies*, vol. 21, no. 3, pp. 199–214.

Steward, F. and Wield, D. (1984) 'Science, planning and the State', Unit 16 of D209 *The State and Society*, Milton Keynes, the Open University.

Thrift, N. (1988) 'Images of social change', in C. Hamnett, L. McDowell and P. Sarre, (eds), ch. 1.

Thrift, N., Leyshon, A. and Daniels, P. (1987) 'Sexy, greedy: the new international financial system, the City of London and the South East of England', paper presented to the Urban Change and Conflict Annual Conference (mimeo).

Walby, S. (1985) 'Theories of women, work, and unemployment', in The Lancaster Regionalism Group, *Localities, Class and Gender*, London, Pion.

Warde, A. (1985) 'Spatial change, politics and the division of labour', in D. Gregory and J. Urry, (eds) *Social Relations and Spatial Structures*, Basingstoke, Macmillan.

—— (1988) 'Industrial restructuring, local politics and the reproduction of labour power: some theoretical considerations', *Environment and Planning D: Society and Space*, vol. 6, no. 1, pp. 75–95.

Witt, S., Mason, C. and Pinch, S. (1988) 'Industrial change in the Southampton city-region: a study of the electronics and electrical engineering industry', Working Paper, Urban Policy Research Unit, Department of Geography, University of Southampton.

# PART II

*Place and Identity*

# Introduction

Much of the early debate about space had been concerned to argue the importance of thinking in geographically more expansive terms. The stimulus had come, at least in part, from the need to set 'places' (whether seen as the national economy, the region or the inner city) in the wider context of the forces and relations which lay not only within but also beyond them and which played so important a role in determining their fate. One effect of this was to rob places in a certain measure of their individual specificity (of course there was uneven development, which assigned places to different locations and functions within the world economic order, but in the end they were all the products of international capital accumulation). Another effect was to assign virtually all causality to a somehow unlocatable level of 'the global'. The turn to considering the local, to explaining the construction of, and taking seriously the importance of, geographical specificity thus came to some as a shock; and it was in some quarters resisted fiercely.

Yet once again the emergence of this new (in fact renewed) focus on to the academic agenda occurred at least in part out of quite concrete and political issues in the world beyond the universities. It was clear that the highly differentiated local economic and political dynamics were posing quite different issues (in terms both of problems and of political potential) in different places ('The shape of things to come'). It was clear, too, that some political debate – such as that sparked off by Eric Hobsbawm's *Forward March of Labour Halted?* – could not be conducted only at a national level, without taking account of the more localized specificities which went to make up the national picture. And it was becoming evident that subnational places were functioning as highly charged symbols of the major lines of political debate. There was the rise of Canary Wharf and Docklands more generally (highly subsidized symbols of how unelected entrepreneurialism could get things done where local authorities had supposedly failed – the subsequent troubles of the development have therefore been equally symbolic); there was the new urban left in the city councils of many of the major cities, conducting one of the most visible and politically radical challenges to the national government from the quite explicitly recognized specificities of their own political strongholds; there were the clear geographical bases and internal differentiations of the long miners' strike; there was Mrs Thatcher's much-photographed walk, looking so neat and tidy, handbag in hand, across the derelict wastes of Teesside. There were emerging loyalties to place which crossed the political spectrum, most worrying of all were those which centred on the aggressively exclusivist nationalisms of Eastern Europe and the former Soviet Union. And so on. It was hard to live politically through this period without recognizing that geographical specificity, and the meanings and symbolisms which people attach to places, and how these can – and should – be struggled over, are all important issues. It was in many ways a further, and very different, and quite practical demonstration of the argument that geography matters.

And yet the move to analyse these issues in part through reconsidering the notion of place, although welcomed and taken up by many, was fiercely resisted by others. 'The political place of locality studies' was one element of a response to this critique.

This negative reaction by some to 'locality studies', and also the widespread wariness about the notion of place more generally, had understandable roots given geography's history of dealing with the specificity of place through internalized descriptions. But it was also deeply ironical. For one crucial element of what 'geography' is all about is difference and specificity.

A concern for spatial differentiation could indeed be seen as geography's particular slant on the emerging interest in 'difference' at this period more widely within the social sciences. And indeed this coincidence of timing (although it may well also have been rather more than simple coincidence) may have been part of the explanation for the entanglements and confusions into which the debate sometimes fell. For the argument about how geographers should think about place (and indeed in some formulations even *whether* they should do so) got thoroughly mixed up with the issues raised in the discussion of postmodernism.

In fact, the issues of locality studies and of postmodernism are in principle quite separate ones ('The political place of locality studies'). Yet the very fact of their having been confounded pointed to real differences between the protagonists in the localities debate. For those who were dubious about the value of such studies the term 'local' sometimes became one which in itself reverberated with disapproval. To call something a local struggle or a local concern was in this lexicon to designate it with a whole range of characteristics – a kind of particularism, an exclusivity, often an essentialism, and a selfishness which refused to consider the supposedly greater good of some (implicitly or explicitly) supposed universal.

Moreover (and quite apart from all the methodological confusions in which the term became entangled), the negative designation of things as (merely) local slipped out of its geographical meaning to be used in relation to a whole variety of issues and struggles. So anti-racism, feminism and environmental concerns, among others were criticized as being 'only local' issues (see part III, especially 'Flexible sexism'). And the global and universal (and the confusion between the two terms was itself symptomatic) concern against which these issues were being compared was that of class. In practice, therefore, the issues raised by the localities debate did touch on questions which had in the wider social sciences been put on the table by feminism, by post-colonial studies, and by postmodernism. If there was agreement about the need in some sense for unity among 'progressive' struggles, the means by which this could be achieved were disputed. Those who mistrusted the newly emerging 'localisms' saw them as divisive. But in reply it had to be argued that the old coherencies had really been constructed by the smothering of internal diversity – the male dominance of the coalfields, looked back on so fondly by some as an exemplary solidarity, was a clear case in point (see part I, 'The shape of things to come'). Moreover, it was increasingly contended, any real unity of purpose can only be constructed out of a prior recognition of differences (and of their implications), whether these be of place of gender or of ethnicity.

But another strand of resistance to any affirmation of the importance of place came from another direction altogether. This argument drew upon the associations of 'a sense of place' with memory, stasis and nostalgia. 'Place' in this formulation was necessarily an essentialist concept which held within it the temptation of relapsing into past traditions, of sinking back into (what was interpreted as) the comfort of Being instead of forging ahead with the (assumed progressive) project of Becoming. The ways in which, here too, issues of gender though largely buried were really at stake were only gradually to become part of the debate, but the manner in which this characteristic of stable Beingness resonated with ways of characterizing femaleness in our culture could not go unnoticed ('A place called home?' and also part III).[1]

The papers in this part seek to address this debate not by simple refutation of the points made in the critique, but rather by arguing for a rethinking of the concept of place ('A global sense of place'; 'A place called home?').

The papers in part I began to develop an argument for thinking of social space in terms of the articulation of social relations which necessarily have a spatial form in their interactions with one another. If this notion is accepted, then one way of thinking about place is as particular moments in such intersecting social relations, nets of which have over time been constructed, laid down, interacted with one another, decayed and renewed. Some of these relations will be, as it were, contained within the place; others will stretch beyond it, tying any particular locality into wider relations and processes in which other places are implicated too. Indeed, the argument elaborated in the papers in part I – that the fortunes of a place can only be explained by setting that locality within a broader context (the argument against 'blaming the cities', for instance) – entails at least a minimal version of this way of thinking about place. Moreover, conceptualizing place in this way challenges that element of critique which sought to characterize all studies of local areas as being necessarily internalized descriptions (see 'The political place of locality studies'). Although this critique should anyway be in part countered by simply noting that 'theory' is not restricted to the sphere of big, grand phenomena alone (for which read international capitalism), what this formulation of the concept of place also makes clear is that the understanding of any locality must precisely draw on the links beyond its boundaries.

Indeed the point is here taken further, for it is not only the 'changing fortunes' of an area which must be understood by locating it within a wider context, but also the character of the place itself. It is not just that, say, the decline of industry in an area must be explained – rather than by looking at the characteristics of the area itself – by understanding the forces of capital accumulation, of changing markets perhaps, or of external ownership; it is also that the very formation of the identity of a place – its social structure, its political character, its 'local' culture – is also a product of interactions. The 'character of an area' is no more the product of an internalized history than are the recent fortunes of its manufacturing industry. The global is in the local in the very process of the formation of the local. This, then, is an extension to the concept of place of that element of the argument about space which has it that not only is space the product of social relations but that 'it is those relations which constitute the social phenomena themselves' (introduction to part I).

Thinking of places in this way implies that they are not so much bounded areas as open and porous networks of social relations.[2] It implies that their 'identities' are constructed through the specificity of their interaction with other places rather than by counterposition to them.[3] It reinforces the idea, moreover, that those identities will be multiple (since the various social groups in a place will be differently located in relation to the overall complexity of social relations and since their reading of those relations and what they make of them will also be distinct). And this in turn implies that what is to be the dominant image of any place will be a matter of contestation and will change over time. As Ernesto Laclau puts it: 'All articulation is partial and precarious'.[4]

At the period when the debate over locality took place, a significant part of the discussion arose from the growing concern with globalization and with time–space compression. Thinking of space and place in this way, however, also modulates the way in which these concepts may themselves be formulated. It emphasizes that it is necessary to move beyond the characterization in terms of speed-up, instantaneous communication and constant global flows to imagine the process in terms of the spatial reorganization of social relations, where those social relations are full of power and meaning, and where social groups are very differentially placed in relation to this reorganization ('A global sense of place'). What is happening to 'places' is that they are caught up in the reconstitution and increasing spread of those relations.[5]

The importance of arguing all this is that it can be fed into current debates. It is not being posited here that this is how places *are* currently seen (the kinds of defensive and exclusivist place-loyalties which currently abound immediately give the lie to this). But it is being argued that it is how places *could be* seen, and that were this to be the case then certain political arguments might be shifted. In this it shares its aim with Said (quoted in the general introduction), and with Iris Marion Young in her arguments for an unoppressive city.[6] The anti-essentialist construction of this alternative concept of place immediately problematizes, for instance, any automatic associations with nostalgia and timeless stasis. It underscores the lack of basis for any claims for establishing the authentic character of any particular place (whether such claims are used as the grounds for arguing for ethnic exclusivity or for opposing some unwanted development – 'it would be out of place here'). There is, in that sense of a timeless truth of an area, built on somehow internally contained character traits, no authenticity of place. In the 1980s when certain East End communities in the Docklands of London resisted the encroachment of new developments and, quite specifically, of 'yuppies' there was a tendency to make the case on the basis that this was 'a working-class area' (yuppies, in other words, had no place there). This was problematical on (at least) two counts. First it was a claim for timeless authenticity (as a working-class area – implication: it should not be changed); yet a couple of centuries previously the Isle of Dogs was fields and farmland. Second, it was an essentialist claim, and the problematical nature of this aspect of the formulation is best illustrated by going back some fifteen years previously. Then, similar communities in nearby areas had resisted another 'invasion'. This time it had been by ethnic minority groups; and this time the claim was that the place was a *white* working-class area. The political left, on the whole, supported 'the local residents' against the yuppies but had resisted the racist version of their claims to exclusive ownership of/right to live in that place. Yet the conceptual basis of the claim was the same in each case – an essentialist definition of place. The real issue was the politics and social content of the changes under way, including their spatial form, rather than a fight over 'the true nature' of a part of east London.[7]

It is here, in the fruitless search after seamless coherence and timelessness, that the issue of the nature of place links up to that of the concept of identity more generally. When time–space compression is seen as disorientating, and as threatening to fracture personal identities (as well as those of place) then a recourse to place as a source of authenticity and stability may be one of the responses. But just as the notion of single coherent and stable identities has been questioned so too could geographers work to undermine the exactly parallel claims which are made about the identity of place. Thus, for instance, if Robins is correct that in these times 'the driving imperative is to salvage centred, bounded and coherent identities – placed identities for placeless times' (cited in 'A place called home?'), then it must be emphasized that there is no way in which this can legitimately be done through the medium of geographical places. The geography of social relations forces us to recognize our interconnectedness, and underscores the fact that both personal identity and the identity of those envelopes of space-time in which and between which we live and move (and have our 'Being') are constructed precisely through that interconnectedness.

And the question must also be asked, Who is it who is so troubled by time–space compression and a newly experienced fracturing of identity? Who is it *really* that is hankering after a notion of place as settled, a resting place? Who is it that is worrying about the breakdown of barriers supposedly containing an identity? It is at least by no means a coincidence that the exultations in the uncontrollable complexity of the city (Virginia Woolf), the questioning of the very notion that a settled place to call one's own was *ever* a reality (Toni Morrison, bell hooks), the insistence that memory and recovery does not have to take the form of nostalgia (bell hooks), and the celebration of a multiplicity of home-places (Michèle le Dœuff) ... that all this has so often come from those who were 'on the margins' of that old, settled (and anyway mythologized?) coherence.

## Notes

1 This rejection of locality studies as 'local', atheoretical, concerned with nostalgia, and so forth may in other words have been a manifestation of a particular variant of what Gillian Rose labels 'social-scientific masculinity' within the discipline of geography (see her *Feminism and Geography: The Limits of Geographical Knowledge* [Cambridge, Polity, 1993]). It is also worth noting that the acute separation of Being and Becoming in some of the geographical writing in this area (which has led authors into their denigration, and fear, of 'Being') is not an indisputable interpretation of Heidegger (thanks to discussions with Ernesto Laclau for this point). Finally, the recoil from place, given that term's connotational association with the concrete, may be tied in to its consequent insistence on our inevitable embeddedness and embodiedness, thus countering pretensions to intellectual universalism (Kevin Robins, personal communication; Susan Bordo, 'Feminism, postmodernism, and gender-scepticism', in Linda J. Nicholson, *Feminism/Postmodernism* [London, Routledge, 1990]; and Donna J. Haraway, *Simians, Cyborgs, and Women: The Reinvention of Nature* [London, Free Association Books, 1991]).

2 See Doreen Massey, 'Power geometry and a progressive sense of place', in J. Bird, B. Curtis, T. Putnam, G. Robertson and L. Tickner, *Mapping the Futures: Local Cultures, Global Change* (London, Routledge, 1993), pp. 59–69.

3 Just to be clear, this is not to invoke yet another form of spatial fetishism. It is not, of course, the places themselves which interact but social relations which take place between agents 'within' them.

4 Ernesto Laclau, *Reflections on the Revolution of Our Time* (London, Verso, 1990), p. 208. And later, in interview, he reinforces the point, this time precisely in relation to the question of identity (though he is talking of subjective identity, rather than the identity of place): 'Well I think that the main task of a new culture ... is to transform the forms of identification and construction of subjectivity that exist in our civilization. It is necessary to pass from cultural forms constructed as a search for the universal in the contingent, to others that go in a diametrically opposite direction: that is, that attempt to show the essential contingency of all universality, that construct the beauty of the specific, of the unrepeatable, of what transgresses the norm' (p. 190).

5 One of the issues facing 'the new urban left' in the UK in the 1980s was

precisely to analyse the balance of and relationship between social relations which stretched beyond the area in question and those which could more clearly be said to be contained within it. That intersection of scales, the presence of the global in the local, and the continuance of within-place relations all had implications for the amount and nature of the leverage which it was possible to employ at the level of the metropolitan council.

6   Iris Marion Young, 'The ideal of community and the politics of difference', *Social Theory and Practice*, vol. 12, no. 1, spring 1986, pp. 1–26.

7   For a fuller exploration of the issues involved in this, and thoughts on other related cases, see Doreen Massey, 'Double articulation: a place in the world', in Angelika Bammer (ed.), *Displacements* (Indiana University Press, forthcoming).

# 5

# The Political Place of Locality Studies

## Introduction: space, politics and locality research

At a number of points in the rich debate about locality studies in the United Kingdom, various authors have made various assumptions about the *reasons* for pursuing this kind of research in the first place. The different positions of the particular contributors have, however, unlike other aspects of the discussion, rarely been linked together into a debate. Yet it is clearly an important issue. For one thing, it will crucially affect the way locality studies, as a category and individually, are evaluated. It is difficult adequately to assess research without understanding its aims in the first place, both in order to have something to evaluate it against and because the objectives may themselves be open to evaluation. For another thing, this issue of the aims of locality studies links into a wider debate about our role as academics or intellectuals and the relationship of our work to current political issues and debates (Walker, 1989). The purpose of the present paper is simply to reflect upon some of the reasons why the programme of locality studies called the Changing Urban and Regional System (CURS) was first proposed and developed.[1]

One of the most striking things about the assumptions most often made by commentators about the reasons for the programme is that, although most of them come from people who would define themselves as being 'on the left', they almost never refer to politics, and more particularly to the political situation in which the issue of locality studies was being raised. If politics does enter the question, then it usually does so in one of two ways (and sometimes both at once). On the one hand, it is assumed by some that Marxist theory or the mechanics of accumulation at a grand scale are always and everywhere politically 'OK' things to work on. On the other hand, it is argued, or asserted, that studying 'the local' or 'place' is necessarily politically problematic. (Among the few exceptions is the interesting discussion by Jonas [1988].)

The idea for the current focus on locality studies arose in the United Kingdom of the early 1980s. From the end of the 1960s there had been clear intimations that the economy at least, and maybe society more widely, was entering a period of significant change. There was an accelerating shift away from manufacturing, a noticeable increase in registered unemployment, a continuing transformation of the occupational structure, and so on. The major social changes which appeared to be heralded by these economic shifts also provoked political reflection. It was a set of processes which were further heightened by the events of the early 1980s. The debates about flexibilization and 'post-Fordism' and the continued presence in power of a right-wing Conservative government, and the failure of the Labour Party to exercise any hold over the imaginations of the majority, reinforced the feeling that an era was at an end. There was a major political debate, initiated by Eric Hobsbawm, about whether the 'forward march of labour' had been halted, about whether the 'natural' (a term which was anyway highly questionable) social base of the Labour Party was being inexorably eroded, about the fragmentation of the working class (or was it merely that that fragmentation, and internal conflicts of interest, were only now being recognized?), indeed about the role of class as a primary political organizing principle at all. *Marxism Today* was developing its analyses of structural change and their (usually depressing) political implications and outlining its theory of Thatcherism and of the potential new ideological hegemony.

Although these debates did not take place primarily within human geography as an academic discipline, they related to it in a number of ways. For one thing, among the significant changes under way in British society, some of the most important ones were geographical. There was a spatial restructuring as an integral part of the social and economic. The economies of the big manufacturing cities went into severe decline. The bases of the heavy-industry regions were undermined. There was decentralization of both population and employment from big cities outwards to more rural areas and, in some parts of the period, from core regions to the old industrial periphery. The increase in paid employment for women, and the shifts in balance between male and female employment, happened differentially across the country. The so-called high-technology industries, and the hugely expanding banking, finance and professional services sectors transformed the south-east region. More recently, there has been a noticeable, if spatially restricted, transformation of parts of once declining inner cities. Waterfronts everywhere are being revitalized into expensive housing and trendy offices; the Docklands, in London's eastern area, became for a while so much a symbol of the transformative impact of Mrs Thatcher's government that she began her 1987 election campaign there. Indeed, much of what was going on seemed to be about 'places' and their reconstitution in some way or another.

Moreover, and more urgently significant in a political sense for some, the organizational base of the left was being affected by spatial changes as well as by changes in the national economy and society (Lane, 1982; Massey, 1983; Massey and Miles, 1984). Perhaps more than anything else, the very fact that the national structural changes themselves involved a geographical restructuring meant that people in different parts of the country were experiencing highly contrasting shifts, and that even the trajectories of change (for example in class structure) could be quite different in one place from in another. And, especially because it is not simply final outcomes but processes of change which are significant to people's experience of their world, this meant that the political implications of these 'structural changes' were likely also to be highly contrasting between one place and another. Moreover, this spatial variation was reinforced by the fact that people in different parts of the country had distinct traditions and resources to draw on in their interpretation of, and their response to, these changes.

It was also the case that a great deal of immediate politics, both on the part of the government and in terms of oppositional political activity, had a clearly and, more importantly, *explicitly* local base. Perhaps the most obvious example was the rise of what came to be called 'the new urban left'. In a number of major cities, of which London and the Greater London Council were only the most prominent example, a new radical left (both within and independent of the local state) became one of the main foci of opposition both to the government and to the labourist politics of the leadership of the main opposition party.

The complexity of this geography of restructuring, its reverberations, and the political responses to it, had a number of important implications. First, it meant that some of the debates being conducted solely at national level, and some of the conclusions being drawn from them, were quite simply unsubstantiable at that level in any rigorous sense. Across the political spectrum, causal connections were being made between changes in employment and occupational structure and wider social, ideological and political changes. We were facing the end of the working class, the end of class politics, a new ideology of individualism, a politics of consumption, the dominance of what were referred to as 'new social movements'. All this was being argued, most frequently, from national-level statistics. Yet, quite apart from the difficulty of establishing such causal connections in the first place and the dubiousness of the economistic form in which they were usually proposed, the issues of spatial scale and spatial variation were usually ignored. And yet presumptions of cause and effect made at national level were clearly untenable when each of the component causal processes, which were supposedly interacting, was taking place unevenly (and differently so) over the national space. Further, the relation between political, cultural, and economic changes may have an important local level of operation. In other words, some of the causal processes which were being appealed to in the debate could not be seen as operating at national level only.

Second, spatial variation meant that the potential, the problems, and even the style of political response and organization would be different in distinct parts of the country. Conclusions drawn at national level about policy implications and changes in political strategy could not be assumed to be universally applicable, to resonate in the same way with the particular traditions and circumstances in different parts of the country. At perhaps the most trivial, but certainly the most easily documented, political level it was clear that the voting patterns of individual social groups were becoming increasingly geographically differentiated.

Third, recognizing variation in no way implies abandoning wider movements or wider levels of organization. But local contrasts did mean that it was not possible to construct them by simply proclaiming that each local change was underlain by capitalism – that is, by simply asserting 'the general'. It also required, for a solid foundation, a recognition and understanding of the reality and conditions of diversity, and of the actual processes which linked the local particularities (Massey, 1983).

The fact of spatial variation in national change, in other words, had immediate and obvious political importance.[2] It became important to know just how differently national and international changes were impacting on different parts of the country. Something that might be called 'restructuring' was clearly going on, but its implications both for everyday life and for the mode and potential of political organizing were clearly highly differentiated and we needed to know how. It was in this context that the localities projects in the United Kingdom were first imagined and proposed. It was research with an immediate, even urgent, relevance beyond academe.

## The local, the concrete and the postmodern

This history has a number of implications. It contradicts a number of other retrospective interpretations.

It is not, for instance, the case that the study of locality is a necessary vehicle for, nor equivalent to, empirical research or the study of concrete phenomena. This question has generated confusion. The issues of specificity and empirical uniqueness were on the agenda in the same period, and again as part of wider movements, in philosophy, the social sciences beyond geography, and the humanities. Localities are certainly 'specific' in this context in the sense that one of the prime aims, given the social and political background outlined above, was precisely to understand their differences. (This does not, of course, mean that they are unrelated and one of the aims of such locality research has to be – and was in this case – to understand, not just the interdependencies between localities in the sense of direct links, but the ways in which, in part, the changes going on in them were products of a wider restructuring.) In this case, then, the counterposition is between general (meaning wider) and specific (meaning more local). Some commentators, however, have at this point fallen into the trap of eliding the fact of being specific in this sense with that of being 'concrete', the product of many determinations. They then reason that, because localities are in this sense concrete, *only* localities are concrete. Here, the elision is between the dimensions specific–general and concrete–abstract. Duncan (1989) comments that what he calls the 'social' reasons for using the term locality, and which he argues are 'quite as important as its scientific use' are often 'to signify one's concern for the empirical and concrete' (p. 222). Yet the current world economy, for instance, is no less concrete than a local one. The world economy is *general* in the sense of being a geographically large-scale phenomenon to which can be counterposed internal variations. But it is also unequivocally concrete as opposed to abstract. It is not, any more than is a local economy, the simple manifestation of the capitalist mode of production. It is, just as much, a specific product of many determinations. Those who conflate the local with the concrete, therefore, are confusing geographical scale with processes of abstraction in thought.

Moreover, those who make this mistake then frequently rush headlong into another: they confuse the study of the local with description, which they oppose to theoretical work. Smith (1987), for instance, seems to be arguing that locality research is necessarily descriptive in these terms. There are a number of problems with this argument. First, in the form in which Smith puts it, it is an accusation which could only ever be made from a view of the world which equated empirical generalizability with explanation, a position which the theoretical basis of the CURS localities approach most clearly rejected. There is an assumption behind it that 'theory' is 'opposed to a concern with specificity or uniqueness', a position which is untenable 'unless one wants to argue that theory cannot grasp the unique and hence the perception of the unique is theory-neutral – an idea which died at least twenty years ago with the demise of the concept of a theory-neutral observation language' (Sayer, 1989, p. 303). Second, this argument continues the confusion between the dimensions concrete–abstract and local–general. Yet the fact that a phenomenon is 'more general' in the simple sense of being 'bigger' does not make it any more amenable to theoretical analysis. Third, this is true not only because both levels are the product of many determinations, but also because abstract analysis can be just as much about 'small' objects as it is about 'large' ones. As was pointed out above, the fact that in the debate about changes in the United Kingdom some of the conclusions being drawn at national level could not really be drawn at that level, because some of the key significant causal processes were also operative at smaller spatial scales, was one of the reasons behind the locality studies. 'The local' (meaning the small scale) is no less subject to nor useful for theorization than big, broad, general things. The counterposition of general and local is quite distinct from the distinction between abstract and concrete (see Sayer [1991] for expansion of these issues).

Indeed, when locality research came on to the agenda, new insights into understanding and *explanation* of concrete phenomena were central to the debate in human geography (Massey, 1984a; Sayer, 1984), and these provided ways into the question of local variation. So the co-appearance of an interest in methodology and studies of localities was mutually highly beneficial. But they are not equivalent to each other. These points were made in one of the initial public documents about the establishment of the research programme:

> But if there are reasons, both in policy and in analysis, why such a set of local studies is important now, it is also the case that this is a propitious moment because both theory and method have been and are still being developed in ways which make such analyses more possible. These should not be 'case studies', in the sense of idiosyncratic portraits of individual regions. Each study should attempt both to link the fortunes of the local area to the wider national and international scene, which is part of the explanation for the changes taking place, and also rigorously to link together the different levels of change going on within the local area – between economic and social changes for instance. In this context, recent theoretical developments within the field of regional geography will be of major help.

The increasing focus on the analysis of particular regions, on the notion of spatial synthesis, on the relation between general processes at national level and specific local outcomes, and on the analysis of places in the wider context of a national spatial division of labour will all give these studies a rigorous theoretical underpinning. (Massey, 1984b, p. xv)

There is a difference, then, between the *reasons* for the importance of local studies at that time, and the *conditions provided* by theoretical developments which made such analysis more possible.

The same kind of argument must be spelled out (because it seems to be so widely misunderstood) in relation to that oft-quoted slogan 'geography matters'. Duncan (1989), for instance, rests a large part of his case against the adoption of a notion of locality precisely on the idea that locality research grew out of arguments about the effectivity of spatial form. It is certainly true, as I have already said, that this was a period in which it was increasingly argued that 'place' was important. Moreover, the methodologies adopted for the study of localities, for the explanation of uniqueness, emphasized the point in a different way. For it was stressed that, not only was the character of a particular place a product of its position in relation to wider forces (the more general social and economic restructuring, for instance), but also that that character in turn stamped its own imprint *on* those wider processes. There was *mutual* interaction (Massey, 1984a). Moreover, the nature of the interaction, of the impact of local specificities on the operation of wider processes, may vary in kind. It may be that it occurs through self-conscious social activity. In the United Kingdom of the early 1980s, it was this which was the political focus of attention and inquiry. As the local political activists aimed to demonstrate in practice and as the localities projects showed in their research, there was a huge variety – of varying effectiveness – of local activity, resistance and promotion (Cooke, 1989; 1990; Harloe et al., 1990). In these cases the focus of the 'local impact' was the local government, but it could of course be other agencies, social movements, or constellations of them. Moreover, the mutual conditioning of local and wider processes need not be a product of conscious social agency. Local impact may equally well, indeed more frequently, come about through the structural interaction of social processes without any deliberate local social agency. So studies of localities *may* certainly endorse the idea that geography matters, but it is an empirical question. Moreover, localities do not by any means exhaust the idea that geography matters. Even at the level of the social and political issues being raised in the early 1980s this was evidently the case. Not just the character of individual places themselves, but the fact, nature and degree of the differences and interdependencies between them were also having their effect on the wider economy and society. The north–south divides both within the United Kingdom and internationally were (and still are) perhaps the most obvious examples. Within the United Kingdom, uneven development had important impacts both on the national economy (see Massey, 1988) and even on the country's electoral political future. At an international level, Arrighi (1990) has recently presented an interesting argument in relation to socialist politics. Thus, the spatial organization of social relations, and the interpretation of that spatial organization, has effects in more ways than through the impact of processes related to locality. The facts of distance, between-ness, unevenness, nucleation, co-presence, time–space distanciation, settings, mobility and differential mobility, all these affect how specified social relations work; they may even be necessary for their existence or prevent their operation. As we have just seen, the fact of spatial variation itself, and of interdependence – of uneven development – has major implications. 'Geography matters' does not just mean 'locality matters' – it has much wider implications, greater claims to make, than this.

Finally, in this brief tour through things which locality studies are *not*, or not necessarily, they are not *necessarily* part of the turn to the postmodern. That is to say, the debate about locality studies is in principle distinct from the debate about postmodernism. There are, of course, many apparent points of contact (Cooke [1990] has recently explored some of them), but many of these are more the result of the accidents of language than real connections, and none of them amount to real equivalences. Perhaps what a focus on localities can share with the shifts towards postmodernism is a recognition of, and a recognition of the potential significance of, both the local and variety. This, it seems to me, is unequivocally positive. Gregory, in another context, has argued tellingly that

> one of the *raisons d'être* of the human sciences is surely to comprehend the 'otherness' of other cultures. There are few tasks more urgent in a multicultural society and an interdependent world, and yet one of modern geography's greatest betrayals was its devaluation of the specificities of place and of people. (1989, p. 358)

Even those who are critical of the philosophical arguments of the postmodernists also recognize at least this characteristic to be potentially progressive. Thus, Harvey writes:

> How, then, should postmodernism in general be evaluated? My preliminary assessment would be this. That in its concern for difference, for the

difficulties of communication, for the complexity and nuances of interests, cultures, places, and the like, it exercises a positive influence. (1989 p. 113)

The problem, of course, is that postmodernism in its current guise rarely lives up to the democratic potential opened by this move. On the other hand, as Harvey recognizes, the recognition of difference is a characteristic which a reformed modernism could take on board. Thus, first among the developments which he argues should be attended to, to respond to the current difficulties and criticisms of the progressive modernist project is

> The treatment of difference and 'otherness' not as something to be added on to more fundamental Marxist categories (like class and productive forces), but as something that should be omnipresent from the very beginning in any attempt to grasp the dialectics of social change. (1989, p. 355)

However, there are other ways in which locality studies are sometimes thought to be closer to postmodernism than they are. One confusion arises over the term 'local' itself. The meaning of the term in the context of 'locality studies' is not the same as its meaning when used for instance by Lyotard in his arguments for 'local determinisms' and the abandonment of grander theories.

(There seem, suitably enough, to be numerous confusions over words. The problems provoked by the multiple meanings of the term 'specific' were pointed to above, and Sayer [1991] follows up this issue further. Here it is the term 'local' which is at issue.) Neither a focus on the empirically local (in terms of geographical scale) nor an insistence that not all theorizable causal processes operate at the level of global accumulation, implies local determinism in the sense meant by Lyotard. 'Local' in locality is not opposed to 'meta' as in 'metatheory'. Once again, there is a potential confusion between the question of level in terms of geographical scale and level of abstraction in thought. Let us take one example where the confusion can arise. Harvey (1989, p. 117) writes:

> Postmodernism has us accepting the reifications and partitionings ... all the fetishisms of locality, place or social grouping, while denying that kind of metatheory which can grasp the political-economic processes (money flows, international divisions of labour, financial markets, and the like) that are becoming ever more universalizing in their depth, intensity, reach and power over daily life.

There are a number of points here. First, studying localities does not amount to fetishizing them (I shall address this point again later); nor is

Harvey necessarily saying it does. There is perhaps no disagreement here. Second, locality studies as I see them most definitely do not deny the kind of theory which can grasp political-economic processes such as the international division of labour. The CURS programme was of course founded on precisely such concepts, and it was axiomatic that studying local areas necessarily required theories which were wider than their application to that area both in the sense that they had a broader spatial reach and in the sense of being more abstract. Such theories need not, though, only relate, as the quotation seems to imply, to economic phenomena. Third, this seems to be, precisely, a misuse of the term 'metatheory', confusing the philosophical meaning with the question of scale. The same confusion arises later in the book when an acceptance of grand narratives is opposed to an emphasis on community and locality (p. 351). Yet, if they are needed at all, grand narratives are needed just as much in the study of the local as of the international. Fourth, and more politically, it is difficult to reconcile this quotation's dismissive treatment of 'fetishisms of ... social groupings' (women, for instance?) with the apparent commitment to a democratic recognition of the existence of difference cited above. Although postmodernism certainly has its difficulties in doing anything more democratic than recognizing the existence of others, modernism seems to have problems in really, in the end, taking seriously the autonomy of others. Thus, just before this quotation, Harvey writes, 'Postmodernist philosophers tell us not only to accept but even to revel in the fragmentations and the cacophony of voices through which the dilemmas of the modern world are understood' (p. 116). He opposes such a position absolutely. I know what he means, and I have some sympathy. But I also have real reservations about this formulation. At one, very practical level, there seems to me to be not *enough* fragmentation at the moment. At least in the context of some political debates, there seems sometimes to be one megaphone – that of reaction. But that raises the second point in relation to Harvey's position: you cannot argue for the right to oppose when others are in power (and that includes being in power even within 'the left') if you will not allow it when the situation is reversed. Put together, all these quotations seem to say that it is OK to have a background orchestra of others, so long as you yourself are the conductor. Thus to return to the original issue of the meaning of the word 'local', the argument here is not that *some* local studies may not adopt a postmodern approach, indeed as Harvey points out (p. 47), Fish (1980) *has* understood 'local determinism' to mean 'localities' such as interpretative communities and particular places; but it *is* to argue that the one does not necessarily entail the other.

Again, the debate about the postmodern has brought with it a sudden recognition of, indeed a revelling in, the importance of space and place. It is a realization, a sudden discovery, which seems to have dawned on intellectuals across much of the social sciences. Jameson (1984) is only the most obvious theoretician to whom one could point. But yet again it is important to make distinctions. Although it emerged at the same period, the argument of the postmodernists about the importance of space and place is distinct, in its roots and in its nature, from the debate in geography which led to 'geography matters' and 'the difference that space makes'. For one thing, and most trivially, gratifying as it is to geographers, perhaps, to have the dimension which they have always treated as their own now accorded such centrality, it has to be said that some of the claims being made in the postmodern literature about the current importance of the spatial are grandly unsubstantiated. But, more significantly, the claim made in the debate about postmodernity is a historically specific one: it is that space and place are important *now*, and that this is something new. The arguments being made in the debate about 'geography matters' were rather different. They also involved a distinct, and I believe more constructive, engagement with and development of the form of Marxism which had been dominant in the previous decade. Here, the argument was not an empirical one in the sense that it was saying that the world had changed. More, it was an argument about our intellectual focus and about the complexity of the causal processes which we should recognize. This is not incompatible with the argument that space and place have great and real significance in these times, nor that this significance may be increasing, but it is not the same argument.

## Localities, reaction and progressiveness

A wider argument has, however, been made by Harvey in the context of the debate over *The Condition of Postmodernity*. This argument is that a focus on place and the local is, by its very nature, anti-progressive. It is necessary to be clear here. Harvey is not saying that all foci on localities are necessarily reactionary; nor certainly am I saying that a focus on the local is necessarily progressive (far from it!), and even more certainly I am not saying that it is any more than one among many potential ways of studying for geographers (for a further development of this argument see Massey, 1990). So, in broad terms we probably agree. None the less, Harvey's argument is interesting and important to consider.

There are two interweaving strands. The first begins from the philosophical arguments of such as Heidegger and Bachelard that whereas Time connotes Becoming (which is assumed, in modernist terms, to be progressive), Space connotes Being. And this in turn implies fixity, stasis. The second thread is that a concern with place leads inexorably to an aesthetic mode, and that in turn virtually inevitably to reaction. Both of these lines of argument are interesting. But they both also have weaknesses. First, both of them involve internal slippages and leaps of logic. Second, both singly and together they imply a concept of 'locality' which is certainly not the only one available and, I would argue, is at odds with the one which is implied by at least some locality studies.

The first argument, then, equates Space with Being; 'Space contains compressed time. That is what space is for' (Harvey, 1989, p. 217). The implication, immediately, is that spaces, such as localities, are essentially simultaneities. Moreover, and more importantly, they are static.

> Being, suffused with immemorial spatial memory, transcends Becoming . . . Is this the foundation for collective memory, for all those manifestations of place-bound nostalgias that infect our images of the country and the city, of region, milieu, and locality . . . And if it is true that time is always memorialized not as flow, but as memories of experienced places and spaces, then history must indeed give way to poetry, time to space . . . (1989, p. 218)

This notion is closely tied to what Harvey sees as important dilemmas, most particularly for capital: 'the most serious dilemma of all: the fact that space can be conquered only through the production of space' (p. 258). When placed in the context of capital accumulation this leads, of course, to the crucial contradiction of 'the spatial fix', and Harvey is here essentially generalizing that concept to a wider field. But there are real difficulties in such an attempt at generalization. The problem with the idea of spatial fix is that it really is about fixity, about immobility. The spatial fix is the physical forms of buildings and infrastructure; it is the prison-house of capital tied up. But this imagery is not transferable to wider fields nor, in particular, to localities. There is clearly a tension between trying on the one hand to capture a synchronicity and attempting to follow a process on the other. But localities, as I see them, are not just about physical buildings, nor even about capital momentarily imprisoned; they are about the intersection of social activities and social relations and, crucially, activities and relations which are necessarily, by definition, dynamic, changing. There is no stable moment, in the sense of stasis, if we *define* our world, or our localities, *ab initio* in terms of change. The CURS programme has 'Change' in the first word of its title. As was argued in the opening section of this paper, its empirical focus was precisely on the quite contrasting ways in which local sets of social relations were being transformed: *how* they were 'becoming'. It is an accepted argument that capital is not a thing, it is a process. Maybe it ought to be more clearly established that places can be conceptualized as processes, too.[3] If that were so, then it would be possible not only to agree that 'the present is valid only by virtue of the potentialities of the future' (Poggioli, 1968, p. 73, cited in Harvey, 1989, p. 359), but to apply it to localities as well.

The second thread of Harvey's argument is that place inexorably brings with it aesthetics and, in its turn, political reaction. One starting point for the staking out of this position is the close connection made between place and identity. The next step is to endow both place and identity with some kind of seamless coherence. A sense of identity is needed because of the unsettling flux of modern times (more on this later); a sense of identity means something stable, coherent, uncontradictory; places have already been identified as means of constructing identities, hence places are coherent, uncontradictory – a characterization which is of course further reinforced by (indeed is integral to) the attribution of stasis already discussed.

Now, there are a number of comments to be made at this point in the argument. First, this *is* certainly one way in which the notion of 'place' is commonly used, and I would agree with Harvey that it has potential dangers (see below). The problem is that Harvey seems to elide this version of the concept 'place' with any and every notion of locality and the local. Second, this way of thinking of identity is curiously solid in an age of recognition of the decentred subject and of multiple identities. Individuals' identities are not aligned with *either* place *or* class; they are probably constructed out of both, as well as a whole complex of other things, most especially 'race' and gender. The balance between these constituents, and the particular characteristics drawn upon in any one encounter or in any one period, may of course vary. And, third, this applies to places too. They do not have single, pregiven, identities in that sense. For places, certainly when conceptualized as localities, are of course *not* internally uncontradictory. Given that they are constructed out of the juxtaposition, the intersection, the articulation, of multiple social relations they could hardly be so. They are frequently riven with internal tensions and conflicts. Places are shared spaces: you could not think about London's Docklands at the moment without precisely that conflictual sharing and the conflict between interests and views of what the area is, and what it ought to *become*. This is not an idiosyncratic view, although there is horrendous terminological confusion. Thrift (1983, p. 40) for instance, writes that 'the region, initially, at least, must not be seen as a *place*; that is a matter for investigation. Rather, it must be seen as made up of a number of different but connected *settings for interaction*'. In the argument in the present paper the term 'locality' could be substituted for 'region' in this quotation. Moreover, if the term 'place' is to have the extra endowment of meaningfulness implied in that quotation, then it must be understood (as Thrift makes clear) as different from other spatial terms, including locality. Chouinard (1989) argues that localities are not bounded areas but spaces of interaction. Sayer points out that spatial juxtaposition may mean that localities contain many quite unrelated elements:

> Yet, despite this lack of functional integrity, they may still be distinctive and even derive their identity from the lack of unity ... The awkward aspect of this property of localities is that people can actually be shaped by factors which, among themselves, are totally unrelated. (Sayer, undated, p. 3)

Precisely, and to misquote a current lager advert, 'only spatial juxtaposition can do this!' (although, of course – just in case I should be misunderstood – only by virtue of the social phenomena thus juxtaposed).

Moreover, this crucial aspect of internal differentiation, of articulation, and of potential contradiction and conflict applies even more strongly when analysis turns to how actors actively draw upon localities as a basis for interpretation. Wright (1985) has written of the variety of meanings and interpretations of Hackney, many of them implicitly if not always overtly, though indeed sometimes quite actively, in conflict with each other. For each the 'meaning' of Hackney is distinct – for the old white working class, for the variety of ethnic minorities, for the new monied gentrifiers. Each has its view of what the essential place is, each partly based on the past, each drawing out a different potential future. For the analyst of the locality this intersection is surely precisely one of the things which must be addressed. Hackney *is* Hackney only because of the coexistence of all those different interpretations of what it is and what it might be. There are, of course, many definitions of locality in the literature at the moment, but, given the argument in this paper, it would seem that any requirement that an intersection of social relations in a particular space can only graduate to locality status if there is a shared local consciousness is inordinately (and arbitrarily) restrictive (and also potentially more open to the arguments about reaction put by Harvey – see below). McArthur (1989), in contrast, argues strongly that any local consciousness, should it exist, will anyway be likely to vary widely in degree and nature between different groups in an area.

All of this relates strongly back to deeper issues of conceptualization. Perhaps localities may be conceptualized as, in one aspect at least, the intersection of sets of (Giddens-type) locales. But, whatever else they are, localities are *constructions* out of the intersections and interactions of concrete social relations and social processes in a situation of co-presence.

Whether that co-presence matters, and whether it leads to new emergent powers, is an open question which will not have an empirically generalizable answer. Moreover, the particular social relations and social processes used to define a locality will reflect the research issue (which in turn means that any locality so defined will *not* be the relevant spatial area for the investigation of all and every social process deemed in some way to have a local level of variation or operation). But all this does mean that localities are not simply spatial areas you can easily draw a line around. They will be defined in terms of the sets of social relations or processes in question. Crucially, too, they are about *interaction*. Such interaction, moreover, is likely to include conflict. Localities will 'contain' (indeed in part will be *constituted by*) difference and conflict. They may also include interaction between social phenomena which may not be 'related' in any immediate way in terms of social relations a-spatially. It may be only the fact of co-presence which makes them have quite direct impacts upon each other. Moreover, the constellations of interactions will vary over time in their geographical form (see Massey, 1984a, p. 123, 196, 299). And the definition of any particular locality will therefore reflect the question at issue.

But all this returns us to the very originating view of Space-as-Being which Harvey adopts. This definition, and its counterposition with the equation Time – Becoming, is a curious mode of argument for him to follow. In most of the other major conceptualizations in the book there is a dynamic tension, sometimes a constructive contradiction. The initiating and powerful definition of modernism, which forms the framework for much of the argument in the book, is precisely of this nature. So why at this point relapse into this simple static dichotomy? Heidegger's is not the only approach to space which could have been adopted, and indeed in other parts of his argument (see below) Harvey is clearly critical of Heidegger precisely for his potentially romantic/reactionary views.

Indeed, the next steps in Harvey's argument are that 'The assertion of any place-bound identity has to rest at some point on the motivational power of tradition' (1989, p. 303) and that such place-relating structures of feeling and action are (almost – it varies) always reactionary: 'Geographical and aesthetic interventions always seem to imply nationalist, and hence unavoidably reactionary, politics' (pp. 282–3). Now, it has already been argued that the concept of locality is not, or need not be, the same as Harvey's concept of place in his argument here. So many points of potential disagreement between the lines of argument may simply evaporate if clear distinctions are made. None the less, there are wider issues to consider. Harvey exemplifies his logic of place ⇒ aestheticization ⇒ reaction at a number of points in his book, and the examples he gives, of reactionary nationalisms, most obviously of Nazism, or even the urban designs of Sitte, are very telling. But it is never quite clear just how *necessary* this chain of connections is supposed to be. Thus, of Sitte he writes:

> Under conditions of mass unemployment, the collapse of spatial barriers, and the subsequent vulnerability of place and community to space and capital, it was all too easy to play upon sentiments of the most fanatical localism and nationalism. I am not even indirectly blaming Sitte or his ideas for this history. But I do think it important to recognize the potential connection between projects to shape space and encourage spatial practices of the sort that Sitte advocated, and political projects that can be at best conserving and at worst downright reactionary in their implications. These were, after all, the sorts of sentiments of place, Being, and community that brought Heidegger into the embrace of national socialism. (1989, p. 277)

Yet if a reactionary outcome is not inevitable, but only a likely danger, still almost no examples of progressive possibilities are given by Harvey (Nicaragua gets a mention). But 'tradition' and an awareness of history can also be strengthening in an oppositional sense. Just within the United Kingdom, examples from the Little Moscows to Red Clydeside, Poplar, Clay Cross, and the 'Socialist Republic of South Yorkshire', show how local bases and traditions can be used. (The last of these was the name accredited to that part of the country for its attempts to combat national policies, most particularly over public transport!) It does not always only work for capital; we have our own traditions, too, and they are not simply to be sentimentalized, they are also to be built on. Moreover, building on traditions can also mean being critical of them. The labour-movement tradition of Sheffield, for instance, has been a strength in many ways, a resource to be drawn upon; but it has also delivered an understanding of gender relations, and of the meanings of masculinity and femininity, which have had to be challenged head on for there to be any chance of maintaining a contemporary radical political culture in the local area. Localities, in that sense, are part of the conditions not of our own making. There are, of course, dangers even here. Even labour-movement history can be commodified, commercialized, romanticized, and sold off. Yes, it can, and it often is. But the consistency with which Harvey points to this kind of outcome (in the case of local history, in the case of local economic strategies, in relation to attempts to create spaces and places to celebrate the French Revolution), indicates a wider problem. This is that, in Harvey's account, capital always wins and, it seems, only capital can ever win. Thus, in the discussions of locally based economic strategies most of the discussion is of capitalist strategies (trying to attract private capital, creating competitive images, etc., etc.), and where 'municipal socialism' is referred to it is labelled 'defensive' (p. 302) without any further explanation.

Moreover, if as I have argued there are indeed multiple meanings of places, held by different social groups for instance, then the question of which identity is dominant will be the result of social negotiation and conflict. In Wright's account of Hackney the different social groups had distinct interpretations, not just of Hackney's present, but also of its past, its 'traditions'. The past is no more authentic than the present; there will be no one reading of it. And 'traditions' are frequently invented or, if they are not, the question of which traditions will predominate can not be answered in advance. *It is people, not places in themselves, which are reactionary or progressive.* Unless, then, *any* notion of the past, any consciousness of any tradition, is *ipso facto* reactionary, the reactionary meaning of places focused on by Harvey is itself a result of conflict and not in principle necessary. Moreover, that means it must be opposed; it cannot simply be ignored.

Harvey writes, ' "Regional resistances", the struggles for local autonomy, place-bound organization, may be excellent bases for political action, but they cannot bear the burden of radical historical change alone' (p. 303). This is certainly correct in the sense that none of them are world revolution. But there are problems with the slippage of terms; place-*based* action gets conflated with place-*bound* action. Yet, to give one example, the wide range of policies from left-wing Labour councils and associated groups in recent years in the United Kingdom, running the gamut from anti-racism to energy policy, was devised at least as much in an attempt to demonstrate a political argument of wider relevance as to impact immediately and directly on the local area. Even the flurry of radical economic strategies (quite different from the local economic strategies discussed by Harvey, but the most difficult area of policy in which to be non-parochial) was a case in point (see Cochrane, 1987). There has been considerable debate about the degree to which parts of the policies were, in the end, competitive between areas. Certainly there were attempts made for this *not* to be the case (there were joint strategies between areas, there was no advertising, in the more radical cases the emphasis shifted away from simply financial viability and/or the numbers of jobs created for instance to improving the quality of work, etc.), and within the best of those local authorities the debate was continuous about how *not* to be parochial. Certainly those days of the 'new urban left' were not about the identity of place in the sense meant by Harvey. They also used local bases to address wider issues. The GLC was particularly extrovert in this sense. It backed workers in local branches of multinationals in their forging of links with workers in other parts of the United Kingdom, in Europe, and in Latin

America. It established a progressive Third World trading institution (Twin Trading) which is still going and is highly successful. Indeed, there was probably little that exasperated and infuriated the Thatcher government more than the GLC's maintenance of its own 'foreign policy', especially on Ireland. And here the debate links back to that about postmodernism.

> This is the progressive angle to postmodernism which emphasizes community and locality, place and regional resistances, social movements, respect for otherness, and the like . . . But it is hard to stop the slide into parochialism, myopia, and self-referentiality in the face of the universalising force of capital circulation. (Harvey, 1989, p. 351)

This is true, but any strategy has its dangers. Harvey opposes to local-based action a very abstract universalism. The danger of *his* strategy is that one sits in one's university and urges the world proletariat to unite. Surely in these postmodern days we should, and could, be actively promoting a conceptualization and a consciousness of place which is precisely about movement and linkage and contradiction. A sense of place which is extra-verted as well as having to deal with and build upon an inheritance from the past. That is surely the meaning of the joint existence of uniqueness and interdependence. Harvey argues (also p. 351) that locally based action can lead to fragmentation. Again, it may. But is it not also a necessary condition for building real unity? We can only build unity if we have the confidence to face diversity without it frightening us and to analyse the *real* conditions for solidarity. This returns us again to the debate about difference, and how to conceptualize localities. At minimum we can say that localities are not internally introspective bounded unities. They have to be constructed through sets of social relations which bind them inextricably to wider arenas, and other places.

## Conclusions

The point of this paper has in no way been to glorify the local level, either as object of analysis or as arena of political action. There are great dangers in an overemphasis on its importance, its significance to 'daily life', its relation to the constitution of identity (Massey, 1990). Nor is the issue whether we *only* do locality studies or *only* do something else. One of the problems with the current debate is that it has been understood by some as being about a new 'orthodoxy' on what geographers ought to be studying. By others, with equally little understanding, it has been dismissed as a fashion. Both of these positions are crippled by thinking of the development of foci of study as happening entirely as a product of events in the academic world or intellectual debate. But things are not (or should not be) so.

Other explanations of the current focus on localities do set the shifts in a wider, and historically specific, context. Thus Harvey, who is addressing a much wider issue than simply the current locality studies, interprets an increasing focus on place as deriving from the unsettling nature of the times in which we live, the current perturbations being a result of a heightened process of time–space compression. There are many paragraphs evoking the ephemerality, confusion, uncertainty, the shifting and the fragmentation, the disruption. 'In periods of confusion and uncertainty, the turn to aesthetics (of whatever form) becomes more pronounced' (p. 328). Apart from the serious question of how one can begin to evaluate such a claim, there is a further point. If people *are* beginning to turn to localities in reactionary ways, then it may precisely be important to study them. Such phenomena are themselves – or should be – amenable to historical materialist analysis. To study something is not necessarily to glorify it; indeed it can be an important part of exposing myths, of locality and place as much as of anything else.

But I also find mystifying the idea, argued by many, that time–space compression is somehow psychologically disturbing. Such flux and disruption is, as Harvey says, part of modernity. Why should the construction of places out of things from everywhere be so unsettling? Who is it who is yearning after the seamless whole and the settled place? A global sense of place – dynamic and internally contradictory and extra-verted – is surely potentially progressive.

None the less, it *is* true that the current programme of locality studies was proposed for reasons which were historically specific.[4] They arose from the situation *then* and *there*. And, moreover, that situation was not one only, nor even primarily, defined by academic or intellectual debate. It was a situation defined by what was happening in society more widely, and by important questions which were raised as a result of those changes. Such a history, in other words, does *not* imply that locality research, the study of particular places, should in some more general sense, always and everywhere, be the focus of human geographical inquiry. Sometimes we may want to study particular localities for particular, strategic, reasons. Most often, indeed, we may find that other foci of research will be more important.

Milton Keynes
published in 1991

# Notes

1 The author was the initiator of the original proposal, and responsible for drawing up the original outline. The funders and the participants subsequently developed and implemented the programme in greater detail and as a product of their own ideas and research.
2 The argument here is directed to 'the left' because that is the debate which I am addressing. But parallel points could be made about relevance across the political spectrum. Government departments, for instance, displayed interest in the geographical variation in penetration of the 'enterprise culture'.
3 Pred (1984; 1989) has of course for a time argued something along those lines, although from a rather different perspective. Perhaps ironically given the context of the present paper, I would argue that he greatly overemphasizes the significance of 'the local' (see Massey, 1990).
4 There are, of course, other more transhistorical claims made by some authors. These are discussed in Massey (1990).

# References

Arrighi, G., 1990, 'Marxist century, American century: the making and remaking of the world labour movement', *New Left Review*, no. 179, pp. 29–63.
Chouinard, V., 1989, 'Explaining local experiences in state formation: the case of cooperative housing in Toronto', *Environment and Planning D: Society and Space*, 7, pp. 51–68.
Cochrane, A. (ed.), 1987, *Developing Local Economic Strategies* (Open University Press, Milton Keynes).
Cooke, P. (ed.), 1989, *Localities* (Unwin Hyman, London).
——, 1990, *Back to the Future: Modernity, Postmodernity and Locality* (Unwin Hyman, London).
Duncan, S., 1989, 'What is locality?', in R. Peet and N. Thrift (eds), *New Models in Geography: The Political Economy Perspective*, vol. II, (Unwin Hyman, London), pp. 221–52.
Fish, S., 1980, *Is There a Text in this Class? The Authority of Interpretive Communities* (Harvard University Press, Cambridge, MA).
Gregory, D., 1989, 'The crisis of modernity? Human geography and critical social theory', in *New Models in Geography: The Political Economy Perspective*, vol. II, ed. R. Peet and N. Thrift (Unwin Hyman, London), pp. 348–85.
Harloe, M., Pickvance, C. and Urry, J., 1990, *Place, Policy and Politics: Do Localities Matter?* (Unwin Hyman, London).
Harvey, D., 1989, *The Condition of Postmodernity* (Basil Blackwell, Oxford).
Jameson, F., 1984, 'Postmodernism, or the cultural logic of late capitalism', *New Left Review* no. 146, pp. 53–92.
Jonas, A., 1988, 'A new regional geography of localities?', *Area* 20, pp. 101–10.

Lane, T., 1982, 'The unions: caught on an ebb-tide', *Marxism Today*, September, pp. 6–13.

Massey, D., 1983, 'The shape of things to come', *Marxism Today*, April, pp. 18–27; this vol. ch. 3.

——, 1984a, *Spatial Divisions of Labour: Social Structures and the Geography of Production* (Macmillan, Basingstoke).

——, 1984b, 'Industrial location: some thoughts and observations', *ESRC Newsletter* no. 51, supplement, p. xv.

——, 1988, 'A new class of geography', *Marxism Today*, May, pp. 12–17.

——, 1990, 'L"estudi de localitats" en geografia regional', *Treballs de la Societat Catalana de Geografia* 21, pp. 73–87.

Massey, D. and Miles, N., 1984, 'Mapping out the unions', *Marxism Today*, May, pp. 19–22.

McArthur, R., 1989, 'Locality and small firms: some reflections from the Franco-British project, "Industrial systems, Technical Change and Locality"', *Environment and Planning D: Society and Space* 7, pp. 197–210.

Poggioli, R., 1968, *The Theory of the Avant-garde* (Harvard University Press, Cambridge, MA).

Pred, A., 1984, 'Place as historically contingent process: structuration and the time-geography of becoming places', *Annals of the Association of American Geographers* 74, pp. 279–97.

——, 1989, 'The locally spoken word and local struggles', *Environment and Planning D: Society and Space* 7, pp. 211–33.

Sayer, A., 1984, *Method in Social Sciences: A Realist Approach* (Hutchinson, London).

——, 1989, 'Dualistic thinking and rhetoric in geography', *Area* 21, pp. 301–5.

——, 1991, 'Behind the locality debate: deconstructing geography's dualisms', *Environment and Planning A* 23, pp. 283–308.

—— (undated), 'Locales, localities, and why we want to study them', mimeo, School of Social Sciences, University of Sussex, Brighton, Sussex.

Smith, N., 1987, 'Dangers of the empirical turn: some comments on the CURS initiative', *Antipode* 19, pp. 59–68.

Soja, E., 1989, *Postmodern Geographies: The Reassertion of Space in Critical Social Theory* (Verso, London).

Thrift, N., 1983, 'On the determination of social action in space and time', *Environment and Planning D: Society and Space* 1, pp. 23–57.

Walker, R., 1989, 'What's left to do?', *Antipode* 21, pp. 133–65.

Wright, P., 1985, *On Living in an Old Country: The National Past in Contemporary Britain* (Verso, London).

# 6

## *A Global Sense of Place*

This is an era – it is often said – when things are speeding up, and spreading out. Capital is going through a new phase of internationalization, especially in its financial parts. More people travel more frequently and for longer distances. Your clothes have probably been made in a range of countries from Latin America to South-East Asia. Dinner consists of food shipped in from all over the world. And if you have a screen in your office, instead of opening a letter which – care of Her Majesty's Post Office – has taken some days to wend its way across the country, you now get interrupted by e-mail.

This view of the current age is one now frequently found in a wide range of books and journals. Much of what is written about space, place and postmodern times emphasizes a new phase in what Marx once called 'the annihilation of space by time'. The process is argued, or – more usually – asserted, to have gained a new momentum, to have reached a new stage. It is a phenomenon which has been called 'time–space compression'. And the general acceptance that something of the sort is going on is marked by the almost obligatory use in the literature of terms and phrases such as speed-up, global village, overcoming spatial barriers, the disruption of horizons, and so forth.

One of the results of this is an increasing uncertainty about what we mean by 'places' and how we relate to them. How, in the face of all this movement and intermixing, can we retain any sense of a local place and its particularity? An (idealized) notion of an era when places were (supposedly) inhabited by coherent and homogeneous communities is set against the current fragmentation and disruption. The counterposition is anyway dubious, of course; 'place' and 'community' have only rarely been coterminous. But the occasional longing for such coherence is none the less a sign of the geographical fragmentation, the spatial disruption, of our times. And occasionally, too, it has been part of what has given rise to defensive and reactionary responses – certain forms of nationalism, senti mentalized recovering of sanitized 'heritages', and outright antagonism to newcomers and 'outsiders'. One of the effects of such responses is that place itself, the seeking after a sense of place, has come to be seen by some as necessarily reactionary.

But is that necessarily so? Can't we rethink our sense of place? Is it not possible for a sense of place to be progressive; not self-enclosing and defensive, but outward-looking? A sense of place which is adequate to this era of time–space compression? To begin with, there are some questions to be asked about time–space compression itself. Who is it that experiences it, and how? Do we all benefit and suffer from it in the same way?

For instance, to what extent does the currently popular characterization of time–space compression represent very much a western, colonizer's, view? The sense of dislocation which some feel at the sight of a once well-known local street now lined with a succession of cultural imports – the pizzeria, the kebab house, the branch of the middle-eastern bank – must have been felt for centuries, though from a very different point of view, by colonized peoples all over the world as they watched the importation, maybe even used, the products of, first, European colonization, maybe British (from new forms of transport to liver salts and custard powder), later US, as they learned to eat wheat instead of rice or corn, to drink Coca-Cola, just as today we try out enchiladas.

Moreover, as well as querying the ethnocentricity of the idea of time–space compression and its current acceleration, we also need to ask about its causes: what is it that determines our degrees of mobility, that influences the sense we have of space and place? Time–space compression refers to movement and communication across space, to the geographical stretching-out of social relations, and to our experience of all this. The usual interpretation is that it results overwhelmingly from the actions of capital, and from its currently increasing internationalization. On this interpretation, then, it is time space and money which make the world go round, and us go round (or not) the world. It is capitalism and its developments which are argued to determine our understanding and our experience of space.

But surely this is insufficient. Among the many other things which clearly influence that experience, there are, for instance, 'race' and gender. The degree to which we can move between countries, or walk about the streets at night, or venture out of hotels in foreign cities, is not just influenced by 'capital'. Survey after survey has shown how women's mobility, for instance, is restricted – in a thousand different ways, from physical violence to being ogled at or made to feel quite simply 'out of place' – not by 'capital', but by men. Or, to take a more complicated example, Birkett, reviewing books on women adventurers and travellers in the nineteenth and twentieth centuries, suggests that 'it is far, far more demanding for a woman to wander now than ever before'.[1] The reasons she gives for this argument are a complex mix of colonialism, ex-colonialism, racism, changing gender relations and relative wealth. A simple resort to explanation in terms of 'money' or 'capital' alone could not begin to get to grips with the issue. The current speed-up may be strongly determined by economic forces, but it is not the economy alone which determines our experience of space and place. In other words, and put simply, there is a lot more determining how we experience space than what 'capital' gets up to.

What is more, of course, that last example indicated that 'time–space compression' has not been happening for everyone in all spheres of activity. Birkett again, this time writing of the Pacific Ocean:

> Jumbos have enabled Korean computer consultants to fly to Silicon Valley as if popping next door, and Singaporean entrepreneurs to reach Seattle in a day. The borders of the world's greatest ocean have been joined as never before. And Boeing has brought these people together. But what about those they fly over, on their islands five miles below? How has the mighty 747 brought them greater communion with those whose shores are washed by the same water? It hasn't, of course. Air travel might enable businessmen to buzz across the ocean, but the concurrent decline in shipping has only increased the isolation of many island communities . . . Pitcairn, like many other Pacific islands, has never felt so far from its neighbours.[2]

In other words, and most broadly, time–space compression needs differentiating socially. This is not just a moral or political point about inequality, although that would be sufficient reason to mention it; it is also a conceptual point.

Imagine for a moment that you are on a satellite, further out and beyond all actual satellites; you can see 'planet earth' from a distance and, unusually for someone with only peaceful intentions, you are equipped with the kind of technology which allows you to see the colours of people's eyes and the numbers on their numberplates. You can see all the movement and tune in to all the communication that is going on. Furthest out are the satellites, then aeroplanes, the long haul between London and Tokyo and the hop from San Salvador to Guatemala City. Some of this is people moving, some of it is physical trade, some is media broadcasting.

There are faxes, e-mail, film-distribution networks, financial flows and transactions. Look in closer and there are ships and trains, steam trains slogging laboriously up hills somewhere in Asia. Look in closer still and there are lorries and cars and buses, and on down further, somewhere in sub-Saharan Africa, there's a woman – amongst many women – on foot, who still spends hours a day collecting water.

Now, I want to make one simple point here, and that is about what one might call the *power geometry* of it all; the power geometry of time–space compression. For different social groups, and different individuals, are placed in very distinct ways in relation to these flows and interconnections. This point concerns not merely the issue of who moves and who doesn't, although that is an important element of it; it is also about power in relation *to* the flows and the movement. Different social groups have distinct relationships to this anyway differentiated mobility: some people are more in charge of it than others; some initiate flows and movement, others don't; some are more on the receiving-end of it than others; some are effectively imprisoned by it.

In a sense at the end of all the spectra are those who are both doing the moving and the communicating and who are in some way in a position of control in relation to it – the jet-setters, the ones sending and receiving the faxes and the e-mail, holding the international conference calls, the ones distributing the films, controlling the news, organizing the investments and the international currency transactions. These are the groups who are really in a sense in charge of time–space compression, who can really use it and turn it to advantage, whose power and influence it very definitely increases. On its more prosaic fringes this group probably includes a fair number of western academics and journalists – those, in other words, who write most about it.

But there are also groups who are also doing a lot of physical moving, but who are not 'in charge' of the process in the same way at all. The refugees from El Salvador or Guatemala and the undocumented migrant workers from Michoacán in Mexico, crowding into Tijuana to make a perhaps fatal dash for it across the border into the US to grab a chance of a new life. Here the experience of movement, and indeed of a confusing plurality of cultures, is very different. And there are those from India, Pakistan, Bangladesh, the Caribbean, who come half way round the world only to get held up in an interrogation room at Heathrow.

Or – a different case again – there are those who are simply on the receiving end of time–space compression. The pensioner in a bed-sit in any inner city in this country, eating British working-class-style fish and chips from a Chinese take-away, watching a US film on a Japanese television; and not daring to go out after dark. And anyway the public transport's been cut.

Or – one final example to illustrate a different kind of complexity – there are the people who live in the *favelas* of Rio, who know global football like the back of their hand, and have produced some of its players; who have contributed massively to global music, who gave us the samba and produced the lambada that everyone was dancing to last year in the clubs of Paris and London; and who have never, or hardly ever, been to downtown Rio. At one level they have been tremendous contributors to what we call time–space compression; and at another level they are imprisoned in it.

This is, in other words, a highly complex social differentiation. There are differences in the degree of movement and communication, but also in the degree of control and of initiation. The ways in which people are placed within 'time–space compression' are highly complicated and extremely varied.

But this in turn immediately raises questions of politics. If time–space compression can be imagined in that more socially formed, socially evaluative and differentiated way, then there may be here the possibility of developing a politics of mobility and access. For it does seem that mobility, and control over mobility, both reflects and reinforces power. It is not simply a question of unequal distribution, that some people move more than others, and that some have more control than others. It is that the mobility and control of some groups can actively weaken other people. Differential mobility can weaken the leverage of the already weak. The time–space compression of some groups can undermine the power of others.

This is well established and often noted in the relationship between capital and labour. Capital's ability to roam the world further strengthens it in relation to relatively immobile workers, enables it to play off the plant at Genk against the plant at Dagenham. It also strengthens its hand against struggling local economies the world over as they compete for the favour of some investment. The 747s that fly computer scientists across the Pacific are part of the reason for the greater isolation today of the island of Pitcairn. But also, every time someone uses a car, and thereby increases their personal mobility, they reduce both the social rationale and the financial viability of the public transport system – and thereby also potentially reduce the mobility of those who rely on that system. Every time you drive to that out-of-town shopping centre you contribute to the rising prices, even hasten the demise, of the corner shop. And the 'time–space compression' which is involved in producing and reproducing the daily lives of the comfortably-off in First World societies – not just their own travel but the resources they draw on, from all over the world, to feed their lives – may entail environmental consequences, or hit constraints, which will limit the lives of others before their own. We need to ask, in other words, whether our relative mobility and power over mobility and communication entrenches the spatial imprisonment of other groups.

But this way of thinking about time–space compression also returns us to the question of place and a sense of place. How, in the context of all these socially varied time–space changes do we think about 'places'? In an era when, it is argued, 'local communities' seem to be increasingly broken up, when you can go abroad and find the same shops, the same music as at home, or eat your favourite foreign-holiday food at a restaurant down the road – and when everyone has a different experience of all this – how then do we think about 'locality'?

Many of those who write about time–space compression emphasize the insecurity and unsettling impact of its effects, the feelings of vulnerability which it can produce. Some therefore go on from this to argue that, in the middle of all this flux, people desperately need a bit of peace and quiet – and that a strong sense of place, of locality, can form one kind of refuge from the hubbub. So the search after the 'real' meanings of places, the unearthing of heritages and so forth, is interpreted as being, in part, a response to desire for fixity and for security of identity in the middle of all the movement and change. A 'sense of place', of rootedness, can provide – in this form and on this interpretation – stability and a source of unproblematical identity. In that guise, however, place and the spatially local are then rejected by many progressive people as almost necessarily reactionary. They are interpreted as an evasion; as a retreat from the (actually unavoidable) dynamic and change of 'real life', which is what we must seize if we are to change things for the better. On this reading, place and locality are foci for a form of romanticized escapism from the real business of the world. While 'time' is equated with movement and progress, 'space'/'place' is equated with stasis and reaction.

There are some serious inadequacies in this argument. There is the question of why it is assumed that time–space compression will produce insecurity. There is the need to face up to – rather than simply deny – people's need for attachment of some sort, whether through place or anything else. None the less, it is certainly the case that there is indeed at the moment a recrudescence of some very problematical senses of place, from reactionary nationalisms, to competitive localisms, to introverted obsessions with 'heritage'. We need, therefore, to think through what might be an adequately progressive sense of place, one which would fit in with the current global–local times and the feelings and relations they give rise to, *and* which would be useful in what are, after all, political struggles often inevitably based on place. The question is how to hold on to that notion of geographical difference, of uniqueness, even of rootedness if people want that, without it being reactionary.

There are a number of distinct ways in which the 'reactionary' notion of place described above is problematical. One is the idea that places have single, essential, identities. Another is the idea that identity of place – the sense of place – is constructed out of an introverted, inward-looking history based on delving into the past for internalized origins, translating the name from the Domesday Book. Thus Wright recounts the construction and appropriation of Stoke Newington and its past by the arriving middle class (the Domesday Book registers the place as 'Newtowne'): 'There is land for two ploughs and a half . . . There are four villanes and thirty seven cottagers with ten acres'. And he contrasts this version with that of other groups – the white working class and the large number of important minority communities.[3] A particular problem with this conception of place is that it seems to require the drawing of boundaries. Geographers have long been exercised by the problem of defining regions, and this question of 'definition' has almost always been reduced to the issue of drawing lines around a place. I remember some of my most painful times as a geographer have been spent unwillingly struggling to think how one could draw a boundary around somewhere like the 'east midlands'. But that kind of boundary around an area precisely distinguishes between an inside and an outside. It can so easily be yet another way of constructing a counterposition between 'us' and 'them'.

And yet if one considers almost any real place, and certainly one not defined primarily by administrative or political boundaries, these supposed characteristics have little real purchase.

Take, for instance, a walk down Kilburn High Road, my local shopping centre. It is a pretty ordinary place, north-west of the centre of London. Under the railway bridge the newspaper stand sells papers from every county of what my neighbours, many of whom come from there, still often call the Irish Free State. The postboxes down the High Road, and many an empty space on a wall, are adorned with the letters IRA. Other available spaces are plastered this week with posters for a special meeting in remembrance: Ten Years after the Hunger Strike. At the local theatre Eamon Morrissey has a one-man show; the National Club has the Wolfe Tones on, and at the Black Lion there's Finnegan's Wake. In two shops I notice this week's lottery ticket winners: in one the name is Teresa Gleeson, in the other, Chouman Hassan.

Thread your way through the often almost stationary traffic diagonally across the road from the newsstand and there's a shop which as long as I can remember has displayed saris in the window. Four life-sized models of Indian women, and reams of cloth. On the door a notice announces a forthcoming concert at Wembley Arena: Anand Miland presents Rekha, live, with Aamir Khan, Salman Khan, Jahi Chawla and Raveena Tandon. On another ad, for the end of the month, is written, 'All Hindus are cordially invited'. In another newsagents I chat with the man who keeps it, a Muslim unutterably depressed by events in the Gulf, silently chafing at having to sell the *Sun*. Overhead there is always at least one aeroplane – we seem to be on a flight-path to Heathrow and by the time they're over Kilburn you can see them clearly enough to tell the airline and wonder as you struggle with your shopping where they're coming from. Below, the reason the traffic is snarled up (another odd effect of time–space compression!) is in part because this is one of the main entrances to and escape routes from London, the road to Staples Corner and the beginning of the M1 to 'the North'.

This is just the beginnings of a sketch from immediate impressions but a proper analysis could be done of the links between Kilburn and the world. And so it could for almost any place.

Kilburn is a place for which I have a great affection; I have lived there many years. It certainly has 'a character of its own'. But it is possible to feel all this without subscribing to any of the static and defensive – and in that sense reactionary – notions of 'place' which were referred to above. First, while Kilburn may have a character of its own, it is absolutely not a seamless, coherent identity, a single sense of place which everyone shares. It could hardly be less so. People's routes through the place, their favourite haunts within it, the connections they make (physically, or by phone or post, or in memory and imagination) between here and the rest of the world vary enormously. If it is now recognized that people have multiple identities then the same point can be made in relation to places. Moreover, such multiple identities can either be a source of richness or a source of conflict, or both.

One of the problems here has been a persistent identification of place with 'community'. Yet this is a misidentification. On the one hand, communities can exist without being in the same place – from networks of friends with like interests, to major religious, ethnic or political communities. On the other hand, the instances of places housing single 'communities' in the sense of coherent social groups are probably – and, I would argue, have for long been – quite rare. Moreover, even where they do exist this in no way implies a single sense of place. For people occupy different positions within any community. We could counterpose to the chaotic mix of Kilburn the relatively stable and homogeneous community (at least in popular imagery) of a small mining village. Homogeneous? 'Communities' too have internal structures. To take the most obvious example, I'm sure a woman's sense of place in a mining village – the spaces through which she normally moves, the meeting places, the connections outside – are different from a man's. Their 'senses of the place' will be different.

Moreover, not only does 'Kilburn', then, have many identities (or its full identity is a complex mix of all these) it is also, looked at in this way, absolutely *not* introverted. It is (or ought to be) impossible even to begin thinking about Kilburn High Road without bringing into play half the world and a considerable amount of British imperialist history (and this certainly goes for mining villages too). Imagining it this way provokes in you (or at least in me) a really global sense of place.

And finally, in contrasting this way of looking at places with the defensive reactionary view, I certainly could not begin to, nor would I want to, define 'Kilburn' by drawing its enclosing boundaries.

So, at this point in the argument, get back in your mind's eye on a satellite; go right out again and look back at the globe. This time, however, imagine not just all the physical movement, nor even all the often invisible communications, but also and especially all the social relations, all the links between people. Fill it in with all those different experiences of time–space compression. For what is happening is that the geography of social relations is changing. In many cases such relations are increasingly stretched out over space. Economic, political and cultural social relations, each full of power and with internal structures of domination and subordination, stretched out over the planet at every different level, from the household to the local area to the international.

It is from that perspective that it is possible to envisage an alternative interpretation of place. In this interpretation, what gives a place its specificity is not some long internalized history but the fact that it is constructed out of a particular constellation of social relations, meeting and weaving together at a particular locus. If one moves in from the satellite towards the globe, holding all those networks of social relations and movements and communications in one's head, then each 'place' can be seen as a particular, unique, point of their intersection. It is, indeed, a *meeting* place. Instead then, of thinking of places as areas with boundaries around, they can be imagined as articulated moments in networks of social relations and understandings, but where a large proportion of those relations, experiences and understandings are constructed on a far larger scale than what we happen to define for that moment as the place itself, whether that be a street, or a region or even a continent. And this in turn allows a sense of place which is extroverted, which includes a conscious-ness of its links with the wider world, which integrates in a positive way the global and the local.

This is not a question of making the ritualistic connections to 'the wider system' – the people in the local meeting who bring up international capitalism every time you try to have a discussion about rubbish-collection – the point is that there are real relations with real content – economic, political, cultural – between any local place and the wider world in which it is set. In economic geography the argument has long been accepted that it is not possible to understand the 'inner city', for instance its loss of jobs, the decline of manufacturing employment there, by looking only at the inner city. Any adequate explanation has to set the inner city in its wider geographical context. Perhaps it is appropriate to think how that kind of understanding could be extended to the notion of a sense of place.

These arguments, then, highlight a number of ways in which a progres-sive concept of place might be developed. First of all, it is absolutely not static. If places can be conceptualized in terms of the social interactions which they tie together, then it is also the case that these interactions themselves are not motionless things, frozen in time. They are processes. One of the great one-liners in Marxist exchanges has for long been, 'Ah, but capital is not a thing, it's a process.' Perhaps this should be said also about places; that places are processes, too.

Second, places do not have to have boundaries in the sense of divisions which frame simple enclosures. 'Boundaries' may of course be necessary, for the purposes of certain types of studies for instance, but they are not necessary for the conceptualization of a place itself. Definition in this sense does not have to be through simple counterposition to the outside; it can come, in part, precisely through the particularity of linkage *to* that 'outside' which is therefore itself part of what constitutes the place. This helps get away from the common association between penetrability and vulnerabil-ity. For it is this kind of association which makes invasion by newcomers so threatening.

Third, clearly places do not have single, unique 'identities'; they are full of internal conflicts. Just think, for instance, about London's Docklands, a place which is at the moment quite clearly *defined* by conflict: a conflict over what its past has been (the nature of its 'heritage'), conflict over what should be its present development, conflict over what could be its future.

Fourth, and finally, none of this denies place nor the importance of the uniqueness of place. The specificity of place is continually reproduced, but it is not a specificity which results from some long, internalized history. There are a number of sources of this specificity – the uniqueness of place.[4] There is the fact that the wider social relations in which places are set are themselves geographically differentiated. Globalization (in the economy, or in culture, or in anything else) does not entail simply homogenization. On the contrary, the globalization of social relations is yet another source of (the reproduction of) geographical uneven development, and thus of the uniqueness of place. There is the specificity of place which derives from the fact that each place is the focus of a distinct *mixture* of wider and more local social relations. There is the fact that this very mixture together in one place may produce effects which would not have happened otherwise. And finally, all these relations interact with and take a further element of specificity from the accumulated history of a place, with that history itself imagined as the product of layer upon layer of different sets of linkages, both local and to the wider world.

In her portrait of Corsica, *Granite Island*, Dorothy Carrington travels the island seeking out the roots of its character.[5] All the different layers of peoples and cultures are explored; the long and tumultuous relationship with France, with Genoa and Aragon in the thirteenth, fourteenth and fifteenth centuries, back through the much earlier incorporation into the Byzantine Empire, and before that domination by the Vandals, before that being part of the Roman Empire, before that the colonization and settlements of the Carthaginians and the Greeks . . . until we find . . . that even the megalith builders had come to Corsica from somewhere else.

It is a sense of place, an understanding of 'its character', which can only be constructed by linking that place to places beyond. A progressive sense of place would recognize that, without being threatened by it. What we need, it seems to me, is a global sense of the local, a global sense of place.

Mexico City
published in 1991

# Notes

1   D. Birkett, *New Statesman & Society*, 13 June 1990, pp. 41–2.
2   D. Birkett, *New Statesman & Society*, 15 March 1991, p. 38.
3   P. Wright, *On Living in an Old Country* (London, Verso, 1985), pp. 227, 231.
4   D. Massey, *Spatial Divisions of Labour: Social Structures and the Geography of Production* (Basingstoke, Macmillan, 1984).
5   D. Carrington, *Granite Island: A Portrait of Corsica* (Harmondsworth, Penguin, 1984).

# 7

# A Place Called Home?

In the debates about such concepts as 'home', 'place', 'location-locality', identity and sense of place, and so on, one of the prime contributions of geographers so far, and most particularly of economic geographers, has been to provide a kind of backcloth, more precisely an economic rationale, for some of the senses of dislocation, fragmentation and disorientation that are currently being expressed by so many.

The argument is that we are living through a period (the precise dating is usually quite vague) of immense spatial upheaval, that this is an era of a new and powerful globalization, of instantaneous worldwide communication, of the break-up of what were once local coherencies, of a new and violent phase of 'time–space compression'.

It is certainly true that these things are going on. The world economy, and the local, regional and national economies (if one can still indeed talk of such things) which make it up, look very different from the way they looked, say, as the world emerged from war in 1945.

## Changes in the world economy

The changes even in the last twenty years have been enormous. They are characterized in a variety of ways: as a move from organized to disorganized capitalism, from modern to postmodern, from industrial to postindustrial, manufacturing to service, from Fordist to post-Fordist. The frequency of use of the prefix 'post' indicates the prevailing uncertainty about the positive shape of the new (and indicates also, therefore, the fact that it is open to contestation), but one of the key processes universally agreed to be at the heart of it all is globalization. In spite of all the rhetoric (and to some extent the reality) of small firms and of individual entrepreneurship, of flexibility, niche-marketing and decentralization, of the potential importance of local economies and of economies of scope rather than scale, the reality is that within the economic system power is related to size.[1] The key movers within the world economy remain the multinational, now increasingly transnational and global, corporations, and their power is increasing.[2] The internationalization of capital is a process with old roots, but in recent decades it has increased in intensity and scope and changed in its nature. The total flow of international direct investment (that is, investment directly into production facilities, from one country to another) increased by about 15 per cent *per annum* (in current US dollar terms) through the 1970s, more than trebled overall between 1970 and 1980, and has continued to increase, in spite of slowdowns and looming crises in the world economy, since then.[3] The form which this investment takes has also shifted. The earliest important form of capital export was aimed at obtaining raw materials for processing and production 'back home'. Later the investment in processing and production was itself done overseas, to capture foreign markets, to get round tariff barriers and trade restrictions, and so forth. This is the form which is still, in volume terms, most significant today. More recently, however, capital export has also been into production overseas, but not to serve the markets in which the production is located, but for re-export, either to the home country or to third markets. Here, the stimulus behind the push to multinationalization is the ability to take advantage of the specificities of conditions of production (whether these be cheap labour, lack of unionization, or the availability of particular skills and cultural traditions).

It is important to recognize what these forms of capital export represent. They are more than the increasing spatial reach of a particular group of companies, though of course they *are* that. But they are also – and more helpfully – understood as the stretching out of different kinds of social relationships over space. And that means also the stretching out over space of relations of power, and of relations imbued with meaning and symbolism. It is not just, in the rather straightforward economic cases which we have just been discussing, that capitalist relations of production have been exported. It is that they have taken on a new spatial form. Accumulation, through the extraction of surplus, takes an internationalized form. And, in each of the three cases mentioned above, it does so in a different way, whether that be through the internationalization of the supply of raw materials; through the multiplication of basically similar branch plants of a particular corporation in a range of countries to sell to their local markets; or through the organization of different plants in different countries each producing, according to their own 'comparative advantage', components to be assembled into a global product to be exported elsewhere. Each of these cases represents a different 'spatial structure of production',[4] a different way in which capitalist social relations of production may be stretched over space. The most recent, quite newly emerging, form of spatial structure is that of the 'global corporation' – a massively multinationalized entity, frequently incorporating not only the above forms of international spatial structure but others as well, which spans a vast variety of sectors of production (both manufacturing and services) and which is organized not so much from a centre in one country from which the tentacles of relations of power spread out to others, but on a more truly international basis, with a global profits strategy, a view of a world divided for this purpose into regions, each with their own operational headquarters, and with – this is as yet a tendency on the horizon rather than a fully fledged achievement – no particular country called 'home'.

For most companies, however, there is still an identifiable national origin and in that sense a clear geographical 'direction' to the flows of foreign direct investment. But the geography of these flows has been changing and becoming more complex.[5] While before 1970 it was US corporations which incontrovertibly dominated, both in size and in number, this is no longer so clearly the case. Before 1970, more than two-thirds of foreign direct investment was accounted for by US multinationals; today the figure is way below half. Japan, (West) Germany and Canada have grown in importance as sources of foreign investment and the number of multinationals based in the 'South' has increased. The bulk of the flows remains between First World countries, but with the big change that there is now significant foreign investment *into* the USA, and from First World countries to a handful of 'developing' economies.

The final big change has been the massively increasing internationalization of finance, and of services more generally. The creation of the Eurodollar market, the internationalization of the banks and of capital markets, the fact of twenty-four-hour trading (as Tokyo closes, London opens, and some hours later New York picks up the baton), the multinational spread of everything from accountancy firms, to tourism, to property companies, to cleaning services – all these reflect the way in which globalization has been deepened in recent years, to penetrate into ever more sectors of national and regional economies.

Little of this would have been possible without new technologies of communication, of image-processing and transmission and of information systems.[6] And it is the internationalization of some of these systems themselves which brings home most clearly the fact of the globalization of the inputs to daily life. The burgeoning communications empires of a handful of corporations (Paramount, Sony, Disney) and individual 'players' (Murdoch, Berlusconi, Bertelsman), and the oft-quoted example of CNN are at the focus of it all. Their own national identities become confused or irrelevant (Murdoch operates far from his home shores; Sony takes over companies like CBS and Columbia Pictures, for long regarded as part of – and certainly important influences on – US identity). Powerful forces for forging a sense of what is 'home' are produced by capital which comes from somewhere else entirely. Their messages flow across old earth boundaries in ways in which no national government can easily prevent. There is emerging, it is argued, a new 'global space of electronic information flows'.[7] And complex and intersecting as it is, there are again – as in the case of manufacturing, services and finance – clear, broad geographies of power. Once again, the presence of the US is dominating. By the end of the 1980s, its entertainments industry was second only to aerospace as a foreign-trade earner for the US national economy.[8] More generally, it is argued that culture is being globalized through the emergence of 'global products', the popularity of World Music and the organization of endless World Cups.[9] The link between culture and place, it is argued, is being ruptured.

Before we evaluate the reality of all this, and the implications that are drawn from it for the meaning of home and locality, there are a few important points which ought to be registered. Thus, globalization can in no way be equated with homogenization. The spanning of the globe by economic relations has led to new forms and patterns of inequality not simply to increasing similarity. Even the 'global products', apart from the obvious and perhaps too often quoted examples of Coca-Cola and McDonalds, penetrate different national markets in different ways. Their globality, and the consequent ability of companies to produce them on a mass scale, comes from their finding numerous different niche-markets in all corners of the earth. The companies can thereby combine economies of scope (variety in the range of their production) with economies of scale. Moreover, along with the chaos and disorder which characterizes the new relations there is also a new ordering of clear global-level hierarchies. The few global cities which dominate the world economy, such as New York, London and Tokyo, do so because they are the foci, the points of intersection, of vast numbers of these 'social-relations-stretched-over-space', and because they are at the end of those relations where power is lodged. There is clearly emerging a global hierarchy as social and economic power seem inexorably to be increasingly geographically centralized. And these forms of organization extend down below the national, to the regional and the local. Regional and local economies are increasingly locked in, not so much to national economies, but directly to the world economy. Indeed it becomes ever more doubtful how valid it is to speak even of coherent national economies in some cases, but certainly of subnational ones. Local, regional and national are increasingly drawn into, and constituted by, a logic which exists at international level. Thus there is a series of tensions: a world characterized on the one hand by complexity and potential disorder, but on the other hand very clear and consistent directions in the geography of power; and the continuance of geographical diversity but one formed, not so much out of a home-grown uniqueness, as out of the specificity of positioning within the globalized space of flows.

There are also, within the wider context of globalization, some counter-tendencies. It is argued that certain characteristics of the post-mass-production flexible specialization lend themselves to the development of relatively coherent and internally networked local economies. The most frequently cited examples of these 'industrial districts', as they are called, are 'the third Italy' (Emilia-Romagna), Baden-Württemberg in Germany, and Jutland in Denmark. It is this view of the possibilities of local economies which has lain at the basis of some of the recent flurry of local industrial strategies – such as that of the Greater London Council in the early 1980s.[10] Less potentially radical local councils and institutions, in contrast, further contributed to the fragmentation of their local economies by trying to attract investment from outside, but ironically by designing and presenting coherent images of themselves through which to market their advantages to mobile capital.

But whatever the importance of these new localisms – and it *is* disputed – they are occurring in a context of a truly major reshaping of the spatial organization of social relations at every level, from local to global. Each geographical 'place' in the world is being realigned in relation to the new global realities, their roles within the wider whole are being reassigned, their boundaries dissolve as they are increasingly crossed by everything from investment flows, to cultural influences, to satellite TV networks. Even the different geographical scales become less easy to separate – rather they constitute each other: the global the local, and vice versa. Moreover, as distance seems to be becoming meaningless, so relations in time, too, are altered. Before the 1970s companies made major investment decisions every few years and reviewed prices once a year; exchange rates changed roughly every four years, interest rates perhaps twice a year. All this now seems incredibly slow and ponderous – we get news of exchange-rate changes four or more times a day; prices are highly mobile; investment decisions (which may mean whole factories opening and closing) are made at least once a year.[11] Communications round the world, by electronic mail, by fax, are virtually instantaneous. It is this combination of changes in our experience of space and time which has given rise to the powerful notion that the age we are living in is one of a new burst of 'time–space compression'.

## Postulated implications – and some reservations

Moreover, it is argued that this new round of time–space compression has produced a feeling of disorientation, a sense of the fragmentation of local cultures and a loss, in its deepest meaning, of a sense of place. The local high street is invaded by cultures and capitals from the world over; few areas remain where the majority of industry is locally owned; places seem to become both more similar and yet lacking in internal coherence; home-grown specificity is invaded – it seems that you can sense the simultaneous presence of everywhere in the place where you are standing. Conceptualized in terms of the geography of social relations, what is happening is that the social relations which constitute a locality increasingly stretch beyond its borders; less and less of these relations are contained within the place itself.

It has indeed clearly unnerved a lot of people. There is much talk of postmodern geographies of fragmentation, depthlessness and instantaneity. Emberley writes of a new world where 'the notions of space as enclosure and time as duration are unsettled and redesigned as a field of infinitely experimental configurations of space–time' where 'the old order of prescriptive and exclusive places and meaning-endowed durations is dissolving'.[12] Baudrillard speaks of delirium and vertigo in the face of a world of images and flows. Harvey argues that the disorientation of present times is giving rise to a new – and in his view almost necessarily reactionary – search for stability through a sense of place.[13] Robins writes that 'the driving imperative is to salvage centred, bounded and coherent identities – placed identities for placeless times.'[14] Jameson calls for cognitive mapping, expressing a longing to get his bearings, to orientate himself in what are clearly for him and others disorientating times, to reassert some feeling of a control which seems to have been lost. And indeed there is today all too much evidence of the emergence of disquieting forms of place-bound loyalties. There are the new nationalisms springing up in the east of Europe. There are also burgeoning exclusive localisms, the constructions of tightly bounded place-identities. There is talk of 'the new enclosures', and yuppies build walls around their new inner-urban enclaves to protect themselves, physically and by simple spatial definition, from the others who also live in inner-urban areas. Nor is this appeal to an unproblematized identity of place confined to the right wing of the political spectrum. In the long battle over London's Docklands, some of the notions of place-identity constructed by those defending themselves against the new invaders were equally static, self-enclosing and defensive. A main argument of this paper is that notions of a sense of place do not have to be so.

The most commonly argued position, then, is that the vast current reorganizations of capital, the formation of a new global space, and in particular its use of new technologies of communication, have undermined an older sense of a 'place-called-home', and left us placeless and disorientated.

But is it really so? Clearly something is going on, but before we get carried away by the simplicity and appeal of this argument, we would be wise to stop and think more clearly about its form. First, there are reservations about how the argument is usually posed. Second, there are debates to be had about how, anyway, we think about space and place.

The reservations move from relatively trivial to really quite serious. Beginning, then, at the beginning, there is the question of language. A special style of hype and hyperbole has been developed to write of these matters. The same words and phrases recur; the author gets carried away in a reeling vision of hyperspace. For that reason I have deliberately tried to be downbeat in the opening section of this paper. For amid the Ridley Scott images of world cities, the writing about skyscraper fortresses, the Baudrillard visions of hyperspace ... most people actually still live in places like Harlesden or West Brom. Much of life for many people, even in the heart of the First World, still consists of waiting in a bus-shelter with your shopping for a bus that never comes. Hardly a graphic illustration of time–space compression. There is also the question of how new it all is. The oft-quoted Saatchi remark that there are now more cultural contrasts between the Bronx and midtown Manhattan than between midtown Manhattan and the 7th *arrondissement* of Paris is convincing until one remembers, say, the social gulf that separated, even in the nineteenth century, the West End from the East End of London, for example, and how the denizens of the former viewed the inhabitants of the latter as exotic and as potentially threatening as the indigenous populations of the farthest-flung outposts of empire. So, quite simply, a preliminary word of caution. We must not get too carried away in our own excitement.

Again, it has for long been the exception rather than the rule that place could be simply equated with community, and by that means provide a stable basis for identity. In the United Kingdom, with the exception of a few small mining towns and cotton towns and (maybe) parts, for instance, of the Docklands of London, 'places' have for centuries been more complex locations where numerous different, and frequently conflicting, communities intersected.[15] Nor do 'communities' necessarily have to be spatially concentrated. The strong distinction which Giddens and Jameson make between presence and absence, and the greater problems of effective understanding encountered as time–space distanciation is increased, raise more questions about their assumptions of the directness of face-to-face communication than about the impact of distance on interpretation. Of course geography makes a difference – it is a point which geographers have been arguing for a decade[16] – but 'presence-availability' does not somehow do away with issues of representation and interpretation. That place called home was never an unmediated experience.

Further, there are potential problems of deep economism in some of these accounts, and also of class reductionism. It is not only capital which moulds and produces changes in our understanding of and access to space and time. The recent changes in space–time have clearly been propelled by shifts in capitalism and developments in technology. But that is not all. To reduce them to the cultural logic of late capitalism (Jameson) or of flexible accumulation (Harvey) is severely to reduce their meaning and their variety. Although such groundings in a material base may come as a relief after years of analysis which seemed ready to blow away in a whirl of rhetorical self-referencing, these economic interpretations come far too close to depriving the cultural (or the non-economic more generally) of any autonomy at all. Nor is our experience and interpretation of all these changes dependent only upon our place within, or without, capitalist class relations. Ethnicity and gender, to mention only the two most obvious other axes, are also deeply implicated in the ways in which we inhabit and experience space and place, and the ways in which we are located in the new relations of time–space compression.

Which begins to bring us to more serious reservations about the normal formulation of the argument about the new, disturbing placelessness. There is reference to *the* condition of postmodernity, but in fact there are many such conditions. Different social groups, and different individuals belonging to numbers of social groups, are located in many different ways in the new organization of relations over time–space. From jet-setters, to pensioners holed up in lonely bed-sits, to Pacific Islanders whose air and sea links have been cut, to international migrants risking life and livelihood for the chance of a better life ... all in some way or another are likely to be affected by the shifting relations of time–space, but in each case the effect is different; each is placed in a different way in relation to the shifting scene.[17] Even as you wait, in a bus-shelter in Harlesden or West Brom, for a bus that never comes, your shopping bag is likely to contain at least some products of the global raiding party which is constantly conducted to supply the consumer demands of the world's relatively comfortably-off. The point, however, is that much, if not all, of what has been written has seen this new world from the point of view of a (relative) elite. Those who today worry about a sense of disorientation and a loss of control must once have felt they knew exactly where they were, and that they *had* control.

For who is it in these times who feels dislocated/placeless/invaded? To what extent, for instance, is this a predominantly white/First World take on things? There are a number of ways in which this question can be addressed, but one of them concerns the newness of the changes under discussion. The assumption which runs through much of the literature is that this openness, this penetrability of boundaries is a recent phenomenon. It has already been argued that even in the First World some aspects of the newness have been exaggerated. But the point is even clearer when, as is more fitting, a global perspective is taken. Thus, even Robins, one of the more perceptive writers on the subject, finds himself lured into the rhetoric. He writes, for instance, that 'Globalization, as it dissolves the barriers of distance, makes the encounter of colonial centre and colonized periphery immediate and intense'.[18] While there is clear recognition here that the 'periphery' has been colonized, there is no such recognition that *from the point of view of* that colonized periphery that encounter has for centuries been 'immediate and intense'. Or again:

> Whereas Europe once addressed African and Asian cultures across vast distances, now that 'Other' has installed itself within the very heart of the western metropolis. Through a kind of reverse invasion, the periphery has infiltrated the colonial core. The protective filters of time and space have disappeared, and the encounter with the 'alien' and 'exotic' is now instantaneous and immediate. The western city has become a crucible in which world cultures are brought into direct contact ... Time and distance no longer mediate the encounter with 'other' cultures.[19]

Once again there is both recognition and slippage within this formulation. There is recognition of a past colonialism, that the present 'invasion' is a 'reverse' of a previous one. And yet ... did Europe once address its colonies, formal and informal, only across vast distances? To those living in those colonies it cannot have seemed so. To say that 'Time and distance *no longer* mediate the encounter with "other" cultures' is to see only the present form of that encounter, and implicitly to read the history from a First World/colonizing country perspective. For the security of the boundaries of the place one called home must have dissolved long ago, and the coherence of one's local culture must long ago have been under threat, in those parts of the world where the majority of its population lives. In those parts of the world, it is centuries now since time and distance provided much protective insulation from the outside.

That is one way of looking at these changes: that certainly there has been in recent years a quickening of globalization, a new stretching of social relations over space, but that what is also at issue is a change in the nature and direction of those relations. It is often commented that the UK economy is extremely open. But this has been so for centuries. What has changed in the last two decades is the nature of that openness, its directionality, and the power relations which are embedded in it. In the past the openness was represented by the UK being 'the workshop of the world' (i.e., a major exporter of manufactured goods – frequently undermining local production elsewhere), a major participant in the plunder of the world's natural resources, and the chief financier and insurer for much of the world's production and exchange. Today, as Nissan, Toyota, Hitachi and others invest within these shores the openness is, and is seen as, very different. As was pointed out in the opening section, one of the main changes in the flow of foreign direct investment in recent years has been that the US, too, is no longer almost exclusively a source of such investment; it is also a recipient.

But there are also questions at what might be called a more 'local' level. bell hooks argues that the very meaning of the term 'home', in terms of a sense of place, has been very different for those who have been colonized, and that it can change with the experiences of decolonization and of radicalization.[20] Toni Morrison's writing, especially in *Beloved*, undermines for ever any notion that everyone once had a place called home which they could look back on, a place not only where they belonged but which belonged to them, and where they could afford to locate their identities. The nature of the impact of the current phase of globalization has so far perhaps – and ironically – been analysed from a very *un*-global perspective.

Moreover, if one accepts that the identification of a current feeling of disorientation and placelessness has to be restricted primarily to the First World and even then differentially, and in different ways, to different strata of the population, there is still another curious anomaly to be investigated. Much of the current disorientation, as we have seen, is put down to the arrival in one form or another of the 'Other'. Yet some 'Others' of the dominant definers in First World society have always been there – women. It is interesting to note how frequently the characterization of place as home comes from those who have left, and it would be fascinating to explore how often this characterization is framed around those who – perforce – stayed behind; and how often the former was male, setting out to discover and change the world, and the latter female, most particularly a mother, assigned the role of personifying a place which did not change. Moreover, it is not simple spatial proximity but the relations of power in which that proximity is embedded which are crucial. Thus Wilson argues that in small-scale settlements, where social control can be relatively tight, women have represented little threat to men – although of course there have always been honourable exceptions. The scale and the complexity of life in the big city, however, makes such regulation and control more difficult. 'Almost from the beginning, the presence of women in cities, and particularly in city streets, has been questioned, and the controlling and surveillance aspects of city life have always been directed particularly at women. Urban life potentially challenged patriarchal systems.'[21] The point to draw from this is that it is not proximity in itself which is unsettling but also the nature of the social relations, and most particularly in their aspect of power relations, of which proximity is the geography. Just to talk of the collapse of time and distance, or to see it in terms only of movement and flows, is insufficient; what is at issue is the changing geography of (changing) social relations. And to analyse the impact of those changes it is necessary to take account of both sides of the formulation. *Both* the geography (proximity, time–space distanciation, etc.) *and* the content of the social relations themselves (full of the implications of sexism, or of the power relations of colonialism present or past, or of the relations of capital accumulation) must be taken into account. Moreover, each aspect – spatial form and social content – will affect the other. It is through this lens, too, that statements about the 'newness' of the encounter with a colonial past must be interpreted. It is not only time and distance (after noting the ethnocentricity of even this formulation) which have changed.

## Identity and place

There is, then, an issue of whose identity we are referring to when we talk of a place called home and of the supports it may provide of stability, oneness and security. There are very different ways in which reference to place can be used in the constitution of the identity of an individual, but there is also another side to this question of the relation between place and identity. For while the notion of personal identity has been problema-tized and rendered increasingly complex by recent debates, the notion of *place* has remained relatively unexamined.

The most common formulations of the concept of geographical place in current debate associate it with stasis and nostalgia, and with an enclosed security. Harvey, for example, sees all place-based politics (which he significantly conflates with place-*bound* politics) as suffused with aestheticization (which he sees as almost necessarily 'bad') and a longing for stability and coherence. Equating Time with Becoming and Space with Being (and dichotomizing and opposing them in a way that Heidegger never did) he rejects the latter in favour of the former.[22] In political and social life, also, recent years have seen the emergence of many arguments, policies and movements which indeed, in their attempts to establish a relationship between a place and an identity, a place and a sense of belonging, do depend precisely on such notions – of recourse to a past, of a seamless coherence of character, of an apparently comforting bounded enclosure. Such views of place have been evident in a whole range of settings – in the emergence of certain kinds of nationalisms, in the marketing of places, whether for investment or for tourism, in the new urban enclosures, and even – on the other side of the social divide – on occasion by those defending their communities against yuppification by recourse to concepts such as 'the real Isle of Dogs'. All of these have been attempts to fix the meaning of places, to enclose and defend them: they construct singular, fixed and static identities for places, and they interpret places as bounded enclosed spaces defined through counterposition against the Other who is outside.

Yet this is not the only way in which the notion of 'place' can be conceived. If *space* is conceptualized in terms of a four-dimensional 'space–time' and, as hinted at above, as taking the form not of some abstract dimension but of the simultaneous coexistence of social interrelations at all geographical scales, from the intimacy of the household to the wide space of transglobal connections, then *place* can be reconceptualized too. This was the point of the stress laid earlier on seeing phenomena such as globalization and time–space compression as changing forms of the spatial organization of social relations. Social relations always have a spatial form and spatial content. They exist, necessarily, both *in* space (i.e., in a locational relation to other social phenomena) and *across* space. And it is the vast complexity of the interlocking and articulating nets of social relations which is social space. Given that conception of space, a 'place' is formed out of the particular set of social relations which interact at a particular location. And the singularity of any individual place is formed in part out of the specificity of the interactions which occur at that location (nowhere else does this precise mixture occur) and in part out of the fact that the meeting of those social relations at that location (their partly happenstance juxtaposition) will in turn produce new social effects.

On this reading, the 'identity of a place' is much more open and provisional than most discussions allow. First, what is specific about a place, its identity, is always formed by the juxtaposition and co-presence there of particular sets of social interrelations, and by the effects which that juxtaposition and co-presence produce. Moreover, and this is the really important point, a proportion of the social interrelations will be wider than and go beyond the area being referred to in any particular context as a place. Second, the identities of places are inevitably unfixed. They are unfixed in part precisely because the social relations out of which they are constructed are themselves by their very nature dynamic and changing. They are also unfixed because of the continual production of further social effects through the very juxtaposition of those social relations. Moreover, that lack of fixity has always been so. The past was no more static than is the present. Places cannot 'really' be characterized by the recourse to some essential, internalized moment. Virtually all the examples cited above – from forms of nationalism, to heritage centres, to ascriptions of 'the real Isle of Dogs' – seek the identity of a place by laying claim to some particular moment/location in time–space when the definition of the area and the social relations dominant within it were to the advantage of that particular claimant group. When black-robed patriarchs organize ceremonies to celebrate a true national identity they are laying claim to the freezing of that identity at a particular moment and in a particular form – a moment and a form where they had a power which they can thereby justify themselves in retaking. All of which means, of course, that the identity of any place, including that place called home, is in one sense for ever open to contestation. What is going on in London's 'Docklands' now includes precisely a contest over the identity of that area – whether it is Docklands or the Isle of Dogs.

But, finally and most importantly, on this reading of space and place the identity of place is in part constructed out of positive interrelations with elsewhere. This is in contrast to many readings of place as home, where there is imagined to be the security of a (false, as we have seen) stability and an apparently reassuring boundedness. Such understandings of the identity of places require them to be enclosures, to have boundaries and – therefore and most importantly – to establish their identity through negative counterposition with the Other beyond the boundaries. An understanding of the socio-economic geography of any place, certainly in those parts of the world where the debate is now rife, reveals that such a view is untenable. The identity of a place does not derive from some internalized history. It derives, in large part, precisely from the specificity of its interactions with 'the outside'.

It is here that the debate about place, and particularly about place and belonging, place and home, links up to discussion about identity more generally. While it is frequently accepted that identities are relational, the possibilities are often closed down by the assumption that such relations must be those of bounded, negative counterposition, of inclusion and exclusion. Yet, as has been seen, it has in principle always been difficult, and has over the centuries become more so, to distinguish the inside of a place from the outside; indeed, it is precisely in part the presence of the outside within which helps to construct the specificity of the local place.

The question of the extent to which this is a gender-related issue must at least be asked. It is often argued, for instance within object-relations theory, that in societies where early child-rearing is almost entirely in the hands of women, the project of identity construction is different for little girls and little boys. In particular it is different in relation to the issue of boundaries. Thus, Hartsock writes, 'women and men, then, grow up with personalities affected by different boundary experiences, differently constructed and experienced inner and outer worlds, and preoccupations with different relational issues. This early experience forms an important ground for the female sense of self as connected to the world and the male sense of self as separate, distinct and even disconnected.'[23] It is the boy's need, growing up in a society in which genders are constructed as highly differentiated, and as unequal, to differentiate himself from his mother, which encourages in him an emphasis, in the construction of a sense of identity, on counterposition and on boundary-drawing. Only by this means, it seems, can his identity be securely established. And, given the dominant place of masculine views in this society, it is this – defensive and potentially so vulnerable – way of establishing a sense of self which becomes generalized in social relations.

> Thus, the boy's construction of self in opposition to unity with the mother, his construction of identity as differentiation from the other, sets a hostile and combative dualism at the heart of both the community men construct and the masculinist world view by means of which they understand their lives ... The construction of the self in opposition to another who threatens one's very being reverberates throughout the construction of both class society and the masculinist world view ...[24]

It also reverberates, I would argue, through our currently dominant notions of place and of home, and very specifically through notions of place as a source of belonging, identity and security. Moreover, it reverberates – and most importantly – in the fear which is apparently felt by some, including many writers on the subject, when the boundaries dissolve (or are felt to do so), when the geography of social relations forces us to recognize our interconnectedness. On the one hand, then, that kind of boundedness has not for centuries really been characteristic of local places. A large component of the identity of that place called home derived precisely from the fact that it had always in one way or another been open; constructed out of movement, communication, social relations which always stretched beyond it. In one sense or another most places have been 'meeting places'; even their 'original inhabitants' usually came from somewhere else. This does not mean that the past is irrelevant to the identity of place. It simply means that there is no internally produced, essential past. The identity of place, just as Hall argues in relation to cultural identity,[25] is always and continuously being produced. Instead of looking back with nostalgia to some identity of place which it is assumed already exists, the past has to be constructed. bell hooks, in *Yearning*, returns again and again to the phrase 'our struggle is also a struggle of memory against forgetting', but she is talking of 'a politicization of memory that distinguishes nostalgia, that longing for something to be as once it was, a kind of useless act, from that remembering that serves to illuminate and transform the present'.[26]

Yet, on the other hand, it is also true that the balance between the internally focused and externally connected social relations which construct a place has shifted dramatically, in recent years and in certain parts of the world, towards the latter. Yet the argument that this necessarily produces fear and disorientation depends on a very particular view of both personal identity and the identity of place, and one which is contestable. Wilson writes of the way in which the big city – a 'place' which is by its very nature open and in flux – has produced in many a feeling of fear; fear of the disorder, the uncontrollable complexity, the chaos. But not all have felt this fear. Women, argues Wilson, have often appeared less daunted by city life than have men. While

> most of the male modernist literary figures of the early twentieth century drew ... a threatening picture of the modern metropolis (an exception being James Joyce) ... modernist women writers such as Virginia Woolf and Dorothy Richardson responded with joy and affirmation. In *Mrs Dalloway*, Virginia Woolf exulted in the vitality of a summer's morning in London, in the 'swing, tramp and tread; in the bellow and uproar ... in the triumph and the jingle and the strange high singing of some aeroplane overhead'. Acknowledging the unstable and uncertain nature of personal identity, she does not find this alarming, as did Kafka and Musil.[27]

bell hooks writes of how at times of estrangement and alienation

> home is no longer just one place. It is locations. Home is that place which enables and promotes varied and everchanging perspectives, a place where one discovers new ways of seeing reality, frontiers of difference. One

confronts and accepts dispersal and fragmentation as part of the constructions of a new world order that reveals more fully where we are, who we
can become. . .[28]

In other words, for the new complexities of the geography of social
relations to produce fear and anxiety, both personal identity and 'a place
called home' have had to be conceptualized in a particular way – as
singular and bounded. Of course places can be home, but they do not
have to be thought of in that way, nor do they have to be places of
nostalgia. You may, indeed, have many of them. Michèle le Dœuff has
written:

> I was born just about everywhere, under the now shattered sky of the
> Greeks, in a Brittany farmer's clogs, in an Elizabethan theatre, in my
> grandmother's famines and destitution, and in the secular, compulsory and
> free schooling that the state was so good to make available to me, but also
> in the rebellions that were mine alone, in the slaps that followed or
> preceded them, in Simone de Beauvoir's lucid distress and in Descartes'
> stove. And there is more to come.[29]

And what is more, each of these home-places is itself an equally complex
product of the ever-shifting geography of social relations present and past.

London
published in 1992

# Notes

1  K. Robins, 'Tradition and translation: national culture in its global context', in
   J. Corner and S. Honey (eds). *Enterprise and Heritage*, Routledge, London
   1991.
2  N. Thrift, 'The geography of international economic disorder', in D. Massey
   and J. Allen (eds), *Uneven Re-Development: Cities and Regions in Transition*,
   Hodder & Stoughton in association with the Open University, London 1988.
3  Ibid.
4  D. Massey, *Spatial Divisions of Labour: Social Structures and the Geography
   of Production*, Macmillan, Basingstoke 1984.
5  Thrift, op. cit.
6  D. Morley and K. Robins, 'Spaces of identity: communications technologies
   and the reconfiguration of Europe', *Screen*, vol. 30, no. 4, autumn, 1989, pp.
   10–34.
7  Ibid.
8  C. Hoskins and R. Mirus, 'Reasons for the US dominance of the international
   trade in television programmes', *Media, Culture and Society*, vol. 10, no. 4,
   1988, cited in Morley and Robins, op. cit.

9  See, for instance, the special issue of *Theory, Culture & Society*, vol. 7, 1990.
10  See, for instance, *The London Industrial Strategy*, produced by the GLC in 1985.
11  Thrift, op cit., p. 10.
12  P. Emberley, 'Places and stories: the challenge of technology', *Social Research*, vol. 5, no. 3, 1989, pp. 741–85.
13  D. Harvey, *The Condition of Postmodernity*, Basil Blackwell, Oxford 1989.
14  Robins, op. cit., p. 41.
15  D. Massey, 'A global sense of place', *Marxism Today*, June 1991, pp. 24–9; this vol. ch. 6.
16  See, for instance, Massey, 1984, op. cit.
17  Massey, 1991, op. cit.
18  Robins, op. cit., p. 25.
19  Ibid., pp. 32, 33.
20  bell hooks, *Yearning: Race, Gender, and Cultural Politics*, Turnaround, London 1991.
21  E. Wilson, *The Sphinx in the City: Urban Life, the Control of Disorder, and Women*, Virago, London 1991.
22  See Harvey, 1989, op. cit. and the critique in D. Massey, 'The political place of locality studies', *Environment and Planning A*, no. 23, 1991, pp. 267–81; this vol. ch. 5.
23  N.C.M. Hartsock, 'The feminist standpoint: developing the ground for a specifically feminist historical materialism', in S. Harding and M.B. Hintikka (eds), *Discovering Reality*, Reidel, Dordrecht and London 1983, pp. 283–310. The quotation is from p. 295. Hartsock's is one of a number of articles in this collection which develop this theme, although not in relation to the specific issue of place. See also some of the contributions to L. Nicholson (ed.), *Feminism/Postmodernism*, Routledge, London 1990.
24  Ibid., p. 296.
25  S. Hall, 'Cultural identity and diaspora', in J. Rutherford (ed.), *Identity: Community, Culture, Difference*, Lawrence & Wishart, London 1990.
26  hooks, op. cit., p. 147.
27  Wilson, op. cit., p. 157.
28  In 'Choosing the margin', p. 148; in bell hooks, op. cit.
29  M. le Dœuff, *Hipparchia's Choice: An Essay Concerning Women, Philosophy, etc.*, Blackwell, Oxford 1991, p. 172.

# PART III
*Space, Place and Gender*

# Introduction

The intersections and mutual influences of 'geography' and 'gender' are deep and multifarious. Each is, in profound ways, implicated in the construction of the other: geography in its various guises influences the cultural formation of particular genders and gender relations; gender has been deeply influential in the production of 'the geographical'. There is now a very considerable literature in feminist geography which spans the range from attempts simply to get the issue on to the agenda to highly sophisticated theoretical and methodological arguments which should (though whether they will or not remains to be seen) change the very nature of geographical inquiry.[1] The opening paper in this part ('Space, place and gender') traces some of the developments which took place in the early years within feminist (or, more generally, gender-aware) approaches in that small corner of geography which deals with regional employment change and regional economic policy. As a group, the papers presented in this part explore just one or two threads within this increasingly complex field. The aim is to highlight some of the specific interconnections of geography and gender where these relate particularly to space and place. Some of the conceptual intersections between the terms have been highlighted in the general introduction; the notes here begin from rather more concrete connections. The influences run both ways.

In the first instance, and in what might be interpreted as yet a further extension of the theme that geography matters (for which, in a very general form, see also 'Politics and space/time'), is the argument that geography matters to gender. And it does so in a whole variety of ways.

One of the earliest observations highlighted by feminists within geography was that gender relations vary over space (it had long been recognized that they vary over time). Thus 'A woman's place?' (written with Linda McDowell) uses the views of space and place outlined in parts I and II to examine the variations in the construction, and the reconstruction over time, of gender relations in four different parts of the United Kingdom. The evidence of variation is dramatic (and this is just within one small country), and it is a variation which persists, although in continually altering form, up to this day. Moreover, to the four areas investigated in this paper could be added the high-technology-professional patriarchal gender relations being put in place right now in Cambridge – that is, in one of the symbolic sectors and places of 'the future' (see 'Space, place and gender', and 'Uneven development'). In other words, not just in the past but also today and not just across major cultural differences but also between quite closely related 'local cultures', gender relations can vary quite systematically.

The importance of the existence of this variable construction of gender relations in different local-cultural space/places, and the importance of documenting and analysing it, is not merely to revel once again in the fact of geographical variation. Rather it is that such a finding underlines even more sharply the necessity for a thoroughgoing theoretical anti-essentialism at this level (what it means to be masculine in the Fens is not the same as in Lancashire) and that that in turn undermines those arguments (whether they be in industrial location theory – those nimble fingers – or in gender politics more widely) which rely on attributions of characteristics as 'natural' to men and women. The demonstration of geographical variation adds yet another element to the range of arguments that these things are in fact socially constructed.

The complement of this is, of course, that geographical variations in the construction of gender relations also point, if in a relatively minor way compared with other axes of contrast, to the fact of differences among women (and indeed among men), not only in their construction as gendered people but also in the way in which they relate to particular political struggles, including those around gender itself. The discussion of nineteenth- and early twentieth-century Lancashire in 'A woman's place?' focuses on an example of this, and an example in which the organization of space/place was of particular salience. On the one hand, the particular nature of the local economy, and the concentration and dominance there of certain parts of cotton-textile production, were a condition for the development and solidarity of the suffragette movement. On the other hand, when the battle in which they were engaged moved to national level (because of the necessity of parliamentary action) the regionally based movement found itself relatively isolated. The demands which the women of Lancashire found so important either did not strike the same chord or could not be mobilized around in the same way in other parts of the country.

This links back to the wider argument about identity laid out in the general introduction. If identity is thought in terms of an articulation of the social relations in which a person/group is involved, as is proposed by Chantal Mouffe and Teresa de Lauretis among others (and as is here being extended to the concept of place), then (political) alliances have to be positively constructed across and between these varying articulations. However, the same reasoning implies that any one social relation may have distinct meanings and interpretations when combined into different articulations. Thus, in the case here the distinct articulations, in different regions, of gender relations with other social relations made the meaning of 'the gender issue' itself change form, and any assumption of easy alliances among women in different parts of the country was consequently untenable.[2]

But there are other ways, too, in which space and place are important in the construction of gender relations and in struggles to change them. From the symbolic meaning of spaces/places and the clearly gendered messages which they transmit, to straightforward exclusion by violence, spaces and places are not only themselves gendered but, in their being so, they both reflect and affect the ways in which gender is constructed and understood. The limitation of women's mobility, in terms both of identity and space, has been in some cultural contexts a crucial means of subordination. Moreover the two things – the limitation on mobility in space, the attempted consignment/confinement to particular places on the one hand, and the limitation on identity on the other – have been crucially related (see also the general introduction).

One of the most evident aspects of this joint control of spatiality and identity has been in the West related to the culturally specific distinction between public and private. The attempt to confine women to the domestic sphere was both a specifically spatial control and, through that, a social control on identity. Again, 'A woman's place?' illustrates this theme, by pointing to the specific (though not unique) importance of the *spatial separation* of home and workplace in generating dismay in certain quarters at women becoming 'economically active'. It was certainly not the only factor – the fact of women having access to an independent income was itself a source of anxiety – but in the comparison between Lancashire and Hackney it is clear that the fact of escape from the spatial confines of the home is in itself a threat (the reference to the dangers of 'gregarious employment' and the specific concern about travelling gangs in the

Fenlands case allude to the same phenomenon). And it was a threat in (at least) two ways: that it might subvert the willingness of women to perform their domestic roles and that it gave them entry into another, public, world – 'a life not defined by family and husband'.

The construction of 'home' as a woman's place has, moreover, carried through into those views of place itself as a source of stability, reliability and authenticity. Such views of place, which reverberate with nostalgia for something lost, are coded female.[3] Home is where the heart is (if you happen to have the spatial mobility to have left) and where the woman (mother, lover-to-whom-you-will-one-day-return) is also. The occasional idealizations of home by the working-class lads (the Angry Young Men) who came south in the middle decades of this century, and who looked back north with an unforgiveable romanticism, often constructed that view around 'Mum', not as herself a living person engaged in the toils and troubles and pleasures of life, not actively engaged in her own and others' history, but a stable symbolic centre – functioning as an anchor for others. Raymond Williams's *Border Country* has many of the same characteristics. In this way of looking at the world, the identities of 'woman' and of the 'home-place' are intimately tied up with each other. It is little wonder that Elizabeth Wilson's analysis leads her to conclude that as, over time, women in big cities were less and less easy to contain in heterosexuality and in the domestic sphere (and here of course capitalism and patriarchy have had an uneasy relationship) metropolitan life itself seemed to throw up such a threat to patriarchal control (see 'Politics and space/time'). In general terms what is clear is that spatial control, whether enforced through the power of convention or symbolism, or through the straight-forward threat of violence, can be a fundamental element in the constitution of gender in its (highly varied) forms.

Moreover, the influences also run the other way. Gender has been deeply implicated in the construction of geography – geography as uneven development or regional variation and local specificity (and in the con-struction of these, not merely the fact of them), geography as an academic/intellectual discourse and set of social institutions,[4] and geography in terms of its founding concepts and systems of knowledge. In particular – the concern here – gender is of significance to geographical constructions of space and place.

Most simply perhaps, and as papers throughout this collection indicate, gender and the fact of spatial variation in gender relations are a significant component in an understanding of the organization and reorganization of the national economic space. In 'A woman's place?' to the more specifically economically and class-orientated analyses of earlier papers concerned with the construction of place is articulated consideration of patriarchal relations. 'Capitalism' and 'patriarchy' are considered as autonomous and of equal weight. The question at issue is their mutual accommodation and the kinds of synthesis which result. The final paragraph in 'A woman's place?' brings together the intersection of local and global, of space and place, with the highly differentiated forms and forces of capitalist indust-rialism, with ethnicity and with the geographical variability of certain aspects of gender relations, in 1980s Hackney. Both 'A woman's place?' and 'Space, place and gender' argue that British industry has actively used geographical differences in systems of gender relations in attempts to remain competitive. It is not, therefore, just that spatial variation, and the use of it in industrial location, was important in the (ultimately vain) attempt to preserve certain elements of British Fordism within the national space (see the introduction to part I), but that it was a highly gendered spatial variation. It is not, in other words, just that geography matters but that it is a gendered geography which matters. And what that means in turn is that taking gender seriously produces a different analysis. Both 'Space, place and gender' and 'A woman's place?' make the same point in relation to the analysis and evaluation of regional policy. From the designation of the area to which it applied (and the significant non-designation of others), through the processes of spatial industrial change in which it became involved, through the greater and lesser attractions of particular areas for industrial investment, to the social and political response to the nature of the incoming investment, to the gradually evolving nature of the evaluation of the policy by politicians and academics – in all these ways, and probably many more, the story of the period of regional policy in the decade from the mid-1960s was a thoroughly gendered one. And recognizing *that* changes every aspect of our analysis of it and our response to it. Moreover, it is not only the actions and activities of capital to which such an analysis can be applied; the same points hold true for the labour movement, for instance. 'A woman's place?' instances a number of occasions in which the labour movement played a role in the local structuring of gender relations. And both 'Space, place and gender' and (in part I) 'The shape of things to come' argue that the resultant geography of gender relations, and the particular form it took in certain regions has come back to haunt the labour movement itself: 'it is interesting to speculate on the degree to which this highly patriarchal past has been one of the conditions for the threat currently posed to it ... To the extent that it was complicit in the rigidity of the sexual division of labour in these [mining] regions, and in the exclusion of women from so many social activities, the old traditional heart of the (male) labour movement may well itself have been party to the creation of the new super-cheap labour-forces industry was searching out in the sixties and seventies.' Moreover, this geography of gender relations was in turn an important element in the debate over whether there was 'a decline of the working class' and if so what form it was taking ('The political place of locality studies'). The symbolic association of 'old-fashioned patriarchy', a strong labour movement, and the declining sectors of the economy – and the concentration of this constellation of characteristics into certain parts of the country – became a significant vulnerability ('Space, place and gender').

This approach, therefore, underscores that it is necessary to understand not only class relations but also (for instance) gender relations as significant in the structuring of space and place, spaces and places. It is arguing that gender is not somehow a 'local' concern (and therefore, for reasons themselves associated with gender, to be seen of lesser importance) but that, along with other axes of the constructed divisions in the societies we currently inhabit, it takes its place in principle alongside other divisions, such as class, whose relative significance in practice needs to be evaluated in each particular context (see 'Flexible sexism').

But adopting such an approach has implications. It means that time–space compression, for example, and the way in which space, place and spatiality are experienced cannot be understood as simply the product of shifts in the nature of capital accumulation ('A global sense of place', and 'Flexible sexism'). It means that spatiality cannot be analysed through the medium of a male body and heterosexual male experience, but without recognizing these as important and highly specific characteristics, and then generalized to people at large ('Flexible sexism'). It means that some of the concepts central to recent debate need reconsideration in the light of gender specificity and oppressive gender constructions and relations. 'Modernity' and 'modernism' are cases in point ('Flexible sexism'), warranting reconsideration in terms of their definition (see, for instance, the arguments of *Feminist Arts News*), both in terms of the gendering of their spatialities and in terms of the gendered spaces in which they were formed.

Thus when Henri Lefebvre writes of the space of modernity he is concerned centrally with its very particular gendering and sexualization:

> Picasso's space *heralded* the space of modernity ... What we find in Picasso is an unreservedly visualized space, a dictatorship of the eye – and of the phallus; an aggressive virility, the bull, the Mediterranean male, a *machismo* (unquestionable genius in the service of genitality) carried to the point of self-parody – and even on occasion to the point of self-criticism. Picasso's cruelty toward the body, particularly the female body, which he tortures in

a thousand ways and caricatures without mercy, is dictated by the dominant form of space, by the eye and by the phallus – in short, by violence.[5]

And this space of modernity is based on a wider notion of 'abstract space' in which 'critical analysis ... is ... able to distinguish three aspects': the geometric, the optical (or visual) and the phallic.[6] Lefebvre's analysis traces the history of what he calls the male and female principles within transformations of space. This is not an essentialism, for he sees the content of these principles as 'differently formulated from one society to another'.[7] And one aspect which he traces in this history of space is the demise of the body, which he relates to the female principle but which – as here – he is critical of in its formulation of a simple dualism with a polar opposite of 'mind'. 'Over abstract space', he writes, 'reigns phallic solitude and the self-destruction of desire'.[8] The hegemonic spaces and places which we face today are not only products of forms of economic organization but reflect back at us also – and in the process reinforce – other characteristics of social relations, among them those of gender.

# Notes

1   For an extremely thorough review of the literature, debates and developments within feminist geography in the UK, North America and the Antipodes see Linda McDowell's two contributions to *Progress in Human Geography*, vol. 17, 2 (1993), pp. 157–9, and vol. 17, 3 (1993), forthcoming. And for a challenging argument that the dominant nature of geographical inquiry in those regions is masculinist see Gillian Rose's *Feminism and Geography: The Limits of Geographical Knowledge* (Cambridge, Polity, 1993).

2   Once again, however, what is at issue here is a tension between generalities and the playing out of relations in specific situations. As Susan Bordo writes: 'gender never exhibits itself in pure form but in the context of lives that are shaped by a multiplicity of influences, which cannot be neatly sorted out. This doesn't mean, however ... that abstractions or generalizations about gender are methodologically illicit or perniciously homogenizing of difference' ('Feminism, postmodernism, and gender-scepticism', in Linda J. Nicholson (ed.), *Feminism/Postmodernism* (London, Routledge, 1990), pp. 133–56; here p. 50).

3   Gillian Rose also discusses this in ch. 4 of *Feminism and Geography*.

4   On 'geography' as an institution, and some of the practices of academic geography, see Linda McDowell and Linda Peake, 'Women in British geography revisited: or the same old story', *Journal of Geography in Higher Education*, 14 (1990), pp. 19–30; and Linda McDowell, 'Sex and power in academia', *Area*, 22 (1990), pp. 323–32.

5   Henri Lefebvre, *The Production of Space* (Oxford, Blackwell, 1991; first pub-

lished in French in 1974). The quotation is from p. 302. It is perhaps worth noting that the many renderings and explications which there have been of the work of Lefebvre to an English-speaking geographical audience have almost all been blind to this matter, which is central to his argument and his politics, of space's gendering and its implicit but forceful sexuality.

6   Ibid., p. 285.
7   Ibid., p. 248.
8   Ibid., p. 309.

# 8

# *Space, Place and Gender*

I can remember very clearly a sight which often used to strike me when I was nine or ten years old. I lived then on the outskirts of Manchester, and 'Going into Town' was a relatively big occasion; it took over half an hour and we went on the top deck of a bus. On the way into town we would cross the wide shallow valley of the River Mersey, and my memory is of dank, muddy fields spreading away into a cold, misty distance. And all of it – all of these acres of Manchester – was divided up into football pitches and rugby pitches. And on Saturdays, which was when we went into Town, the whole vast area would be covered with hundreds of little people, all running around after balls, as far as the eye could see. (It seemed from the top of the bus like a vast, animated Lowry painting, with all the little people in rather brighter colours than Lowry used to paint them, and with cold red legs.)

I remember all this very sharply. And I remember, too, it striking me very clearly – even then as a puzzled, slightly thoughtful little girl – that all this huge stretch of the Mersey flood plain had been entirely given over to boys.

I did not go to those playing fields – they seemed barred, another world (though today, with more nerve and some consciousness of being a space-invader, I do stand on football terraces – and love it). But there were other places to which I did go, and yet where I still felt that they were not mine, or at least that they were designed to, or had the effect of, firmly letting me know my conventional subordination. I remember, for instance, in my late teens being in an Art Gallery (capital A capital G) in some town across the Channel. I was with two young men, and we were hitching around 'the Continent'. And this Temple of High Culture, which was one of The Places To Be Visited, was full of paintings, a high proportion of which were of naked women. They were pictures of naked women painted by men, and thus of women seen through the eyes of men. So I stood there with these two young friends, and they looked at these pictures which were of women seen through the eyes of men, and I looked at them, my two young friends, looking at pictures of naked women as seen through the eyes of men. And I felt objectified. This was a 'space' that clearly let me know something, and something ignominious, about what High Culture thought was my place in Society. The effect on me of being in that space/place was quite different from the effect it had on my male friends. (I remember that we went off to a café afterwards and had an argument about it. And I lost that argument, largely on the grounds that I was 'being silly'. I had not then had the benefit of reading Griselda Pollock, or Janet Wolff, or Whitney Chadwick ... maybe I really *was* the only person who felt like that ...)

I could multiply such examples, and so I am sure could anyone here today, whether woman or man. The only point I want to make is that space and place, spaces and places, and our senses of them (and such related things as our degrees of mobility) are gendered through and through. Moreover they are gendered in a myriad different ways, which vary between cultures and over time. And this gendering of space and place both reflects *and has effects back on* the ways in which gender is constructed and understood in the societies in which we live.

When I first started 'doing geography' these things were just not talked about. What I want to do here is simply to give one example of how issues of gender began to creep into our subject matter. The example is perhaps quite mundane; it concerns empirical issues of regional development which are now well established in debate; but in spite of that some interesting lessons can be drawn.

The example, then, is from studies of regional employment in the United Kingdom. It concerns the story of the regional decentralization of jobs which took place in this country between the mid-1960s and the early 1970s. There are some facts which ought to be known before the story begins. This was a period largely of Labour government, with Harold Wilson as Prime Minister. There were major losses of jobs in coal mining, in the north-east of England, in south Wales and in central Scotland. It was the great era of regional policy, when there were numerous incentives and inducements to firms to invest in the regions where job loss was taking place. And it was also an era of the decentralization of jobs from the high employment areas of the south-east and the west midlands to these 'northern' regions of high *un*employment. And the question which preoccupied many of us at that time was: how were we to put these facts together? Or, specifically, how were we to explain the decentralization of jobs to the regions of the north and the west?

The argument went through a series of stages. Or, at least, I shall present it as a series of stages – there are many occupants in what I label as the early stages who will doubtless disagree with what I say. Intellectual change is just not as linear as that.

The analysis, then, in 'stage one' was led primarily by people with computers and statistical packages, who correlated the timing and size of the decentralization of employment with the timing and distribution of regional policy. They found a high correlation between the two, and deduced that they were causally related: namely (although this was of course not directly shown by the statistics themselves) that regional policy was the cause of the decentralization of jobs. Thus regional policy, on this reading, was seen as having been quite successful.

But then came stage two. It was provoked by political rumblings of discontent, from male-dominated trade unions and local councils, and from evidence given to a parliamentary sub-committee. For jobs were not just jobs, it seemed: they were gendered. While the jobs which had been lost had been men's, the new jobs, arriving on the wave of decentralization, were largely being taken by women. And within academe, a whole new line of inquiry started as to *why* these jobs were for women. The answers which were found are now well known. Women workers were cheap; they were prepared to accept low wages, the result of years of negotiating in terms of 'the family wage'. Women were also more available than men for part-time work, an effect of the long established domestic division of labour within the household. Both of these reasons were characteristic of male/female relations, within the home and within the employment market, across the country. But some reasons were more specific, or at least more important, to these particular regions to which the jobs had been decentralized. Thus, the women in these regions had very low rates of organization into trade unions, a result of the very low levels of their previous incorporation into paid employment. The female economic activity rates there were indeed amongst the lowest in the country. These women, in other words, were classic 'green labour'.

With this development of the argument a slightly more complex story evolved which recognized some differences within the labour market, which recognized certain constraints and specificities of women as potential employees, which, in brief, recognized that women and women's jobs were different. Such a revised understanding led also to a revised evaluation of the effectivity of regional policy. It was now clearly necessary to be more muted in any claims for its success. There were two versions of this re-evaluation. One, clearly sexist, persisted in its claim that the new jobs being made available in the regions should be criticized for being 'not real jobs', or for being 'only for women'. There was, however, also another form of re-evaluation, more academically respectable although still worrying in its implications: that the fact that the new jobs were for women was unfortunate in the sense that, because women's jobs were less well paid than were men's, aggregate regional income was still lower.

And yet there was a further stage in the development of this argument: stage three. For the more that one thought about it, the more the story seemed more complicated than that. Why, for example, had the economic activity rate for women in these regions been historically so low? This raised the whole question of local gender cultures. Many people, writing in both geography and sociology, commented upon the domestic labour burden of being a wife or mother to miners. They commented also on how the length and irregularity of shift-work made it problematical for the other partner in a couple also to seek paid employment outside the home. There was much detailed investigation of the construction of particular forms of masculinity around jobs such as mining. And all these investigations, and others besides, pointed to a deeper explanation of why, more than in most other regions of the country, there was in these areas a culture of the man being the breadwinner and of the women being the homemaker.

We had, in other words, moved through a series of approaches; from not taking gender into account at all, we had moved first to looking at women, and from there to looking at gender roles, men, and locally constructed gender relations. Moreover this gave us, once again, both a different story of what had happened and a different evaluation of regional policy. The new story was again more complicated and more nuanced. Harold Wilson had come to power in 1964 on a programme of modernizing social democracy, part of which centred on the rationalization of old industries such as coal mining. Contradictorily for him, however, the loss of jobs which would be consequent upon that rationalization would occur precisely in the regions which were his main geographical power base – regions such as the north-east of England, south Wales, and the central area of Scotland. In order, therefore, to proceed with this reconstruction of the old basic sectors of these regions, it was necessary to have as the other side of the deal a strong regional policy. Given this, acquiescence might be won from the trade unions and their members. However, it was the very fact that the men in the region were being made redundant which was important in creating the availability of female labour. For women were now for the first time in decades 'freed' on to the labour market. They needed paid employment, most particularly now in the absence of work for men, and there was less of a domestic labour burden upon them

restraining them from taking it. Moreover these women had been constructed over the years, precisely by the specificity of the local gender
culture, into just the kind of workforce the decentralizing industries were
looking for.

Moreover, there was yet again a different evaluation of regional policy.
For regional policy could no longer be accepted as the single dominant
factor in the explanation of decentralization of employment because the
labour-force which had been part of the attraction to the incoming
industries had been created not by regional policy but by the simultaneous
decline of men's jobs and as a result of the previous gender culture. It
certainly remained true that regional policy had brought with it only low-
paid jobs, but on the other hand there were some positive aspects to the
jobs it did bring, which previously had been unrecognized. Most importantly, it did bring some independent income for women, and for the first
time in decades. Moreover, as the very fact of the initial complaints
indicated, precisely by bringing in those jobs it began to disrupt some of
the old gender relations. In other words, on this score (though not on
many others) regional policy can be seen to have had some quite positive
effects – though in a wholly different way from that initially claimed in
stage one of the development of the argument.

There are a number of reflections which can be drawn from this story of
a developing analysis. First, and most obviously, taking gender seriously
produced a more nuanced evaluation of regional policy, a far better
understanding of the organization and reorganization of our national
economic space, and indeed – since these decentralizing industries were
moving north to cut costs in the face of increasing international competition – it has shown us how British industry was actively *using* regional
differences in systems of gender relations in an early attempt to get out
of what has become the crisis of the British economy. Second, this
understanding was arrived at not just by looking at women – although that
was a start – but by investigating geographical variations in the construction of masculinity and femininity and the relations between the two.
Feminist geography is (or should be) as much about men as it is about
women. Third, moreover, the very focus on geographical variation means
that we are not here dealing with some essentialism of men and women,
but with how they are constructed as such.

The fourth reflection is a rather different one. It is easy now to look
back and criticize this old-time patriarchy in the coalfields. Indeed it has
become a stick with which to beat 'the old labour movement'. But that
should not let us slide into an assumption that because the old was bad
the new is somehow unproblematical. So, partly in response to the last
three reflections (the need to look at men and masculinity, the importance

of recognizing geographical variations and of constructing a non-essentialist analysis, and the feeling that it is important to look at new jobs as well as at old) I am now involved in research on a 'new' region of economic growth – Cambridge. Cambridge: the very name of the place gives rise to thoughts of 'the Cambridge phenomenon' of high-technology growth, of science and innovation, and of white-collar work. It is all a million miles from coal mines, geographically, technologically, and – you would think – socially. In fact the picture is not as clear as that.

It is the highly qualified workers in high technology sectors on which this new research is concentrating. Well over 90 per cent of these scientists and technologists are men. They frequently love their work. This is no bad thing, until one comes across statements like 'the boundary between work and play disappears', which immediately gives pause for thought. Is the only thing outside paid employment 'play'? Who does the domestic labour? These employees work long hours on knotty problems, and construct their image of themselves as people around the paid work that they do. But those long hours, and the flexibility of their organization, is someone else's constraint. Who goes to the launderette? Who picks up the children from school? In a previous project, from which this one derived, and from which we have some initial information, only one of these employees, and that one of the few women whom we found, mentioned using the flexibility of work hours in any relation to domestic labour – in this case she said that on occasions she left work at six o'clock to nip home to feed the cat![1] The point is that the whole design of these jobs requires that such employees do not do the work of reproduction and of caring for other people; indeed it implies that, best of all, they have someone to look after *them*. It is not therefore just the old labour movement, it is also the regions of the 'new man' which have their problems in terms of the construction of gender relations. What is being constructed in this region of new economic growth is a new version of masculinity, and a new – and still highly problematical – set of gender roles and gender relations.[2]

London, published in 1992

## Notes

1  See Doreen Massey, Paul Quintas and David Wield, *High-Tech Fantasies: Science Parks in Society, Science and Space*, London, Routledge, 1992.

2  This research is being undertaken with Nick Henry at the Open University and with funding from the Economic and Social Research Council (Grant no. R000233004, High status growth? Aspects of home and work around high technology sectors).

# 9

# A Woman's Place?

The nineteenth century saw the expansion of capitalist relations of production in Britain. It was a geographically uneven and differentiated process, and the resulting economic differences between regions are well known: the rise of the coalfields, of the textile areas, the dramatic social and economic changes in the organization of agriculture, and so forth. Each was both a reflection of and a basis for the period of dominance which the UK economy enjoyed within the nineteenth-century international division of labour. In this wider spatial division of labour, in other words, different regions of Britain played different roles, and their economic and employment structures in consequence also developed along different paths.

But the spread of capitalist relations of production was also accompanied by other changes. In particular it disrupted the existing relations between women and men. The old patriarchal form of domestic production was torn apart, the established pattern of relations between the sexes was thrown into question. This, too, was a process which varied in its extent and in its nature between parts of the country, and one of the crucial influences on this variation was the nature of the emerging economic structures. In each of these different areas 'capitalism' and 'patriarchy' were articulated together, accommodated themselves to each other, in different ways.

It is this process that we wish to examine here. Schematically, what we are arguing is that the contrasting forms of economic development in different parts of the country presented distinct conditions for the maintenance of male dominance. *Extremely* schematically, capitalism presented patriarchy with different challenges in different parts of the country. The question was in what ways the terms of male dominance would be reformulated within these changed conditions. Further, this process of accommodation between capitalism and patriarchy produced a different synthesis of the two in different places. It was a synthesis which was clearly visible in the nature of gender relations, and in the lives of women.

This issue of the synthesis of aspects of society within different places is what we examine in the following four subsections of this chapter. What we are interested in, in other words, is one complex in that whole constellation of factors which go to make up the uniqueness of place.

We have chosen four areas to look at. They are places where not only different 'industries' in the sectoral sense, but also different social forms of production, dominated: coal mining in the north-east of England, the factory work of the cotton towns, the sweated labour of inner London, and the agricultural gang-work of the Fens. In one paper we cannot do justice to the complexity of the syntheses which were established in these very different areas. All we attempt is to illustrate our argument by highlighting the most significant lines of contrast.

Since the construction of that nineteenth-century mosaic of differences all these regions have undergone further changes. In the second group of sections we leap ahead to the last decades of the twentieth century and ask, 'Where are they now?' What is clear is that, in spite of all the major national changes which might have been expected to iron out the contrasts, the areas, in terms of gender relations and the lives of women, are still distinct. But they are distinct in different ways now. Each is still unique, though each has changed. In this later section we focus on two threads in this reproduction and transformation of uniqueness. First, there have been different changes in the economic structure of the areas. They have been incorporated in different ways into the new, wider spatial division of labour, indeed the new international division of labour. The national processes of change in the UK economy, in other words, have not operated in the same way in each of the areas. The new layers of economic activity, or inactivity, which have been superimposed on the old are, just as was the old, different in different places. Second, however, the impact of the more recent changes has itself been moulded by the different existing conditions, the accumulated inheritance of the past, to produce distinct resulting combinations. 'The local' has had its impact on the operation of 'the national'.

# The nineteenth century

*Coal is our life: whose life?*

Danger and drudgery; male solidarity and female oppression – this sums up a classic view of life in many colliery villages during much of the nineteenth century. Here the separation of men's and women's lives was virtually total: men were the breadwinners, women the domestic labourers, though hardly the 'angels of the house' that featured so large in the middle-class Victorian's idealization of women. The coal-mining areas of Durham provide a clear example of how changes in the economic organization of Victorian England interacted with a particular view of women's place to produce a rigidly hierarchial and patriarchal society. These villages were dominated by the pits and by the mine owners. Virtually all the men earned their livelihood in the mines and the mines were an almost exclusively male preserve, once women's labour was forbidden from the middle of the century. Men were the industrial proletariat selling their labour power to a monopoly employer, who also owned the home. Mining was a dirty, dangerous and hazardous job. Daily, men risked their lives in appalling conditions. The shared risks contributed to a particular form of male solidarity, and the endowment of their manual labour itself with the attributes of masculinity and virility. The shared dangers at work led to shared interests between men outside work: a shared pit language, shared clubs and pubs, a shared interest in sport. Women's banishment from the male world of work was thus compounded by their exclusion from the dominant forms of local political and social life.

Paid jobs for women in these areas were few. Domestic service for the younger girls; for married women poorly paid and haphazard work such as laundry, decorating or child-care. But most of the families were in the same position: there was little cash to spare for this type of service in families often depending on a single source of male wages. For miners' wives almost without exception, and for many of their daughters, unpaid work in the home was the only and time-consuming option. And here the unequal economic and social relationships between men and women imposed by the social organization of mining increased the subordinate position of women. A miner's work resulted in enormous domestic burdens for his wife and family. Underground work was filthy and this was long before the installation of pithead showers and protective clothing. Working clothes had to be boiled in coppers over the fire which had to heat all the hot water for washing clothes, people and floors. Shiftwork for the men increased women's domestic work: clothes had to be washed, backs scrubbed and hot meals prepared at all times of the day and night:

> 'I go to bed only on Saturday nights', said a miner's wife; 'my husband and our three sons are all in different shifts, and one or other of them is leaving or entering the house and requiring a meal every three hours of the twenty four.' (Webb, 1921, pp. 71–2)

An extreme example, perhaps, but not exceptional.

These miners, themselves oppressed at work, were often tyrants in their own home, dominating their wives in an often oppressive and bullying fashion. They seem to have 'reacted to [their own] exploitation by fighting not as a class against capitalism, but as a gender group against women – or rather within a framework of sex solidarity against a specific woman chosen and caged for this express purpose' (Frankenberg, 1976, p. 40). Men were the masters at home. Here is a Durham man, who himself went down the pits in the 1920s, describing his father:

> He was a selfish man. If there was three scones he'd want the biggest one. He'd sit at the table with his knife and fork on the table before the meal was even prepared . . . Nobody would get the newspaper till he had read it. (Strong Words Collective, 1977, pp. 11–12)

Thus gender relations took a particular form in these colliery villages. National ideologies and local conditions worked together to produce a unique set of patriarchal relations based on the extreme separation of men's and women's lives. Masculine supremacy and male predominance in many areas of economic and social life became an established, and almost unchallenged, fact. Patriarchal power in this part of the country remained hardly disturbed until the middle of the next century.

## Cotton towns: the home turned upside down?

The images of homemaker and breadwinner are of course national ones, common to the whole of capitalist Britain, and not just to coalfield areas. But they were more extreme in these regions, and they took a particular form; there were differences between the coalfields and other parts of the country.

The cotton towns of the north-west of England are probably the best-known example from, as it were, the other end of the spectrum, and a major element in this has been the long history of paid labour outside the home for women. It is often forgotten to what extent women were the first labour-force of factory-based, industrial capitalism. 'In this sense, modern industry was a direct challenge to the traditional sexual division of labour in social production' (Alexander, 1982, p. 41). And it was in the cotton industry around Manchester that the challenge was first laid down.

Maintaining patriarchal relations in such a situation was (and has been) a different and in many ways a more difficult job than in Durham. The challenge was none the less taken up. Indeed spinning, which had in the domestic organization of the textile industry been done by women, was taken over by men. Work on the mule came to be classified as 'heavy', as, consequently, to be done by men, and (also consequently) as skilled (Hall, 1982). The maintenance of male prerogative in the face of threats from women's employment, was conscious and was organized:

> The mule spinners did not leave their dominance to chance ... At their meeting in the Isle of Man in 1829 the spinners stipulated 'that no person be learned or allowed to spin except the son, brother, or orphan nephew of spinners'. Those women spinners who had managed to maintain their position were advised to form their own union. From then on the entry to the trade was very tightly controlled and the days of the female spinners were indeed numbered. (Hall, 1982, p. 22)

But if men won in spinning, they lost (in those terms) in weaving. The introduction of the power loom was crucial. With it, the factory system took over from the handloom weavers, and in the factories it was mainly women and children who were employed. This did present a real challenge:

> The men who had been at the heads of productive households were unemployed or deriving a pittance from their work whilst their wives and children were driven out to the factories. (Ibid., p. 24)

Nor was 'the problem' confined to weavers. For the fact that in some towns a significant number of married women went out to work weaving meant that further jobs were created for other women, doing for money aspects of domestic labour (washing and sewing, for example) that would otherwise have been done for nothing by the women weavers. Further, the shortage of employment for men, and low wages, provided another incentive for women to earn a wage for themselves (Anderson, 1971).

The situation caused moral outrage among the Victorian middle classes and presented serious competition to working-class men. There was

> what has been described as 'coincidence of interests' between philanthropists, the state – representing the collective interests of capital – and the male

working class who were represented by the trade union movement and Chartism – which cooperated to reduce female and child labour and to limit the length of the working day. (Hall, 1982, p. 25)

In the same way, it was at national level that arguments about 'the family wage' came to be developed and refined as a further means of subordinating women's paid labour (for pin-money) to that of men's (to support a family). The transformation from domestic to factory production, a transformation which took place first in the cotton towns,

> provoked, as can be seen, a period of transition and re-accommodation in the sexual division of labour. The break-up of the family economy, with the threat this could present to the male head of household, who was already faced with a loss of control over his own labour, demanded a re-assertion of male authority. (Hall, 1982, p. 27)

Yet in spite of that reassertion, the distinctiveness of the cotton areas continued. There were more women in paid work, and particularly in relatively skilled paid work, in the textile industry and in this part of the country, than elsewhere:

> In many cases the family is not wholly dissolved by the employment of the wife, but turned upside down. The wife supports the family, the husband sits at home, tends the children, sweeps the room and cooks. This case happens very frequently: in Manchester alone, many hundred such men could be cited, condemned to domestic occupations. It is easy to imagine the wrath aroused among the working-men by this reversal of all relations within the family, while the other social conditions remain unchanged. (Engels, 1969 edn, p. 173)

This tradition of waged labour for Lancashire women, more developed than in other parts of the country, has lasted. Of the early twentieth century, Liddington writes, 'Why did so many Lancashire women go out to work? By the turn of the century economic factors had become further reinforced by three generations of social conventions. It became almost unthinkable for women *not* to work' (1979, pp. 98–9).

And this tradition in its turn had wider effects. Lancashire women joined trade unions on a scale unknown elsewhere in the country: 'union membership was accepted as part of normal female behaviour in the cotton towns' (Liddington, 1979, p. 99). In the nineteenth century the independent mill-girls were renowned for their cheekiness; of the women of the turn-of-the-century cotton towns, Liddington writes: 'Lancashire women, trade unionists on a massive scale unmatched elsewhere, were organized, independent and proud' (1979, p. 99). And it was from this base of organized working women that arose the local suffrage campaign of the early twentieth century: 'Lancashire must occupy a special place in the minds of feminist historians. The radical suffragists sprang from an industrial culture which enabled them to organize a widespread political campaign for working women like themselves' (ibid., p. 98).

The radical suffragists mixed working-class and feminist politics in a way which challenged both middle-class suffragettes and working-class men. In the end, though, it was precisely their uniqueness which left them isolated – their uniqueness as radical trade unionists *and* women, and, ironically, their highly regionalized base:

> The radical suffragists failed in the end to achieve the political impact they sought. The reforms for which they campaigned – of which the most important was the parliamentary vote – demanded the backing of the national legislature at Westminster. Thousands of working women in the Lancashire cotton towns supported their campaign, and cotton workers represented five out of six of all women trade union members. No other group of women workers could match their level of organization, their (relatively) high wages and the confidence they had in their own status as skilled workers. Their strength, however, was regional rather than national, and when they tried to apply their tactics to working-class women elsewhere or to the national political arena, they met with little success. Ultimately the radical suffragists' localised strength proved to be a long-term weakness.
> (Liddington, 1979, p. 110)

## The rag-trade in Hackney: a suitable job for a woman?

But there were other industries in other parts of the country where women were equally involved in paid labour, where conditions were as bad as in the cotton mills, yet where at this period not a murmur was raised against their employment. One such area was Hackney, dominated by industries where sweated labour was the main form of labour organization.

What was different about this form of wage relation for women from men's point of view? What was so threatening about women working? Hall (1982) enumerates a number of threads to the threat. The first was that labour was now *waged* labour. Women with a wage of their own had a degree of potentially unsettling financial independence. But Lancashire textiles and the London sweated trades had this in common. The thing that distinguished them was the spatial separation of home and workplace. The dominant form of organization of the labour process in the London sweated trades was homeworking. The waged labour was carried out in the home: in Lancashire, birthplace of the factory system, waged labour by now meant leaving the house and going to the mill. It wasn't so much 'work' as 'going out to' work which was the threat to the patriarchal order. And this in two ways: it threatened the ability of women adequately to perform their domestic role as homemaker for men and children, and it gave them an entry into public life, mixed company, a life not defined by family and husband.

It was, then, a change in the social *and the spatial* organization of work which was crucial. And that change mattered to women as well as men. Lancashire women did get out of the home. The effects of homeworking *are* different: the worker remains confined to the privatized space of the home, and individualized, isolated from other workers. Unionization of women in cotton textiles has always been far higher than amongst the homeworking women in London.

Nor was this all. For the *nature* of the job also mattered in terms of its potential impact on gender relations:

> Only those sorts of work that coincided with a woman's natural sphere were to be encouraged. Such discrimination had little to do with the danger or unpleasantness of the work concerned. There was not much to choose for example – if our criterion is risk to life or health – between work in the mines, and work in the London dressmaking trades. But no one suggested that sweated needlework should be prohibited to women. (Alexander, 1982, p. 33)

Thinking back to the contrast between the coalfields and the cotton towns and the relationship in each between economic structure and gender relations and roles, it is clear that the difference between the two areas was not simply based on the presence/absence of waged labour. We have, indeed, already suggested other elements, such as the whole ideology of virility attached to mining. But it was also to do with the *kind* of work for women in Lancashire: that it was factory work, with machines, and outside the home. In the sweated trades of nineteenth-century London, capitalism and patriarchy together produced less immediate threat to men's domination.

There were other ways, too, in which capitalism and patriarchy interrelated in the inner London of that time to produce a specific outcome. The sweated trades in which the women worked, and in particular clothing, were located in the inner areas of the metropolis for a whole variety of reasons, among them the classic one of quick access to fast-changing markets. But they also needed labour, and they needed cheap labour.

Homeworking, besides being less of an affront to patriarchal relations, was one means by which costs were kept down. But costs (wages) were also kept down by the very availability of labour. In part this was a result of immigration and the vulnerable position of immigrants in the labour market. But it was also related to the predominantly low-paid and irregular nature of jobs for men (Harrison, 1983, p. 42). Women in Hackney *needed* to work for a wage. And this particular Hackney articulation of patriarchal influences and other 'location factors' worked well enough for the clothing industry.

But even given that in Hackney the social organization and nature of women's work was less threatening to men than in the cotton towns, there were still defensive battles to be fought. The labour-force of newly arrived immigrants also included men. Clearly, were the two sexes to do the same jobs, or be accorded the same status, or the same pay, this would be disruptive of male dominance. The story of the emergence of a sexual division of labour within the clothing industry was intimately bound up with the maintenance of dominance by males in the immigrant community. They did not use the confused and contradictory criteria of 'skill' and 'heavy work' employed so successfully in Lancashire. In clothing *any* differentiation would do. Phillips and Taylor (1980) have told the story of the establishment of the sexual division of labour in production, based on the minutest of differences of job, changes in those differences over time, and the use of them in whatever form they took to establish the men's job as skilled and the women's as less so.

### Rural life and labour

Our final example is drawn from the Fenlands of East Anglia, where the division of labour and gender relations took a different form again. In the rural villages and hamlets of nineteenth-century East Anglia, as in the Lancashire cotton towns, many women 'went out to work'. But here there was no coal industry, no factory production of textiles, no sweated labour in the rag trade. Economic life was overwhelmingly dominated by agriculture. And in this part of the country farms were large, and the bulk of the population was landless, an agricultural proletariat. The black soils demanded lots of labour in dyking, ditching, claying, stone-picking and weeding to bring them under the 'New Husbandry', the nineteenth-century extension of arable land (Samuel, 1975, pp. 12 and 18). Women were an integral part of this agricultural workforce, doing heavy work of all sorts on the land, and provoking much the same moral outrage as did the employment of women in mills in Lancashire:

> ... the poor wage which most labourers could earn forced their wives to sell their labour too, and continue working in the fields. In Victorian eyes, this was anathema for it gave women an independence and freedom unbecoming to their sex. 'That which seems most to lower the moral or decent tone of the peasant girls', wrote Dr. Henry Hunter in his report to the Privy Council in 1864, 'is the sensation of independence of society which they acquire when they have remunerative labour in their hands, either in the fields or at home as straw-plaiters etc. All gregarious employment gives a slang character to the girls appearance and habits, while dependence on the man for support is the spring of modest and pleasing deportment'. The first report of the Commissioners on The Employment of Children, Young Persons and Women in Agriculture in 1867, put it more strongly, for not only did landwork 'almost unsex a woman', but it 'generates a further very pregnant social mischief by unfitting or indisposing her for a woman's proper duties at home'. (Chamberlain, 1975, p. 17)

The social and spatial structure of the rural communities of this area also influenced the availability and the nature of work. Apart from work on the land, there were few opportunities for women to earn a wage. Even if they did not leave the village permanently, it was often necessary to travel long distances, frequently in groups, with even more serious repercussions in the eyes of the Victorian establishment:

> The worst form of girl labour, from the point of view of bourgeois respectability, was the 'gang' system, which provoked a special commission of inquiry, and a great deal of outraged commentary, in the 1860s. It was most firmly established in the Fen districts of East Anglia and in the East Midlands. The farms in these parts tended to be large but the labouring population was scattered ... The labour to work the land then had to be brought from afar, often in the form of travelling gangs, who went from farm to farm to perform specific tasks. (Kitteringham, 1975, p. 98)

There are here some familiar echoes from Lancashire. And yet things were different in the Fens. In spite of all the potential threats to morality, domesticity, femininity and general female subordination, 'going out to work' on the land for women in the Fens, even going off in gangs for spells away from the village, does not seem to have resulted in the kinds of social changes, and the real disruption to established ways, that occurred in Lancashire. In this area, women's waged labour did not seem to present a threat to male supremacy within the home. Part of the explanation lies in the different nature of the work for women. This farm labour was often seasonal. The social and spatial organization of farmwork was quite different from that of factory work, and always insecure. Each gang negotiated wage rates independently with the large landowners, the women were not unionized, did not work in factories, were not an industrial proletariat in the same sense as the female mill workers in the cotton towns. Part of the explanation too, as in the colliery villages, lies in the organization of male work. Men, too, were predominantly agricultural labourers, though employed on an annual rather than a seasonal basis, and like mining, agricultural work was heavy and dirty, imposing a similar domestic burden on rural women.

A further influence was the life of the rural village, which was overwhelmingly conservative – socially, sexually and politically. Women on the land in this area did not become radicalized like women in the cotton towns. Relations between the sexes continued unchanged. Women served their menfolk, and both men and women served the local landowner; nobody rocked the boat politically:

> When the Coatesworths ruled the village to vote Tory was to get and keep a job. The Liberals were the party of the unemployed and the undeserving ... Concern over politics was not confined to men. The women took an interest, too. They had to. Their man's political choice crucially affected his employment, and their lives. (Chamberlain, 1975, p. 130)

## Where are they now?

What is life like in these areas now? Have the traditional attitudes about women's place in the home in the heavy industrial areas survived postwar changes? Have Lancashire women managed to retain the independence that so worried the Victorian middle class? In this century there have been enormous changes in many areas of economic and social life. The communications revolution has linked all parts of the country together. TV, radio, video and a national press have reduced regional isolation and increased the ease with which new ideas and attitudes spread. Changes in social mores, in the role of the family, in the labour process of domestic work, increased divorce rates and a rapid rise in women's participation in waged labour between the Second World War and the end of the seventies have all had an impact. And yet, we shall argue here, regional differences remain.

There are, as we said in the introduction, two threads which we shall follow in this process of the reproduction of local uniqueness. The first concerns the geographically differentiated operation of national processes. Over 40 per cent of the national paid labour-force in the UK now consists of women: a vast majority of them married. One of the consequences of this growth of jobs 'for women' has paradoxically been both an increase and a reduction in regional differences. The gender division of labour is changing in different ways in different areas, in part in response to previous patterns. Regional disparities in the proportion of women at work are closing, but the corollary of this, of course, is that the highest proportions of new and expanding jobs are in those very regions where previously few women have been involved in waged labour. The four regions are being drawn in different ways into a new national structure of employment and unemployment. We cannot here attempt to explain this new spatial pattern. One thing we do hint at, though, is that the form of gender relations themselves, and the previous economic and social history of women in each of these places, may be one, though only one, thread in that explanation.

The areas, then, have experienced different types of change in their economic structure. In many ways the growth of jobs for women has been of greater significance in the north-east and in East Anglia than in the cotton towns or in Hackney. But that is not the end of the story. For those changes have themselves been combined with existing local conditions and this has influenced their operation and their effect. The impact of an increase in jobs for women has not been the same in the Fens as it has been in the coalfields of the north-east. This, then, is the second thread in our discussion of the reproduction of local uniqueness.

In the rest of this paper we try to show the links between past and present patterns, how changing attitudes to women's and men's roles at work and in the family in different parts of the country (themselves related to previous economic roles) both influence and are influenced by national changes in the nature and organization of paid employment over time. The present gender division of labour in particular places is the outcome of the combination over time of successive phases. Space and location still matter. The structure of relationships between men and women varies between, and within, regions. Life in inner London is still not the same as in the Fenlands, in the coalfields of the north-east, as in the textile towns round Manchester. The current division of labour between women and men is different, paid employment is differently structured and organized, and even its spatial form varies between one part of the country and another.

## Coal was our life?

The decline of work in the pits is a well-known aspect of post-war economic changes in Britain. How have the men and women of the north-east reacted to this decline in their traditional livelihood? Have the changes challenged or strengthened the traditional machismo of the north-eastern male? What is happening in the north-east today in many ways recalls some of the images – and the social alarm – generated by the cotton towns a hundred years earlier. It is now in the north-east that homes are being 'turned upside down' and patriarchy threatened by women going out to work. At the beginning of the 1960s, still something less than a quarter of all adult women in the old colliery areas worked outside their homes for wages. The figure has more than doubled since then. And part of the explanation lies in the local distinctiveness, the uniqueness of these areas that has its origins in the nineteenth century. The women of this area have no tradition of waged labour, no union experience. It was, of course, these very features that proved attractive to the female-employing industries that opened branch plants in increasing numbers in Co. Durham in the sixties and seventies.

The new jobs that came to the north-east, then, were mainly for women. They were located on trading estates and in the region's two New Towns built to attract industrial investment and also to improve housing conditions. The women who moved into the New Towns of Peterlee and Washington provided a cheap, flexible, untrained and trapped pool of labour for incoming firms. And added to this, the loss of jobs for men together with the rent rises entailed by a move to new housing pushed women into the labour market.

Male antagonism to the new gender division of labour was almost universal. Outrage at women 'taking men's jobs', pleas for 'proper jobs', an assumption that the packing, processing and assembly-line work that loomed ever larger in the economic structure of the area was an affront to masculine dignity: 'I think a lot of men feel that assembly work wouldn't be acceptable; they'd be a bit proud about doing that type of work in this area. North East ideas are ingrained in the men in this area' (Lewis, 1983, p. 19). These assumptions appear to be shared by the new employers: 'we are predominantly female labour orientated ... the work is more suited to women, it's very boring, I suppose we're old-fashioned and still consider it as women's work ... the men aren't interested'.

This lack of interest plays right into the hands of the employers: once defined as 'women's work', the jobs are then classified as semi- or unskilled and hence low paid. An advantage that can be further exploited, as this factory director explains:

'we changed from full-time to part-time women(!) ... especially on the packing ... because two part-timers are cheaper than one full-timer ... we don't have to pay national insurance if they earn less than £27.00 a week, and the women don't have to pay the stamp . . . the hours we offer suit their social lives'. (Lewis, 1984)

So if men aren't doing jobs outside the house, what are they doing instead? Are men here, like their Lancashire forebears 'condemned to domestic occupations'? Unlikely. An ex-miner's wife speaking on *Woman's Hour* in 1983 recalled that her husband would only reluctantly help in the home, pegging out the washing, for example, under cover of darkness!

Things *are* changing, though. Men are seen pushing prams in Peterlee, Newcastle-upon-Tyne Council has a women's committee, TV crews come to inquire into the progress of the domestication of the unemployed north-eastern male and the social and psychological problems it is presumed to bring with it. Working-class culture is still dominated by the club and the pub but even their male exclusivity is now threatened. The 1984 miners' strike seems set to transform gender relations even further. New battle-lines between the sexes are being drawn. The old traditional pattern of relations between the sexes, which was an important condition for the new gender division being forged in the labour market, is now under attack.

## *Industry in the country?*

How has life changed in the Fens? In some ways, continuity rather than change is the link between the past and present here. For many women, especially the older ones, work on the land is still their main source of employment:

> hard work, in uncompromising weather, in rough old working clothes padded out with newspaper against the wind . . . Marriage for convenience or marriage to conform . . . Land-worker, home servicer. Poverty and exploitation – of men and women by the landowners, of women by their men. (Chamberlain, 1975, p. 11)

Not much different from their grandmothers and great-grandmothers before them. Gangs are still a common feature and the nature of fieldwork has hardly changed either. Flowers are weeded and picked by hand. Celery and beet are sown and picked manually too. And this type of work is considered 'women's work'. It is poorly paid, seasonal and backbreaking. Male fieldworkers, on the other hand, have the status of 'labourers', relative permanence and the benefits associated with full-time employment. And they are the ones who have machinery to assist them.

Life *has* changed though. Small towns and rural areas such as the Fens have been favoured locations for the new branch plants and decentralizing industries of the sixties and seventies. Labour is cheap here – particularly with so few alternatives available – and relatively unorganized. Especially for younger women, the influx of new jobs has opened up the range of employment opportunities. It provides a means, still, both of supplementing low male wages, and of meeting people – of getting out of the small world of the village.

The impact of such jobs on women's lives, though, even the possibility of taking them, has been structured by local conditions, including gender relations. This is still a very rural area. The new jobs are in the nearby town. So unless factories provide their own transport (which a number do), access is a major problem. Public transport is extremely limited, and becoming more so. There are buses – but only once a week to most places. Not all families have a car, and very few women have daily use of one, let alone own 'their own' car. For many women, a bicycle is the only means of getting about.

This in turn has wider effects. For those who do make the journey to a factory job the effective working day (including travel time) can be very long. The time for domestic labour is squeezed, the work process consequently intensified. Those who remain in the village become increasingly isolated. The industrial workers, be they husbands or women friends, are absent for long hours, and services – shops, doctors, libraries – gradually have been withdrawn from villages.

It seems that the expansion of industrial jobs 'for women' has had relatively little impact on social relations in the rural Fens. In part, this is to do with the local conditions into which the jobs were introduced: the impact back of local factors on national changes. The Fenland villages today are still Conservative – politically and socially. Divorce, left-wing politics, women's independence are very much the exception.

Old cultural forms, transmitted, have remained remarkably intact:

> Although love potions and true-lovers' knots made of straw have disappeared, Lent and May weddings are still considered unlucky. The Churching of Women – an ancient post-natal cleansing ceremony – is still carried on, and pre-marital intercourse and the resulting pregnancy is as much a hangover from an older utilitarian approach to marriage as a result of the permissive society. In a farming community sons are important and there would be little point in marrying an infertile woman. (Chamberlain, 1975, p. 71)

Attitudes to domestic responsibilities also remain traditional:

> No women go out to work while the children are small – tho' there isn't much work anyway, and no facilities for childcare. Few women allow their

children to play in the streets, or let them be seen in less than immaculate dress. Many men come home to lunch and expect a hot meal waiting for them. (Ibid., p. 71)

It takes more than the availability of a few jobs, it seems, substantially to alter the pattern of life for women in this area:

> Although employment is no longer dependent on a correct political line, the village is still rigidly hierarchic in its attitudes, and follows the pattern of the constituency in voting solidly Conservative. And in a rigidly hierarchical society, when the masters are also the men, most women see little point in taking an interest in politics, or voting against the established order of their homes or the community as a whole . . . Most women must of necessity stick to the life they know. Their husbands are still the all-provider. The masters of their lives. (Ibid., pp. 130–1)

Gender relations in East Anglia apparently have hardly been affected by the new jobs, let alone 'turned upside down'.

## A regional problem for women?

The contrast with the cotton towns of Lancashire is striking. Here, where employment for women in the major industry had been declining for decades, was a major source of female labour, already skilled, already accustomed to factory work, plainly as 'dexterous' as elsewhere. And yet the new industries of the sixties and seventies, seeking out female labour, did not come here, or not to the extent that they went to other places.

The reasons are complex, but they are bound up once again with the intricate relationship between capitalist and patriarchal structures. For one thing, here there was no regional policy assistance. There has, for much of this century, been massive decline in employment in the cotton industry in Lancashire. Declines comparable to those in coal mining, for instance, and in areas dominated by it. Yet the cotton towns were never awarded Development Area status. To the extent that Assisted Areas were designated on the basis of unemployment rates, the explanation lies at the level of taxes and benefits which define women as dependent. There is often less point in signing on. A loss of jobs does not necessarily show up, therefore, in a corresponding increase in regional unemployment. Development Areas, however, were *not* designated simply on the basis of unemployment rates. They were wider concepts, and wider regions, designated on the basis of a more general economic decline and need for regeneration. To that extent the non-designation of the cotton towns was due in part to a more general political blindness to questions of women's employment.

So the lack of regional policy incentives must have been, relatively, a deterrent to those industries scanning the country for new locations. But it cannot have been the whole explanation. New industries moved to other non-assisted areas – East Anglia, for instance. Many factors were in play, but one of them surely was that the women of the cotton towns were not, either individually or collectively in their history, 'green labour'. The long tradition of women working in factory jobs, and their relative financial independence, has continued. In spite of the decline of cotton textiles the region still has a high female activity rate. And with this there continued, in modified form, some of those other characteristics. Kate Purcell, doing research in the Stockport of the 1970s, found that:

> It is clear that traditions of female employment and current rates of economic activity affect not only women's activity per se, but also their attitudes to, and experience of, employment. The married women I interviewed in Stockport, where female activity rates are 45 per cent and have always been high, define their work as normal and necessary, whereas those women interviewed in the course of a similar exercise in Hull, where the widespread employment of married women is more recent and male unemployment rates are higher, frequently made references to the fortuitous nature of their work. (Purcell, 1979, p. 119)

As has so often been noted in the case of male workers, confidence and independence are not attributes likely to attract new investment. It may well be that here there is a case where the same reasoning has applied to women.

But whatever the precise structure of explanation, the women of the cotton towns are now facing very different changes from those being faced by the women of the coalfields. Here they are not gaining a new independence from men; to some extent in places it may even be decreasing. Women's unemployment is not seen to 'disrupt' family life, or cause TV programmes to be made about challenges to gender relations, for women do the domestic work anyway. Having lost one of their jobs, they carry on (unpaid) with the other.

## Hackney: still putting out

What has happened in Hackney is an intensification of the old patterns of exploitation and subordination rather than the superimposition of new patterns. Here manufacturing jobs have declined, but the rag trade remains a major employer. The women of Hackney possess, apparently, some of the same advantages to capital as do those of the coalfields and the Fens: they are cheap and unorganized – less than 10 per cent are in a union (Harrison, 1983, pp. 69–70). In inner London, moreover, the spatial organization of the labour-force, the lack of separation of home and work, strengthens the advantages: overheads (light, heat, maintenance of machinery) are borne by the workers themselves; workers are not eligible for social security benefits; their spatial separation one from another makes it virtually impossible for them to combine to force up wage rates, and so on.

So given the clear advantages to capital of such a vulnerable potential workforce, why has there been no influx of branch plants of multinationals, of electronics assembly lines and suchlike? Recent decades have of course seen the growth of new types of jobs for women, particularly in the service sector, if not within Hackney itself then within travelling distance (for some), in the centre of London. But, at the moment, for big manufacturing capital and for the clerical mass-production operations which in the sixties and seventies established themselves in the Development Areas and more rural regions of the country, this vulnerable labour of the capital city holds out few advantages. Even the larger clothing firms (with longer production runs, a factory labour process, locational flexibility and the capital to establish new plant) have set up their new branch plants elsewhere, either in the peripheral regions of Britain or in the Third World. So why not in Hackney? In part the women of Hackney have been left behind in the wake of the more general decentralization, the desertion by manufacturing industry of the conurbations of the First World. In part they are the victims of the changing international division of labour within the clothing industry itself. But in part, too, the reasons lie in the nature of the available labour. Homeworking does have advantages for capital, but this way of making female labour cheap is no use for electronics assembly lines or for other kinds of less individualized production. The usefulness of this way of making labour vulnerable is confined to certain types of labour process.

The influx of service jobs in central London has outbid manufacturing for female labour, in terms both of wages and of conditions of work (see Massey, 1984, ch. 4). But working in service jobs has not been an option available to all. For women in one way or another tied to the home, or to the very local area, homeworking in industries such as clothing has become increasingly the only available option. Given the sexual division of labour in the home, homeworking benefits some women:

> Homework when properly paid, suits many women: women who wish to stay at home with small children, women who dislike the discipline and timekeeping of factory work and wish to work at their own pace. Muslim women observing semi-purdah. (Harrison, 1983, p. 64)

But homework seldom is 'properly paid'. Harrison again, on types of work and rates of pay in Hackney in 1982:

> There are many other types of homework in Hackney: making handbags, stringing buttons on cards, wrapping greeting cards, filling Christmas crackers, assembling plugs and ballpens, sticking insoles in shoes, threading necklaces. Rates of pay vary enormously according to the type of work and the speed of the worker, but it is rare to find any that better the average female hourly earnings in the clothing trade in 1981, £1.75 an hour, itself the lowest for any branch of industry. And many work out worse than the Wages Council minimum for the clothing trade of £1.42 per hour (in 1982). Given these rates of pay, sometimes the whole family, kids and all, are dragooned in ... one mother had her three daughters and son helping to stick eyes and tails on cuddly toys. (Ibid., pp. 67–8)

The involvement of all members of a family in homework or working as a team in small family-owned factories is not uncommon, especially among certain ethnic minorities. For small companies the extended family may be essential to survival:

> the flexibility comes from the family: none of their wages are fixed. When times are good, they may be paid more. When they are bad, they are paid less. They get the same pay whether their hours are short or long.

The fact that women are employed in the context of an extended family is important not only in the organization of the industry but also for the lives of the women themselves. They may have a wage, but they do not get the other forms of independence which can come with a job. They do not get out of the sphere of the family, they do not make independent circles of friends and contacts, nor establish a spatially separate sphere of existence. Within the family itself the double subordination of women is fixed through the mixing in one person of the role of husband or father with that of boss and employer.

But it is not that there have been no changes in recent decades for the homeworkers of Hackney. They too have been caught up in and affected by the recent changes in the international division of labour. The clothing industry of London in the second half of the twentieth century finds itself caught between cheap imports on the one hand and competition for labour from the better working conditions of the service sector on the other. The clothing firms with the ability to do so have long since left. For those that remain, cutting labour costs is a priority, and homeworking a means to do it. So an increasing proportion of the industry's work in the metropolis is now done on this social system while the amount of work overall, and the real wages paid, decline dramatically. For the women who work in this industry there is thus more competition for available work, increasing vulnerability to employers and intensification of the labour process. And this change in employment conditions brings increased pressures on home life too, though very different ones from those in the north-east, or the Fens. For these women in Hackney their workplace is also their home.

Here's Mary, a forty-five-year-old English woman with teenage children describing the pressures she feels:

> I've been machining since I was fifteen, and with thirty years' experience I'm really fast now … But I'm having to work twice as hard to earn the money. The governors used to go on their knees to get you to take work if they had a rush to meet a delivery date. But they're not begging no more. It's take it or leave it. If you argue about the price they say we can always find others to do it. It's like one big blackmail. Three years ago we used to get 35p to 40p for a blouse, but now [1982] you only get 15p to 20p …
>
> I used to get my work done in five hours, now I work ten or twelve hours a day … The kids say, mum, I don't know why you sit there all those hours. I tell them, I don't do it for love, I've got to feed and clothe us. I won't work Sundays though. I have to think about the noise … I'm cooped up in a cupboard all day – I keep my machine in the storage cupboard, it's about three feet square with no windows. I get pains in my shoulders where the tension builds up. I've got one lot of skirts to do now, I've got to do sixteen in an hour to earn £1.75 an hour, that means I can't let up for half a second between each skirt. I can't afford the time to make a cup of tea. With that much pressure, at the end of the day you're at screaming pitch. If I wasn't on tranquillizers, I couldn't cope. I'm not good company, I lose my temper easily. Once I might have been able to tolerate my kids' adolescence, with this I haven't been able to, I haven't been able to help them – I need someone to help me at the end of the day. (Harrison, 1983, pp. 65–7)

Reflected in this woman's personal experience, her sweated labour and family tensions, is a new spatial division of labour at an international scale. Low-wage, non-unionized workers in Hackney are competing directly with the same type of low-technology, labour-intensive industries in the Third World. But it is precisely the history of the rag trade in Hackney, the previous layers of economic and social life, that have forced this competition on them. The intersection of national and international trends, of family and economic relationships, of patriarchy and capitalism have produced this particular set of relationships in one area of inner London.

Milton Keynes
published in 1984

# References

Alexander, S. (1982) 'Women's work in nineteenth-century London: a study of the years 1820–50', pp. 30–40 in E. Whitelegg et al. (eds.), *The Changing Experience of Women*, Martin Robertson, Oxford.

Anderson, M. (1971) *Family and Structure in Nineteenth-Century Lancashire*, Cambridge University Press, Cambridge.

Chamberlain, M. (1975) *Fenwomen*, Virago, London.

Engels, F. (1969 edn) *The Condition of the Working Class in England*, Panther, St Albans.

Frankenberg, R. (1976) 'In the production of their lives, man (?) . . . sex and gender in British community studies', pp. 25–51 in D.L. Barker and A. Allen (eds.), *Sexual Divisions and Society: Process and Change*, Tavistock, London.

Hall, C. (1982) 'The home turned upside down? The working class family in cotton textiles 1780–1850', in E. Whitelegg et al. (eds.), *The Changing Experience of Women*, Martin Robertson, Oxford.

Harrison, P. (1983) *Inside the Inner City*, Penguin, Harmondsworth.

Kitteringham, J. (1975) 'Country work girls in nineteenth-century England', pp. 73–138, in R. Samuel (ed.), *Village Life and Labour*, Routledge & Kegan Paul, London.

Lewis, J. (1983) 'Women, work and regional development', *Northern Economic Review*, no. 7. Summer, pp. 10–24.

—— (1984) 'Post-war regional development in Britain: the role of women in the labour market', Queen Mary College, University of London, Ph. D thesis.

Liddington, J. (1979) 'Women cotton workers and the suffrage campaign: the radical suffragists in Lancashire, 1893–1914', pp. 64–97, in S. Burman (ed.), *Fit Work for Women*, Croom Helm, London.

Massey, D. (1984) *Spatial Divisions of Labour: Social Structures and the Geography of Production*, Macmillan, London.

Phillips, A. and Taylor, B. (1980) 'Notes towards a feminist economics', *Feminist Review*, vol. 6, pp. 79–88.

Purcell, K. (1979) 'Militancy and acquiescence amongst women workers', pp. 98–111, in S. Burman (ed.), *Fit Work for Women*, Croom Helm, London.

Samuel, R. (1975) *Village Life and Labour*, Routledge & Kegan Paul, London.

Strong Words Collective (1977) *Hello, Are You Working?* Erdesdun Publications, Whitley Bay.

—— (1979) *But the World Goes on the Same*, Erdesdun Publications, Whitley Bay.

Webb, S. (1921) *The Story of the Durham Miners*, Fabian Society, London.

# 10

# Flexible Sexism

## Introduction

In the current debate around modernism and postmodernism, which is having its reflection in our field, both sides claim feminism for their own. Moreover, to feminists each offers possibilities. Postmodernism holds out the potential democracy of a plurality of voices and points of view, the end to a notion of science and society which has in fact (to be distinguished from 'by necessity') been unremittingly and tediously male, a patriarchal hierarchy with a claim to truth. Modernism, on the other hand, points to the possibility of progress and change. Things may be patriarchal now (including, OK let's admit it, modernism itself) but they need not always be so; more than that, it is possible to judge between alternatives, and history is on our side.

However, that it may be difficult to choose between the attractions they each at least in their rhetorics appear to offer, has as its other side that both postmodernism and modernism remain so frequently, so unimaginatively, patriarchal. This has been said before about the wider debate (for instance, see Fraser and Nicholson, 1988). If there is one thing which has most certainly demonstrated its flexibility in an age which as a whole is frequently accorded that epithet, it is sexism.

This feature is also disappointingly characteristic of the way in which at least some of the modernism – postmodernism debate has been conducted in our field, and it is the purpose of this paper to examine some of the ways in which this happens and to explore some of its implications. To this end I am focusing on two books which have been published recently: Soja's *Postmodern Geographies* (1989) and Harvey's *The Condition of Postmodernity* (1989). These books have been chosen not because they are in any sense representative of the debate between postmodernism and modernism (indeed there is argument about even how they might be classified) but because they are, or may become, central to the discussion within geography. Nor is this paper meant to be a full review of either book; it simply reports on the thoughts which they aroused in me around one specific issue: feminism. For it seems to me that the absence from, indeed denial by, both these books of feminism and the contributions it has recently made, raise issues which are important for all of us, and which range from our style as academics to the way in which some of the central concepts of the debate are formulated. Indeed, the implications are perhaps in the end even wider than that. For both these books are centrally concerned with the relation between the poles of that impossible dichotomy: space and society. And, as the debate about this relation is crucial in the whole modernism–postmodernism exchange, it seems important to address its shortcomings. As we shall see, introducing feminism into this exchange challenges the views, not just of society but also of space, which these books develop.

I should also like to report that I had some hesitation about writing this paper. I do not like public mud-slinging and have tried not to indulge in it here, but the paper is at times very critical. Nor do I relish gladiatorial combats and I hope that the result of this paper will be more to open (or continue) a wider debate. For it is certainly not just with these two particular authors that I want to take issue. Similar critiques could be made of much of our work, probably including some of my own and other feminists'. These particular books, however, claim a generality and a breadth of scope which others do not, and it is for this reason that they are particularly important to examine. The questions, though, are ones which we should all address. Moreover, these books are also significant because, I am sure, neither of the authors would want to be thought of as anti-feminist. Yet, I want to argue, both books are in fact quite fundamentally so. And if they are so, as it were, in spite of their authors' best intentions it becomes even more important to think through how that comes about. For it should be stressed that what is being argued here is not that women, or even gender, should have been mentioned more often; but that the incredible lack of attention both to feminism and to what feminists have been arguing now for a considerable number of years in the end vitiates both of the wider, and very different, projects which these two books set out to accomplish.

# Postmodern problems for feminists

*Democracy and academic style*

One of the main attractions of the postmodern perspective is that it would seem on initial viewing to offer the prospect of a greater democracy through its recognition of the reality of a variety of viewpoints, a plurality of cultures. This has its underside: those viewpoints and cultures may, for example, run counter to what we have been accustomed, from a modernist perspective, to think of as progressive, and postmodernism forbids us from evaluating. Moreover, as Harvey argues very well, mere recognition of the existence of something does not empower it.

None the less, one of the promises of postmodernism is that it will allow fuller appreciation of those who have for so long been banished to the margins, whether these be non-western societies, women/feminists, or subordinated class strata.

In such a context one of the emancipatory roles of the writer and intellectual could be precisely to help give voice to the previously excluded. This is not itself an unproblematical possibility, as the intricate debates in other disciplines, most particularly anthropology, bear witness (for reviews and debate see, for instance, Clifford and Marcus, 1986; Mascia-Lees et al., 1989). It is a debate which could profitably be further developed within geography. None the less, postmodernism can to some extent be seen as holding out some such progressive possibilities. And to some extent they have been taken up.

There is, however, another view of the role of intellectuals (particularly the paid professional intellectuals of academe) within the postmodernist project/era. And it is this one which I wish to take up here, for it raises important issues about who and how we are as 'academics'. Thus, Bauman (1988) has interpreted the concept of postmodernism as a response by intellectuals to their own discomfiture, their sense of dislodgement from previous authority. (The deliberate ambiguity of 'project/era' was thus apt in the context of this discussion.) Bauman's argument is that the concept of postmodernity has value precisely because it captures and articulates the changing experience of contemporary intellectuals. Intellectuals have become more self-aware – 'In the discourse of "postmodernity" ... The participants ... appear in the role of "organic intellectuals" of the intellectuals themselves' (p. 218), and this turning around of Gramsci's original definition is, so Bauman argues, a response to a growing sense of failure, uselessness and irrelevance. He goes on to develop an analysis of the reasons behind this 'status crisis' of the intellectuals and isolates three determinants as crucial: the end of the assumption of the superiority of the West over the rest ('now at best ridiculed as naivety, at worst castigated as ethnocentric' [p. 220]), the decline of the state's need for legitimation (which 'has been replaced with two mutually complementary weapons: this of *seduction* and that of *repression*' [p. 221]), and the decline of the judgmental hegemony of intellectuals over the expanding sphere of, especially popular, culture ('what hurts ... is not so much an expropria-tion, but the fact that the intellectuals are not invited to stand at the helm of this breath-taking expansion' [p. 224]).

This view has been developed further by other authors. Owens (1985) emphasizes not just the often-referred-to demise of the dominance of western culture but also the challenge to modernity from within the geographical bases of that culture: 'the causes of modernity's demise ... lie as much within as without' (p. 58). And among the many different challenges to modernity from within has been the challenge from femin-ism. Bondi (1990) argues that postmodernism 'may be understood as a crisis in the experience of modernity among white, western men, and as a response centred on that experience' (p. 5). Moreover, it is argued, the nature of the response to the crisis is such as to find, somehow, a way of hanging on to intellectual hegemony, or at least of not letting anyone else have it. Thus Hartsock (1987, p. 196) argues:

> Somehow it seems highly suspicious that it is at this moment in history, when so many groups are engaged in 'nationalisms' which involve redefini-tions of the marginalised Others, that doubt arises in the academy about the nature of the 'subject', about the possibilities for a general theory which can describe the world, about historical 'progress'. Why is it, exactly at the moment when so many of us who have been silenced begin to demand the right to name ourselves, to act as subjects rather than objects of history, that just then the concept of subjecthood becomes 'problematic'? Just when we are forming our own theories about the world, uncertainty emerges about whether the world can be adequately theorised? Just when we are talking about the changes we want, ideas of progress and the possibility of 'mean-ingfully' organizing human society become suspect?

Similarly, Mascia-Lees et al., drawing on Lennox (1987), comment: 'When Western white males – who traditionally have controlled the production of knowledge – can no longer define the truth ... their response is to conclude that there is not a truth to be discovered' (1989, p. 15).

There are a number of issues here. First, if there is anything at all in these interpretations (and I think there is, though it is by no means a whole explanation), then it is inadequate to try to explain the condition of postmodernity and the associated debates about representation simply as the result of 'time–space compression', as Harvey does. The arguments just cited give more autonomy than does Harvey, not only to the sphere of culture and intellectual debate, but also – and more significantly from the point of view of the discussion here – to the sphere of political action. What is more, as Hartsock argues, political action and intellectual activity have been much more closely linked together in fields such as feminist studies, ethnic studies and Third World studies than they have been in more mainstream white male modernism (including much Marxism) for all its claims to political relevance.[1]

But second, if this is a crisis in part within the groves of academe itself then, it has been argued, it is frequently conducted more with an eye to positions of power and influence within the academy than with any liberating project of the full recognition of others. This point has been made most sharply by Sangren. Writing of ethnography, he says,

> whatever 'authority' is created in a text has its most direct social effect not in the world of political and economic domination of the Third World by colonial and neocolonial powers, but rather in the academic institutions in which such authors participate. (1988, p. 411)

And Mascia-Lees et al. add:

> While postmodernist anthropologists such as Clifford, Marcus, and Fisher may choose to think that they are transforming global power relations as well as the discipline of anthropology itself, they may also be establishing first claim in the new academic territory on which this decade's battles for intellectual supremacy and jobs will be waged. (1989, p. 16)

Third, it is necessary in other words to recognize the power relations within academe and within intellectual debate. Thus, Rorty (1979) proposes that philosophy and intellectual activity should be persistently oppositional and that cultural exchange, indeed culture in general, should be conceptualized as a conversation, and a conversation in which the previously marginalized are invited to participate. But as Hartsock acerbically points out:

> From having been constructed as void and lack, and from having been forbidden to speak, we are now expected to join in equal conversation with someone who has just realised that philosophy has been overconfident. (1987, p. 200)

These arguments raise serious issues for all intellectuals/academics about their behaviour within their own social group, about the nature of their writing, about the power structures of academe, and so on. And these issues arise most acutely for those who are already established and, within these, for those who are members of the already dominant group of white males. For them, if ventures into postmodernism are not to represent simply an attempt at the restoration of their shaky authority as purveyors of truth (even if it is that the whole concept is a lot more complicated than it was previously thought to be), and if it is to be more than another play for status within academe on the part of those who already hold, as a group, most of the positions of power, then there has to be a fundamental questioning of the way they go about their craft.

One aspect of this which is highly symptomatic revolves around the question of 'style', and in particular writing-style. Much writing in and about postmodernism verges on the pretentious, and on occasions the virtually incomprehensible to those not in a (fairly small) group. Moreover 'the left' is not immune from this (and not only among the postmodernists) – and indeed has provided over the years some of the worst examples of undemocratic writing. It is an issue which I should like to see debated, and that is why I raise it now.

For it occurred to me again while reading Soja's book. *Postmodern Geographies* has a strong, central argument, one which is extremely important to communicate, and one which might in general terms be accepted at least in part by many social scientists, whether or not they agreed in detail either with the manner of getting there or with whether it was demonstrated in practice by Soja's own examples. The book is full of rich insights and thought-provoking connections and ideas. I learned a lot from reading it. But the presentation of the argument is bemusing.

First, there is the question of structure. The book begins with a section called 'Preface and Postscript' and its opening sentences are:

> Combining a Preface with a Postscript seems a particularly apposite way to introduce (and conclude) a collection of essays on postmodern geographies. It signals right from the start an intention to tamper with the familiar modalities of time, to shake up the normal flow of the linear text to allow other, more 'lateral' connections to be made.

In fact, what follows is a very conventionally structured argument (for which we should perhaps be grateful), the only 'novelty' being that there is overlap between some of the chapters, presumably an effect of this being a (well-reworked) collection of past articles. Most conventionally, the considerable amount of history which the book presents (for instance, about the development of the social/spatial line of thought amongst geographers) is both structured in an extraordinarily linear manner and leads with an ineluctable inexorability to the author and his current argument. Far from 'tampering with the familiar modalities of time', or 'shaking up the normal flow of the linear text' and so forth, it imposes an order, an order which is linear, and of a particular linearity. Its function is to ratify the present, the contribution which is to come. This is not, of course, unusual. There have been a few such 'histories' written recently, with the apparent authority of the overseer, where many of us involved recognize neither our individual roles nor the play as a whole. What makes it particularly jarring in this book, though, is the fact that it contradicts so completely both those opening sentences and the expressed commitment to multiple voices and plurality. One effect of this is that it leads to problems with the construction of Soja's own argument. By focusing so unremittingly on one characteristic (historicism), and homing in on all examples which exemplify his point, he misses other themes, other examples, and indeed counter-examples. Just looking within geography itself, there was surely a long period, in the early and middle decades of this century, when geography as an academic discipline was intellectually immobilized by its exclusive focus on 'space' and its insistence that there was a world of purely spatial laws, spatial causes, and spatial relations.[2] It does not indeed seem so long ago that a great number of us were spending our intellectual energies trying to combat this very characteristic (Massey, 1984)! This was a discipline which could not have been less 'historicist'.[3]

But another effect of the linear way in which Soja constructs his history is that it omits, not just other themes, but other voices. It has a hermetic coherence which excludes deviant contributions. Non-Marxist geographers, for instance, are not heard from very much. Again, in complete contrast with the promise of the first paragraph of the book, there is little simultaneity here, just a procession of those *who are seen to have been* dominant or important. It is a disappointment because it belies the evident democratic intent. It is very un-postmodern in the best sense of postmodern.

In contrast, however, to the conventionality of the overall structure, the language in which the argument is couched is arcane and tortured. Presentations which play with form, which take a delight in their own artistry, are surely to be applauded, but the taste this book left with me was one of pomposity rather than of an attempt to communicate. There has been much debate recently about the construction of texts, and the effects and implications of different modes of construction. The case of the linear history was an example of this, and here we see a similar effect in relation to linguistic style. *Postmodern Geographies* left at least this reader (and I know I am not the only one; it has been the subject of some discussion) wondering what the author was trying to achieve. The concern most often expressed is that this kind of writing is less about communication than about self-presentation. This is a difficult issue, and I realize that to some extent at least it is subjective. Moreover, in this case I have some sympathy in the sense that Soja is trying to get geographical issues on to the agenda of the intellectual left. Writing to one's audience is an important skill, and I can well understand if he felt that the only way to gatecrash those august portals was to write like too many of them do. I suppose all I am arguing is that we should try to resist the temptation. For, if those of us who would in some way or measure sign up under the banner of postmodernism are to avoid the accusation of using the claimed potential democracy of the message simply to show off to each other, then we have to be very careful how, and for whom, we write. This of course applies to all of us, not just those who align with postmodernism. It is just that postmodernists' proclamations against authority, and their explicitly stated concern with the nature of the text, make such writing in their case particularly ironic. Nor am I trying to make the case that everything we write should be 'for the proletariat' otherwise known in the United Kingdom as the man (sic) on the Clapham omnibus. Styles will, and should, vary with the audience addressed (which is not the same as falling into their bad habits). It is not a question of being anti-intellectual, either; indeed it is in part bound up with precisely the distinction between being an *intellectual* and being an *academic*.

Moreover, the issue is reinforced in Soja's book because we are given clues as to what he was trying to establish himself *as*. We are told, for instance, that the author once went for a trip around Los Angeles with Fredric Jameson and Henri Lefebvre. What are we to make of this information? Perhaps what is being communicated is the sense of an in-crowd, and the fact that the author may be part of it. Thus, Soja refers to Jameson: 'Fredric Jameson, perhaps the pre-eminent American Marxist literary critic' (p. 62). Jameson repays the compliment: 'that new spatiality implicit in the post-modern (which Ed Soja's *Postmodern Geographies* now places on the agenda in so eloquent and timely a fashion)' (1989, p. 45). Soja refers to Harvey: 'A brilliant example of this flexible halfway house of Late Modern Marxist geography is Harvey's recent paper ...' (p. 73) and Harvey is duly quoted on the back of Soja's book: 'One of the most challenging and stimulating books ever written on the thorny issue ...'. On the back of Harvey's book we have Soja: 'Few people have penetrated the heartland of contemporary cultural theory and critique as explosively or as insightfully as David Harvey'.

Now, let us be clear what is being argued here. First of all, on the particular issue of quotes on the back of books, it is not sour grapes! Many of us are asked to participate in this kind of thing, and quite a few refuse. I realize that the pressure initially comes from publishers. It is part of the advertising to have ' "I think it is absolutely wonderful" – Big Name' or

'"Best thing since sliced bread" – Important Academic' on a book. It establishes, supposedly, its credentials. I also realize that the competitive pressures towards this kind of thing are probably far worse in the USA than the ones I know in the United Kingdom. But still, ought we to go along with it? My own reasons for refusing in the past to write such plaudits have been based on straightforward dislike of the big-name syndrome and the individualism (and competitiveness) it implies. At least those of us supposedly on the left could refuse to participate on the grounds both of anti-elitism and of the recognition that research and the development of ideas is in reality (and could be even more) more of a collective process than that. Perhaps these are issues which we should debate openly.

But second, neither is it being pretended that this is a new phenomenon or specific to these authors. It is neither; and indeed I am sure that the geographers involved here would share some of my reservations. Nor, third and most certainly, is it being argued that we should not be complimentary to each other, and congratulatory on each other's achievements. (Soja can be very nasty about less eminent figures – 'self-serving' is one adjective he employs, on p. 73.)

The combination of all these characteristics of style and presentation is, however, alienating. It seems designed to create a sense of a centre and a periphery. If the arguments cited earlier are correct and academics (and especially white male academics) today are feeling that there *is* a loss of status, a feeling that we (they) are not being regarded with the customary awe (at least among those from whom most academics are accustomed to receive it – those on the currently fashionable 'margins' never cared much for most of us anyway), then this is not the way to regain any kind of respect. This kind of response to a crisis chimes only too well with that negative aspect of postmodernist analysis which can only confirm the mutual incomprehensibility of self-defining groups, and greet it with a shrug of indifferent shoulders. On the other hand, it is a style which is in total contradiction to that more emancipatory aspect of postmodernism, the pulling down of hierarchies, the entry of the previously marginalized into the central forum of debate.

On page 74 of his book, in the middle of all this, Soja writes:

> This reconstituted critical human geography must be attuned to the emancipatory struggles of all those who are peripheralized and oppressed by the specific geography of capitalism (and existing socialism as well) – exploited workers, tyrannized peoples, dominated women.

The comment in the margin of my copy is unprintable.

## Difference and distance

But that quotation reveals something else as well. For it is not just in terms of style and textual strategy that *Postmodern Geographies* is ambivalent in its relation to postmodernism. So it is in the content of its theoretical stance and its arguments.

That quotation reveals on the one hand the recognition that a simple dualism of capital versus labour is not enough. Notions of peripherality, and of tyrannized peoples and dominated women get a mention. Yet, on the other hand, the thing by which they are peripheralized, tyrannized or dominated is assumed to be – uniquely – the geography of *the mode of production* (capitalism or 'existing socialism'). It recognizes that there are more things in life than can be captured in the classic formulation, but it does not really take them on board.

This is not an ambivalence particular to that quotation. It is present throughout the book. The existence of racism and sexism, and the need to refer to them, is recognized, but it is assumed throughout, either explicitly or implicitly, that the only axis of power which matters in relation to these distinct forms of domination is that which stems fairly directly from the relations of production. No other relations of power and dominance are seriously addressed. The fact that patriarchy, for instance, is not reducible to the terms of a debate on modes of production, is not considered. Indeed, to take the point further, modernity itself is defined entirely in relation to capitalism, at times seeming almost equivalent to it. Thus, in the key section on the deconstruction and reconstruction of modernity, an initially rich and broad-ranging definition is step by step narrowed down. We move from a recognition that 'the experience of modernity captures a broad mesh of sensibilities' (p. 25) and an argument (still very broad in what it potentially encompasses) that 'spatiality, temporality, and social being can be seen as the abstract dimensions which together comprise all facets of human existence' (p. 25). The breadth of this statement is confirmed by the definition of social being as 'revolving around the constitution of society, the production and reproduction of social relations, institutions, and practices' (p. 25). Yet within a few pages this focus has been reduced, and modernization, each accelerated period of which is seen as giving birth to new forms of modernism, and which becomes conflated with modernity, is reduced to capitalism: 'Modernization can be directly linked to the many different "objective" processes of structural change that have been associated with the ability of capitalism to develop and survive ... This defining association between modernization and the survival of capitalism is crucial ... Modernization ... is a continuous process of societal restructuring ... that arises primarily from the historical and geographical dynamics of modes of production' (pp. 26–7).

Yet between the last two of these statements there is a fleeting moment of doubt, of acknowledgement that it is not as simple as this. 'Modernization', it is conceded, 'is not entirely the product of some determinative inner logic of capitalism, but neither is it a rootless and ineluctable idealization of history' (p. 27). Of course, it partly depends on how you want to define modernization, but there is clearly here a drawing-back from the earlier simple equation of it with capitalism. Yet the revised formulation is also unsatisfactory. The alternatives are not, in fact, limited to a single determinative inner logic on the one hand and total rootlessness on the other. For one thing, and quite apart from the ramifications of wider debates, there are other axes of social power relations by which our current societies are characterized, as well as those of class and capitalism. In Soja's formulation structures such as patriarchy are reduced to noises-off which account for the fact that there is no simple deterministic relation between capitalism and modernization. But why cannot such other axes of power and of social structuring be considered in their own right?[4] Patriarchy is not in the index. Feminism gets one mention, and it is in the passage following the quotation cited at the end of the last section. The passage is dealing with the difficulties of politics in these times and much of it is insightful and useful. The pessimism of some of it is surely warranted. But then: 'Opposition to restructuring is made to appear as extremism [agreed], the very hope of resistance becomes tinged with the absurd [unfortunately true]. Marxism is equated only with totalitarianism [yes, we bitterly recognize that one]; radical feminism becomes the destruction of the family' (p. 74). What? Are these supposed to be equivalent statements? Even if the destruction of the family is a misreading of US radical feminism, is it to be equated with totalitarianism? Or even extremism? There are many feminists, including this one, who would not be unhappy to see the end of 'the family' in its current form (though that is not the same as arguing for its 'destruction').

The characterization of modernism mainly in relation to modes of production is paralleled by an unusual definition of postmodernism. Soja produces a carefully modulated argument here, and is careful too, as we shall see later, in stating his own relation to the wider projects of postmodernism, but in the end the most significant axis of his definition seems to be based around the importance of space. This leads to what seem to me to be some unexpected results. Both Harvey and Mandel turn out to be postmodernists, for instance. And, although the arguments in the chapters on Los Angeles do not establish how or why space is more important now, the arguments about the ontological significance of space (which are very interesting) are general ones: they are not specific to the recent period. But apart from these apparent confusions there is a deeper issue, for the postmodern questioning of modernism has involved far more than that. Among other things it has challenged the existence of a single coherent narrative of a causal structure to which everything can be related, it has challenged the authority of the single author or viewer,[5] and it has challenged the notion of a single universal subject, constructed – usually with blithe unintentionality – in the shape of a white western male heterosexual. In particular, it has been related to, though it is not equivalent to, the feminist critiques of modernism (see, among many writings in this area, Nicholson, 1990). None of this receives any attention.

Now, a number of people have already pointed out that *Postmodern Geographies* is, after all, a thoroughly *modern* text (for instance, see Dear, 1990; Gregory, 1990). Moreover, to be fair to Soja it should also be pointed out that he himself explicitly *dis*claims any intention to be thoroughly *post*modern (p. 5). None the less, he also says that he does now feel comfortable with postmodernism's 'intentional announcement of a possibly epochal transition *in* both *critical thought* and material life' (p. 5, my emphasis). Moreover, some of his reticence about postmodernism seems, in my view quite legitimately, to come from its frequent abandonment of any progressive project other than multiplicity. But, given this, it is possible to make use of some of the changes in critical thought (including some of the uncomfortably searching questions posed by postmodernism) both to address the ways in which modernism was also profoundly flawed and to retain a position of political commitment. Yet there is here no recognition that modernism was or is profoundly patriarchal (for instance) nor that there are possible alternatives which can go some way to addressing the central dilemmas of modernism without leaving us floating in an apolitical void. Perhaps the strongest case for an alternative of this sort has been made by feminists (for instance, see Mascia-Lees et al., 1989).

That arguments such as these have not been taken on board is evidenced in Soja's treatment of his central concepts of space and place. The chapters on Los Angeles are crucial here. They are innovative and fun, and they reveal some worthwhile insights (although they do not seem to do any more in the end than move from the socio-economic to the spatial. It is unclear how, in the real content of the relation they posit between the social and the spatial they are distinct from much previous writing, or are an exemplification of the theoretical propositions laid out in the early part of the book). But they are designed in a particular way. They are very much long-distance views, overviews (literally, from a height, whether it be from the air or from City Hall).

This raises two issues. First, this is very much a visual approach, and in modernism, vision was systematically and symptomatically prioritized over other senses. It has been argued to be the sense which allows most mastery; in part deriving from the very detachment which it allows and requires. And second this detachment, and the authority of the viewer which it helps to construct, is underscored in *Postmodern Geographies* by the very vantage points which Soja chooses to look from. The question of how one presents spaces, places and local cultures is a complex and unresolved one, or certainly that is true of how to do it democratically. The stance which Soja adopts is similar to that from which he writes his history. But such a stance ignores the major debates about the difficulties of such an approach. The work of Clifford and others has already been referred to. The collection by Clifford and Marcus (1986) is precisely concerned with how one constructs a text adequately to take account of the problems both of what he (Clifford) calls 'visualism' and of the recognition and reporting of distinct views and interpretations which are not simply absorbed into and re-presented by the 'author'. These writers, and others in the same vein, have in turn been criticized by feminists on a number of grounds:[6] for the degree to which the complexity of the text can lead to such obscurity that few can understand; for the lack of recognition that they still remain unquestionably 'the authors'; for the introspective self-regard which some postmodern strategies can produce among anthropologists themselves; perhaps most of all, and which is related to commitment, for a lack of regard to the question of whom they are speaking *for*. So these issues are complex and certainly unresolved. But they do, none the less, have to be faced. At the very end of 'Taking Los Angeles apart', in the Afterwords, Soja himself says 'I have been looking at Los Angeles from different points of view' (p. 247), but he hasn't, at least not in the way in which many feminist or postmodernist arguments would have us do. The views are all quite clearly his. He argues that 'Totalizing visions, attractive though they may be, can never capture all the meanings and significations of the urban ... There are too many *auteurs* to identify' (p. 247). Yet, in spite of his best intentions, this is what he has produced. Too few *auteurs*, too much *hauteur*!

## Exclusively masculine modernism

*Blue Velvet* and *Blade Runner*

Harvey's *The Condition of Postmodernity* is also, like *Postmodern Geographies*, and especially given the intrinsic difficulty of the argument it is developing, a major achievement.

But here again, reading it as a feminist, I was troubled. In some ways it is difficult to know where to get into this argument, partly because the book is such a seamless whole and partly because the main problem is precisely one of absence.

The absence is that of other points of view. Whereas Soja's ventures into postmodernism at least provoke him into wrestling with the necessity of recognizing the existence of a multiplicity of '*auteurs*', Harvey's modernism is constructed (or perhaps I should say unreconstructed) around an assumed universal whose particular characteristics are not even recognized. Women, for instance, do not figure in the development of the argument, and neither does the possibility of feminist readings of the issues under consideration. The same could be said of other voices currently subordinated in this society and its dominant lines of intellectual debate. The issue is not confined to feminism. Nor is it that there should be a few paragraphs here and there on 'women, ethnic minorities, etc'. It is that the dominant view is assumed to be the universal, and that view is white, male, heterosexual, western.

The analyses of film are symptomatic. Of David Lynch's film *Blue Velvet*, Harvey writes:

> In the more postmodernist format of the contemporary cinema we find, in a film like *Blue Velvet*, the central character revolving between two quite incongruous worlds – that of a conventional 1950s small-town America with its high school, drugstore culture, and a bizarre, violent, sex-crazed underworld of drugs, dementia, and sexual perversion. It seems impossible that these two worlds should exist in the same space, and the central character moves between them, unsure which is the true reality, until the two worlds collide in a terrible denouement. (p. 48)

This is inadequate on a number of grounds. First, in what sense is this an *incongruous* juxtaposition of worlds? Rather than it seeming 'impossible that these two worlds should exist in the same space', they are in fact necessary to each other; they are mutually constitutive, mutually dependent. Male violence, for instance, is a large part of what maintains the institution of marriage and its variants in contemporary society (see Valentine, 1989) and 'monogamy' has frequently been upheld by its negation, by outside interests, whether these took the form of nineteenth-century prostitution for the male, or the more 'egalitarian' (?) something-on-the-side more typical of today's professional middle classes. Prurience is one of the requirements for the existence of pornography. The film makes this mutuality clear itself in a jokey way when at the end it returns to the primary colours, white fences, and nodding flowers of small-town

USA with its waving, smiling, fireman with no fires to put out (is this really any less 'bizarre' than the other world?), and the robin on the window sill (over which they all coo) has in its beak a writhing bug, tortured in the midst of the rural idyll, and necessarily so in order that the robin may live. The question is not the existence of the underside, but whether or not we see it.

However, the meaning of a text is almost always a site of contestation or at least of implicit disagreement (Denzin, 1988; Grossberg, 1986). And so it is with *Blue Velvet*. Indeed, in the case of this film the debate has been explicit and extensive, particularly given Lynch's own admirable refusal to be categorized into any particular genre (for instance see Rabkin, 1986). It is therefore curious that Harvey does not refer to this. In contrast to Harvey's interpretation, Lynch himself has said, for instance:
'*Blue Velvet* is a trip beneath the surface of a small American town' (in Chute, 1986, p. 32)
(no intimations of incongruity here) and:

> It's like saying that once you've discovered there are heroin addicts in the world and they're murdering people to get money, can you be happy? It is a tricky question. Real ignorance is bliss. That's what *Blue Velvet* is about. (Rabkin, 1986, p. 55)

Among the other possible interpretations of the film are feminist ones. The film is not just about the two sides of US (etc.) culture; but, as Lynch has himself said,

> It's also a probe into the subconscious or a place where you face things that you don't normally face. (Chute, 1986, p. 32)

In this regard, Harvey's characterization, in neutral fashion, of 'the central character' fails to catch a crucial, and necessary, fact. This is a *gendered* central character, and it is male. The two worlds are indeed one, and they are two sides of masculine identity. *Blue Velvet*

> operates with a series of simplistic oppositions – pretty-pretty suburbia versus inner-city decay, night versus day, virginal romance versus sadistic sex, purity and horror, and so on. As Jeff makes his Oedipal journey into the underworld, in this cartoon psychoanalytic drama, it soon becomes clear that these two versions of masculinity, the dark and the light, are really two sides of the same coin. (Moore, 1988, p. 187)

What the film is about, here, is 'masculinity having to face up to its darker side' (ibid., p. 187).

It is not casually the fact, nor accidental, that the central character is male (and heterosexual). For, moreover, the two worlds, or sides of masculinity, are crucially represented in the film by – guess what – women. There is Sandy, of the suburban appearance of health and order (although Lynch is true to his theme again and even she has spots under the make-up), and there is Dorothy, of the world of wild sexuality and violence, the kind of thing they speak of in the suburbs, if at all, as disgusting. Woman stands as choices for men; as their Other. Their function is to help some man find his identity. As Moore (1988) points out in her article 'Getting a bit of the Other – the pimps of postmodernism', this is a characteristic which runs through much of postmodernism, from its initiating theorists (Lacan et al.), through Baudrillard (at times quite laughably so – see his writing on New York in *America* [1988]), to film: 'the world of the feminine becomes a way of men exploring, rejecting or reconstructing their masculinity, of "getting a bit of the other" at the expense of women' (pp. 187–8).

Further, the corollary of this is that women themselves are contained within one or the other of the alternative categories; they themselves have no option (Denzin, 1988; Gledhill, 1978). It is not just that *Blue Velvet* presents a world which denigrates women (McGuigan and Huck, 1986 – and I would argue that this is a problem not of the film, which is restrained in its portrayal, but of the world it is depicting), but that it makes the postmodern message of the film, the one drawn out by Harvey, exclusive to men.

Finally, even the postmodernists actually cannot face up to it. 'Although the insecurity of identity that these films offer is pleasurable, it can also be unsettling if security is not restored by the end of the film' (Moore, p. 188). Jeff settles down with Sandy; he is also in some measure instrumental in what he (though not necessarily she) would see as the 'saving' of Dorothy (that old male thing about their individual, special, relation to women of the *demi-monde*). The good thing about *Blue Velvet* is that it does not let us/you/him off the hook. The robin on the window sill is still torturing the beetle. Denzin (1988) argues that all this may reflect the contradictoriness of these postmodern times, but also, perhaps more acutely, observes:

> It seems that postmodern individuals want films like *Blue Velvet* for in them they can have their sex, their myths, their violence and their politics, all at the same time. (p. 472)

And safely, one might add, since it's all in a movie. But even then, 'the Other' cannot be *too* challenging, at least not to the supposed universal – the white, heterosexual male. While, as we have seen:

> This 'getting a bit of the other' seems . . . to depend on women as the gateway to the other world . . .

and while it is also true that

> increasingly black people and black culture is [sic] used to signify something radically different,

on the other hand,

> Some kinds of 'otherness' remain just too threatening to be colonised in this manner – homosexuality for example seems to be seen as far too disturbing and difficult to offer this kind of escapism. (Moore, 1988, p. 186)

But Harvey misses all this. Had he wanted, this would have been an excellent opportunity to demonstrate the problems for feminism of current actually existing postmodernism. But if the problem of the postmodernists is that while celebrating the existence of the Other most of us are consigned to being means of constructing the identity of white, heterosexual men, the problem of the modernists is that they do not see us, really, at all. Or, if they do, it is as somehow deviations from the norm, troubling exceptions to the(ir) rule.

And so it is with Harvey. As Denzin (1988) points out, the hegemonic reading of *Blue Velvet* (by the *New York Times*, the *New Yorker*, *Christian Century*, *National Review*, *Playboy*, etc.) did not analyse these gender issues in the film. Neither does Harvey; and for classically modernist reasons. In these readings of the movie, masculinity is not in question. The male is not even recognized to be gendered. He is the universal.

But it is perhaps unfair to concentrate too much on the analysis of this particular film. Harvey's reference to it was after all quite a brief one, and it occurred in the context of a wider discussion. Let us look, then, at one of the more extended analyses of film which are to be found towards the end of the book and to which a whole chapter (ch. 18) is devoted. Let us take the case of *Blade Runner*. One of the key threads in this movie is the struggle by the female replicant Rachel to prove that she is not a replicant. However, in order to do this, and thereby to survive, replicants have to prove a history, and their relationship to it; they must, most crucially, enter and establish a place in the symbolic order. And the symbolic order used in *Blade Runner* is that of Freud. So Harvey, drawing on this analysis of the film, which as he says is that of Giuliana Bruno (1987), describes Rachel's (ultimately successful) attempt at survival through the establishment of a (human) identity. As he writes,

But she can re-enter the symbolic realm of a truly human society only by acknowledging the overwhelming power of the Oedipal figure, the father ... In submitting to Deckard (trusting him, deferring to him, and ultimately submitting to him physically), she learns the meaning of human love and the essence of ordinary sociality. In killing the replicant Leon as he is about to kill Deckard, she provides the ultimate evidence of the capacity to act as Deckard's woman. (1989, p. 312)

There are a number of points to be made here. First of all, Harvey does not comment on the particularity of this process of a replicant finding an identity as a woman. She learns the meaning of love through submission (Harvey's word) to a man; she establishes an identity – as 'Deckard's woman'. It is not an appetising prospect, and one wonders whether, if survival had not been dependent on it, she would have bothered. This point is a more significant one than it perhaps sounds in that one of the things which Harvey misses is that Rachel is not just establishing *an* identity, she is establishing a sexual and specifically a *female*, identity. In Bruno's terms 'To survive for a time, the android has to accept the fact of sexual difference, the sexual identity which the entry into language requires' (1987, p. 71).

It is interesting, and surely significant, moreover, that it is precisely and only at this point that Harvey disagrees with Bruno (nor, possibly, is it insignificant that he talks of Bruno as 'he' and calls her Giuliano!). Bruno writes:

Of all the replicants, only one, Rachel, succeeds in making the journey. She assumes a sexual identity, becomes a woman, and loves a man ... Rachel accepts the paternal figure and follows the path to a 'normal', adult, female, sexuality: she identifies her sex by first acknowledging the power of the other, the father, a man. But the leader of the replicants, Roy Batty, refuses the symbolic castration which is necessary to enter the symbolic order. (1987, p. 71)

It is precisely this contrast with which Harvey disagrees. He puts Roy's refusal simply down to the fact that survival in his case is unlikely anyway. I do not know which interpretation is more valid in relation to the film, but it is interesting that this disagreement precisely underlines Harvey's unwillingness to engage on the terrain of sexual identity. For that, of course, might further undermine the supposed universality of one fraction of humanity, the heterosexual male.

This disagreement with Bruno, moreover, is linked back to the earlier lack of comment on the manner of Rachel's acquisition of an identity. Bruno makes it clear that what is involved is submission, and that some may go along with it, and others may refuse. Although he recognizes submission, it is not seen as so problematical a process by Harvey, and later he clearly believes that Rachel really does fall in love with Deckard. Thus, for instance, the possibility that she might be feigning, in order to survive, does not seem to occur to him. Yet women have often had to resort to feigning, in various ways, and often with far less at stake than survival (as another recent movie *When Harry Met Sally* recently pointed out). Moreover, not only does Harvey believe that Rachel really falls for Deckard, but he is disappointed because

> The strongest social bond between Deckard and the replicants in revolt – the fact that they are both controlled and enslaved by a dominant corporate power – never generates the slightest hint that a coalition of the oppressed might be forged between them. (1989, p. 313)

Now that quite took my breath away. On page 312 we are reading all this about Rachel having to submit to Deckard, and on page 313 we are wondering why she does not enter into an alliance with him. The wider political implications of this kind of male-based analysis have recently been analysed by Hart (1989), and I shall return to the point in a later section. But wishing for coalitions of the oppressed without first analysing the contradictions and power relations within those potential coalitions is to court political failure.

### What illustrations illustrate

In the chapter on postmodernism in part I of *The Condition of Postmodernity* there are five pictorial illustrations. Every one of them is of a woman, in every case a naked woman. Harvey makes no comment on this.

His commentaries ponder the superimposition of ontologically different worlds, or the difference between Manet and Rauschenberg, but they are oblivious to what is being represented, how it is being represented and from whose point of view, and the political effects of such representations. David Salle's *Tight as Houses* is the most evident case of this, where Harvey gives no indication that he has grasped the simple pun of the title and its clearly sexist content. Whose gaze is this painting painted from and for? Who could get the 'joke'? The painting is treated with deadly seriousness by Harvey, who cites Taylor (1987) on how it is a collage bringing together 'incompatible source materials as an alternative to choosing between them' (Harvey, p. 49). My own response, as someone who was potentially *in* that picture, and who saw it with completely different eyes, was: 'Here we go, another pretentious male artist who still thinks naked women are naughty'. Any deeper meaning in the picture (though it was hardly intellectually startling when revealed) was entirely obliterated, from my reading position, by the sexism of the image used to convey it.[7] The painting assumes a complicit male viewer. For women, in contrast, the position is different: 'to look at and enjoy the sites of patriarchal culture we women must become nominal transvestites. We must assume a masculine position or masochistically enjoy the sight of woman's humiliation' (Pollock, 1988, p. 85).

To push this issue of positionality further, one can consider the interpretation of those who figure in the illustrations. Try, for instance, looking at Harvey's plates 1.7 and 1.8 (Titian's *Venus d'Urbino* and Manet's *Olympia* – dubbed 'seminal' by Harvey) while reading the following:

I shall be represented analytically and hung
in great museums. The bourgeoisie will coo
at such an image of a river-whore. They call it Art.

Maybe. He is concerned with volume, space.
I with the next meal . . .

         . . . It makes me laugh. His name
is Georges. They tell me he's a genius.
There are times he does not concentrate
and stiffens for my warmth.
        (Duffy 'Standing Female Nude', 1985)

But this is a first response, drawn from the anger I felt on first reading the chapter. Let us, therefore, look more seriously. For apart from this very evident level of sexism in the selection and use of illustrations, there is a deeper problem. By not getting to grips with the feminist analyses and critiques of modernism, Harvey both misses an important aspect of its character and, in consequence, fails fully to understand the nature of the criticisms directed against it. Moreover, this whole feminist debate centrally relates to Harvey's core concerns – modernism, postmodernism, space and politics.

It is useful to begin this argument from Manet, who is widely recognized as being one of the founders of modernism in painting. In his analyses of Manet, Harvey follows Crimp (1985), particularly in the comparisons with Titian and with Rauschenberg. Indeed, it is presumably because he is drawing on Crimp's analysis that Harvey selects that particular Rauschenberg (another voyeuristic view of a woman – *Persimmon*) rather than any other combine of his which could be drawn on to make the same points (about collage, reproduction, juxtaposition and unrelatedness) – see, for instance, Hewison (1990). Yet the analysis of Manet's *Olympia* is curiously limited. Neither it, nor the wider consideration of 'time–space compression and the rise of modernism as a cultural force' (ch. 16), analyse a theme which should be central to Harvey's project – the socio-political implications of the spatial organization of the painting itself and of the modernist art of which it is exemplary. This is all the more curious because the article which follows Crimp's in the Foster collection is on precisely this subject. It is called 'The discourse of others; feminists and postmodernism' (Owens, 1985), and it is not referred to by Harvey.

It is now a well-established argument, from feminists but not only from feminists, that modernism both privileged vision over the other senses and established a *way* of seeing from the point of view of an authoritative, privileged, and male, position (Irigaray, 1978; Owens, 1985; Pollock, 1988).[8] The privileging of vision impoverishes us through deprivation of other forms of sensory perception. 'In our culture, the predominance of the look over smell, taste, touch, hearing, has brought about an impoverishment of bodily relations . . . the moment the look dominates, the body loses its materiality' (Irigaray, 1978, p. 50). But, and more important from the point of view of the argument here, the reason for the privileging of vision is precisely its supposed detachment. Such detachment, of course, can have its advantages, but it is also necessarily a 'detached' view from a particular point of view. Detached does not here mean disinterested. One of the aims of some postmodern artists has been precisely to investigate the interests modernist detachment serves. And, in a widely quoted passage, Irigaray has pointed out that 'investment in the look is not privileged in women as in men. More than the other senses, the eye objectifies and masters' (1978, p. 50). And in the illustrations which Harvey has selected the patriarchal content is doubled by the fact that not only do we have here the classic modernist male authoritative gaze but it is looking at – very particular representations of – women.

Now, as Pollock (1988) points out, 'it is a striking fact that many of the canonical works held up as the founding monuments of modern art treat precisely with this area, sexuality, and this form of it, commercial exchange'; 'it is normal to see women's bodies as the territory across which men artists claim their modernity'.[9] And, she goes on, 'we must enquire why the territory of modernism so often is a way of dealing with masculine sexuality and its sign, the bodies of women – why the nude, the brothel, the bar? What relation is there between sexuality, modernity and modernism?' (p. 54; see also Duncan, 1990).[10] Chadwick (1990) and others have made the same point, Chadwick talking of 'the extent to which the major paintings . . . associated with the development of modern art wrest their formal and stylistic innovations from an erotically based assault on the female form' (p. 266).

There are many lines of analysis, argument and debate which run from here. There is the issue of what this form of representation does to women, how it actively produces conceptualizations of what is feminine and what is masculine, how it influences the form of gender relations, how it thereby contributes to the physical and social circumscribing of women's lives (Cowie, 1978; Pollock, 1988). For, *contra* the overall force of Harvey's argument, which itself belies occasional individual statements of resistance to economism, representation is not merely reflection; it is itself an active force in moulding social relations and social understanding.

But there is also the issue of what it means to ignore these debates about modernism and its ways of seeing. For the implications are not 'confined' to the 'specific' and 'local' issue of feminism. Opposition to this authoritarian gaze, and to the claims it makes, is central to the critique of modernism made by some postmodernists. It is, moreover, a crucial point at which issues about theorizing, about the validity of 'master narratives' and so forth relate most intimately to issues concerning spatial organization. There has, further, been substantial work in this area amongst cultural geographers. The writing of Cosgrove (1984) on the use and implications of perspective in the concept of landscape is an obvious example. By not taking account of the feminist literature, therefore, a whole line of argument central to the relationship between modernity, space, and social relations has been closed off.

## 'Other' spaces of modernism

The spaces of modernism which are mostly celebrated are the public spaces of the city. It was in the rapidly growing western cities, especially Paris, that modernism was born. And the standard literature from Baudelaire onwards is replete with descriptions of boulevards and cafés, of fleeting, passing glances and of the cherished anonymity of the crowd. The spatial and social reorganization, and flourishing, of urban life was an essential condition for the birth of the new era. But that city was also gendered. Moreover, it was gendered in ways which relate directly to spatial organization.

First, it was gendered in the very general sense of the distinction between the public and the private (Wolff, 1985). This period of the mid-nineteenth century was a crucial one in the development of the notion of 'the separation of spheres' and the confinement of women, ideologically if not for all women in practice, to the 'private' sphere of the suburbs and the home (Davidoff and Hall, 1983; Hall, 1981). The public city which is celebrated in the enthusiastic descriptions of the dawn of modernism was a city for men. The boulevards and cafés, and still more the bars and brothels, were for men – the women who did go there were for male consumption. Nineteenth-century Paris presented very different impress-ions and possibilities for men and for women.[11] Thus Pollock (1988), in thinking through the relation between 'space and social processes' (her terms) in relation to art history, argues that one possible approach might lie 'in considering not only the spaces represented, or the spaces *of* the representation, but the social spaces from which the representation is made and its reciprocal positionalities' (p. 66).

But the social spaces from which the generally cited central cultural products of modernism were made were the public spaces of the city – the spaces of men. This has a number of implications. First, many of the paintings (even, or perhaps especially, those of women) were set in places where women of the same class as the painter simply could not go. Thus, to pick up again the theme of *Olympia*, Pollock discussing the picture alongside that of the barmaid in Manet's *A Bar at the Folies-Bergères* asks:

> How can a woman relate to the viewing positions proposed by either of these paintings? Can a woman be offered, in order to be denied, imaginary possession of Olympia or the barmaid? Would a woman of Manet's class have a familiarity with either of these spaces and its exchanges which could be evoked so that the painting's modernist job of negation and disruption could be effective? . . . Would it enter her head as a site of modernity as she experienced it? (1988, pp. 54–5; see also Morgan, 1990)

Indeed, could a woman experience modernity, defined in this way, at all?

Second, one of the key figures embodying the experience of this definition of modernity is the *flâneur*, the stroller in the crowd, observing but not observed. But the *flâneur* is irretrievably male. As Wolff (1985) has argued, the *flâneuse* was an impossibility. In part this is so because 'respectable' women simply could not wander around the streets and parks alone. (This was for reasons of socially constructed 'propriety', but for those 'non-respectable' women who did roam the public spaces movement would still be effectively restricted by the threat of male violence.) In part, the notion of a *flâneuse* is impossible precisely because of the one-way-ness and the directionality of the gaze. *Flâneurs* observed others; they were not observed themselves. And, for reasons which link together the debate on perspective and the spatial organization of paint-ing, and most women's exclusion from the public sphere, the modern gaze belonged (belongs?) to men.[12]

Third, moreover, and reinforcing all of this, the *flâneur*'s gaze was frequently erotic. And woman was, and was *only*, the object of this gaze. Baudelaire's embarrassingly awful views on this are probably now too well known to need citing again.[13] But once again, the subject, the author, of the whole performance is – not by chance but necessarily in its very construction – male.

What all this together implies is that the experience of modernism/ modernity as it is customarily recorded, the production of what are customarily assumed to be its major cultural artefacts, and even its customary definition, are all constructed on and are constructive of particular forms of gender relations and definitions of masculinity and of what it means to be a woman. This is not ('just') to say that modernism was or is patriarchal (this would hardly be news, nor differentiate it from many other periods in history); it is to say that it is not possible fully to understand modernism without taking account of this. To return more directly to Harvey, modernism is about more than a particular articulation of the power relations of time, space and money. Harvey has produced a fascinating, if arguably economistic, exploration of the relation between the definition, production and experience of space, on the one hand, and modes of production and class formation, on the other. But it completely misses other ways, other power relations, in which space is also structured and experienced. Harvey mentions none of the arguments which have been addressed in this section. He discusses suburbanization at a number of points, but does not mention the separation of spheres. Or again, he discusses how Frédéric Moreau, hero of Flaubert's *L'Education sentimentale*, 'glides in and out of the differentiated spaces of the city, with the same sort of ease that money and commodities change hands. The whole narrative structure of the book likewise gets lost in perpetual postponements of decisions precisely because Frédéric has enough inherited money to enjoy the luxury of not deciding'. Comments Harvey: 'it was the possession of money that allowed the present to slip through Frédéric's grasp, while opening social space to casual penetration. Evidently, time, space and money could be invested with rather different significances, depending upon the conditions and possibilities of trade-off between them' (pp. 263–4). Well, yes, nearly but not quite. Frédéric, as he casually penetrated these social spaces, did have another little advantage in life too.

As Pollock (1988, p. 5) has very persuasively argued:

> A feminist historical materialism does not ... substitute gender for class but deciphers the intricate interdependence of class and gender, as well as race, in all forms of historical practice. None the less there is a strategic priority in insisting upon recognition of gender power and of sexuality as historical forces of significance as great as any of the other matrices privileged in Marxism or other forms of social history or cultural analysis ... a feminist analysis of the founding conditions of modernism in the

gendered and eroticized terrain of the modern city directly challenges an authoritative social historical account which categorically refuses feminism as a necessary corollary.

The implications of ignoring feminist analyses go beyond the 'local' issue of gender relations.

Moreover, there is a further point, which can be explored by inquiring what happened to women who were painting pictures in and of this period. The point is not that there were some and that they are rarely considered by male art historians and other commentators, though this is true (see Chadwick, 1990). The point is, not that women painted, but that what they painted and the way they painted was different. This occurs in a number of ways, each to do with the relation between space and social organization. First, there is the fact that, as would be expected from the preceding discussion, the paintings are of different places/spaces from those of men. They are not of brothels, or of the apparently endless fascination of the *folies*, they are not of backstage at the theatre; they are much more frequently of the domestic sphere, of balconies and gardens, and, when they move outside, the parts of the public sphere they deal with (a box at the theatre, a park) are distinct from the main preoccupations of male painters. Second, however, the spatial organization of the paintings themselves is sometimes also distinct. Thus, for example, Pollock (1988) points to the fact that they may be organized in such a way that the viewer is drawn more into the picture itself, reducing the feeling of the detachment of the spectator, and reducing also thereby the authority of the spectator's gaze. Moreover, this refocusing is also sometimes brought about by a clear disruption of standard Enlightenment notions of perspective; this is a different way of representing space. Last, it is arguable that this in turn may bring back 'into the picture' the senses other than vision, thus deprioritizing at least a little vision in relation to the other senses and thereby challenging one of the central tenets of modernism-as-it-is-normally-described.

And that extended hyphenation is, of course, the point. It has been argued by a number of women that the usual view of modernism, and perhaps most specifically of its art, is frequently only a partial conception of modernity (for instance, see Wolff, 1985). If that is true of many of the male 'authorities' on the subject, it is *a fortiori* the case with Harvey who, through his whole argument (and this is a more general concern about the discussion) draws only on mainstream (or what was to become mainstream) culture, whether this be gallery art, famous architects, or big-budget movies. This leads to an unnecessarily monolithic view of the modernist period; it shifts the definition of what it was and, by missing out the voices on the margins and in the interstices of what was accepted, it also misses the full force of the critique which those voices, among them feminists, were making of the modernism he does discuss.[14]

All this becomes fully apparent in another way when Harvey considers the work of Cindy Sherman. She is postmodern and female. Harvey clearly does not like what she does and is more than a little disturbed by it. He describes visiting an exhibition of her photographs:

> The photographs depict seemingly different women drawn from many walks of life. It takes a little while to realize, with a certain shock, that these are portraits of the same woman in different guises. Only the catalogue tells you that it is the artist herself who is that woman. The parallel with Raban's insistence upon the plasticity of human personality through the malleability of appearances and surfaces is striking, as is the self-referential positioning of the authors to themselves as subjects. Cindy Sherman is considered a major figure in the postmodern movement. (p. 7)

There is a whole host of problems here. Later, Harvey refers to Sherman and a range of other postmodernists in a discussion of the current crisis of representation. That there *is* such a crisis is not in doubt. But Harvey here (p. 322) and throughout the book identifies the cause of this crisis as 'the experience of time–space compression in recent years, under the pressures of the turn to more flexible modes of accumulation' (p. 322).[15] After all the feminist debate about representation, to which I have just referred, and the directly political critique of modernist representation, it is surely inadequate to put the whole crisis down to time–space compression and flexible accumulation. There was *political* and a specifically feminist criticism of the mode of representation which was dominant prior to the crisis. Much of this postmodern work is thus not just part of a crisis, it is also a social comment. Thus when Harvey writes: 'The interest in Cindy Sherman's photographs (or any postmodern novel for that matter) is that they focus on masks without commenting directly on social meanings other than on the activity of masking itself' (p. 101), he is missing much of the point.[16] Deutsche (1990) in her review of Harvey and Soja has pointed out very clearly that much postmodern art has concerned itself with images precisely to reveal their social importance as sites where meanings, and subjects, are produced. Thus, 'to the extent that this is its goal, postmodernism's concentration on images is emphatically *not* a turn away from, but rather toward, the social' (p. 23). And in this context she refers specifically to the work of Sherman. Crimp (1982) too, whom Harvey cites elsewhere, argues that what Sherman is doing is attacking 'auteurism'.

Moreover, it is not just a general socio-political point which can be drawn from Sherman's photographs, but a specifically feminist one. Harvey says he was shocked to find that all these different images were of 'the same woman'. It is an unintended admission, for that is precisely the effect they are supposed to have on the patriarchal viewer. Thus Owens comments that they

> reflect back at the viewer his own desire (and the spectator posited by this work is invariably male) – specifically the masculine desire to fix the woman in a stable and stabilizing identity. But this is precisely what Sherman's work denies: for while her photographs are always self-portraits, in them the artist never appears to be the same ... while Sherman may pose as a pin-up, she still cannot be pinned down. (1985, p. 75)

It is, precisely, a way of disrupting the normally dominant pleasures of the patriarchal visual field.

Moreover, maybe she *is* all of these things, *and* they are masks. Sherman's work reveals how socially constructed and how unstable 'gender' is and how, indeed, the last few centuries of western culture has produced a 'femininity' which does indeed have a lot to do with self-presentation, in masks for others, in masquerade (Chadwick, 1990, pp. 358–9; Owens, 1985, p. 75).

Finally, Harvey seems to object particularly to the fact that Sherman took these pictures of herself ('the self-referential positioning of the authors to themselves as subjects'). Would it have been less disturbing had a man taken an authoritative picture of this woman? – like Manet painting Olympia, perhaps?[17]

Gender, then, is a determining factor in cultural production. It must be so also in relation to its interpretation. We have seen this, in this section, in specific relation to modernism. At the end of *The Condition of Postmodernity*, Harvey argues for a recuperation of one form of modernism – Marxism. He recognizes, too, that it must be reworked in order to treat more satisfactorily of difference and 'otherness', and that it is not enough simply to add categories on: they should be present in the analysis from the beginning. Yet in his own analysis of modernism and postmodernism one of the most significant of those 'differences' – that which revolves around gender – is absent.

## Politics – and academe

I have great sympathy with the overall projects of both these books. Soja is struggling to be postmodern, but really remaining in many ways modern; Harvey is quite clearly for modernism but wanting, he says, to change it in ways which will respond to certain inadequacies. I, too, would like to retain strong aspects of what characterizes the modernist project, most particularly its commitment to change, hopefully progressive; I also agree strongly with Harvey's defence of much of what has been achieved in its name. But it is necessary also to recognize the inadequacies of the modernist project in its dominant form. One problem of both these books is that they neither fully recognize the issues nor adequately respond to them. The answers which most postmodernism has so far provided may well be mistaken, but the challenges it poses must surely be addressed.

Moreover, one stream of thought which has been raising many of the same issues for far longer, which has been debating a set of answers which do not fall into the traps of postmodernism, which do not disintegrate into localism (in Lyotard's sense, which has nothing to do with the specifically geographical – see Massey, 1991), which do not abandon theories which have sufficient scope to deal with issues such as gender and class, which are historical and sensitive to differentiation ... is feminism. The list of characteristics just mentioned is taken from Fraser and Nicholson (1988), but many others have been debating similar issues. Other than contributions already mentioned there are, for instance, Flax (1986), Harding (1986, 1987 and many others), Haraway (1983), Jardine (1985) and Morris (1988).

This literature is not mentioned by Soja or Harvey. Not one of the above authors is mentioned by either of them.[18] At a number of points in this paper it has been noted that the potential contributions of feminism have simply been ignored. This is perhaps particularly glaring because so many feminists have written on the issues of space and society which are central to the debate in hand. Why, then, are they not considered? Is it that many men feel they do not have to read the feminist literature? Is it seen as a 'specialism'? Harvey has said (1985) that he likes to think of himself as 'a restless analyst'. It is an attractive and appealing image. But maybe he has not been restless enough. It should not be acceptable that a large part of the central literature is simply missing from what sets out to be a comprehensive overview, and that whole lines of debate are simply ignored.

Fraser and Nicholson mention a number of other features which are potentially characteristic of a new mode of theorizing which is neither modern in the old sense nor postmodern in its usual style. The attention to cultural specificity and to differentiation within society and over time is developed into the statement that such theory 'would be non-universalist. When its focus became cross-cultural or transepochal, its mode of attention would be comparativist rather than universalizing, attuned to changes and contrasts instead of to "covering laws"' (1988,

240 Space, place and gender

p. 390–1). I have to say that I am uncertain about this in some ways. (These are confusing times and I think we should be open enough to admit that on some things we may remain undecided.) But this characterization of theory does contrast strongly with Harvey's. Harvey constantly runs together universalism and internationalism. But, often, they are absolutely not the same thing. Indeed in some ways they are potentially antagonistic to each other. A true internationalism is surely a non-starter without the prior recognition of diversity. And the 'universals' on which so much analysis is based are so often in fact quite particular; not universals at all, but white, male, western, heterosexual, what have you. The long attempt to force such universals down unwilling throats is now demonstrating its failure in part precisely by provoking the most reactionary forms of cultural specificity. 'Finally,' write Fraser and Nicholson,

> postmodern-feminist theory would dispense with the idea of a subject of history. It would replace unitary notions of 'women' and 'feminine gender identity' with plural and complexly constructed conceptions of social identity, treating gender as one relevant strand among others, attending also to class, race, ethnicity, age and sexual orientation. (1988, p. 391)

Again, this is easier said than done. But in all kinds of ways, the approaches in the two books which have been discussed here show how poverty-stricken is the analysis, and how open to progressive political criticism is a failure even to wrestle with these problems, and their attendant possibilities. The question of 'authorship' seems to be central. White western men write academic texts and interpret the world for each other; and the universal author of history is understood to be a male, heterosexual and modernizing in the western image. So Harvey fails to understand what Sherman is saying precisely because it is about these things – author(ity), and feminism. Although he discusses perspectivism, for example, and its relation to individualism (for example p. 245) and the modernist 'aura' of the artist as producer (pp. 55 and 245), the full implications are not drawn out and explored. Yet those implications are political, in the widest sense of the word. As Deutsche concludes:

> Postmodernists who problematize the image – artists like Cindy Sherman, Barbara Kruger, Silvia Kolbowski, Mary Kelly, Connie Hatch – reject such vanguard roles. They have been saying for years that, thanks to the recognition that representations are produced by *situated* – not universal – subjects, the world is not so easily mapped anymore. (1990, p. 23)

Feminists, as Pollock points out, 'have nothing to lose with the desecration of Genius. The individualism of which the artist is a prime symbol is gender exclusive' (1988, p. 11).

There are implications also, therefore, for the way we are, and could be, as academics. There are huge questions being raised, in parts of geography, in anthropology and elsewhere, about our role as interpreters of the world. Yet neither of these books addresses these questions. There are issues about the hierarchies within our own fields, and whether we really need to take ourselves *quite* so seriously. *The V-Girls* poke fun at the way we can get out of control. Their subject in this sketch is . . .

## Manet's Olympia: posed and skirted

*The panel assembles behind a cloth-covered table, a water pitcher, plastic glasses, and sits down. Five dark-haired women, probably in their mid to late twenties: Martha Baer, Jessica Chalmers, Erin Cramer, Andrea Fraser, Marianne Weems. Four wear tailored suits, heavy-framed glasses: the signifiers of High Seriousness. It is time for a panel discussion on 'Manet's Olympia: Posed and Skirted.'*

*The moderator, fluttery and apologetic, wears a dress.*

MW:  I will open with a note Manet penned just as he began *Olympia* to M. Moron, a florist located a few blocks from his studio.

Monsieur Moron,
I cannot stand the geraniums. Please send something pink, and less expensive.
Yours sincerely,
Edouard Manet.

This telling reference to money, a worry throughout his life, is echoed in the repetition of the notes to follow.

MB:  It wasn't until very recently, in 1983, that the art historian M.R. Frank made the staggering critical discovery regarding Manet's *Olympia* for which I think we will all be hereafter indebted. In his paper entitled 'Hidden Elements', Frank first noted that there was 'a black person in this painting'. Just two years later, in 1985, S.L. Park wrote 'and we can also see in the near background, just behind the nude, a black person.'

Since that time only one critic, C.M. Paine, has attempted to explicate the extreme belatedness of this discovery. Paine has argued that this tardiness on the part of *Olympia*'s critics follows directly from the fact that so few black people have actually *seen* the painting and that thus museum-goers most versed in this type of analysis have been scanty.

AF:   In his May 11, 1865, letter to Manet, Charles Baudelaire wrote of *Olympia* and I quote: '. . . and the cat (is it a cat, really?) . . .' In my paper today, I would like to return to this fundamental question.

Among the many interpretations of the cat in Manet's *Olympia*, the interpretation by Sir Finding of Hisownimage is here supported with further evidence.

(Grover, 1989, pp. 13–14)

Let me repeat, lest I be misunderstood. This is emphatically *not* to be anti-intellectual. (*The V-Girls* themselves are writers and teachers.) But it *is* to be anti the games of academe. What *The V-Girls* are criticizing are the power relations implicit in the transmission of knowledge and in our institutions of learning.

All this finds its reflection in the wider politics which these books advocate. Here too the difficulties of difference – perhaps, at its simplest, the fact of complexity – are simply erased by the steamroller of an analysis which insists that capital and labour (and in fact mainly capital, for neither book allows much space for resistance, even from labour) are all there is to it. Soja is the more reticent about setting out a political position, though it is implicit throughout and the quotation cited earlier demonstrated his conviction that what we should be fighting in the West is capitalism, and only capitalism, for via that the problems of sexism and racism would also be confronted. At one point he argues that: 'The political challenge for the postmodern left, as I see it, demands first a recognition and cogent interpretation of the dramatic and often confusing fourth modernization of capitalism' (p. 5). This is necessary, surely, but it is not enough (and though this is labelled 'first' we are not given any more). If there is one thing to be taken on board by the political and social shifts of recent decades it is that, unfortunately maybe, things are just not that simple.

Harvey is much more explicit about his politics. It is absolutely stated that everything must be subordinated to – just as, theoretically, it is reduced to – a question of class. Thus on p. 46 he is discussing ideas, such as Foucault's, which 'appeal to the various social movements that sprang into existence during the 1960s (feminists, gays, ethnic and religious groupings, regional autonomists, etc.)'[!]. But, he argues, such movements leave open 'the question of the path whereby such localized struggles might add up to a progressive, rather than regressive, attack upon the central forms of capitalist exploitation and repression. Localized struggles . . . have not generally had the effect of challenging capitalism . . .' There are two major points here. First, in what sense, precisely, is feminism (to take the case under discussion in this paper) a 'local' struggle while class struggle, it is to be presumed, is 'general'? One can only argue such a position if it is held that there are no patriarchal structures not reducible to class. Second, and consequently, why is there an assumption that what these 'local' struggles are fighting is capitalism? Surely what feminists are fighting is patriarchy. People, such as myself, may be both feminists and socialists and see themselves trying to struggle on both fronts (though sometimes with despair, as when reading passages such as these). One's identity, and the struggles we are engaged in, are far more multifaceted than Harvey's position is capable of conceiving.

At the end of his book, Harvey pulls together his theoretical and his political positions, arguing for a further development of Marxist formulations. This, surely, is a positive step, and one which I would whole-heartedly support. But as it is spelled out it becomes clear that what this would mean in Harvey's formulation is continued subordination for all those people in parentheses, those who do not in their complex identities match the postulated, uncomplicated-because-unanalysed, universal. Thus, consider the following:

> The importance of recuperating such aspects of social organization as race, gender, religion, within the overall frame of historical materialist enquiry (with its emphasis upon the power of money and capital circulation) and class politics (with its emphasis upon the unity of the emancipatory struggle) cannot be overestimated. (p. 355)

How to have your cake and eat it too! There are four comments. First, I am absolutely in favour of thinking through issues of gender 'within the overall frame of historical materialist enquiry'. Second, however, we have to be sure what that means. Materialism is far wider than an 'emphasis upon the power of money and capital circulation'. This is less materialism than economism; and it simply could not deal even with many of the gender issues raised earlier in this paper. Third, again yes – we need to think through ways of constructing 'the unity of the emancipatory struggle'; but, fourth, this emphatically cannot be achieved by forcing all struggles under 'the overall frame of ... class politics'. What Harvey's position means is a unity enforced through the tutelage of one group over others. As Hadjimichalis and Vaiou have recently written, in the context precisely of debates within our field,

> In a contradictory way, by advocating 'unity' and ignoring divisions (theoretically, practically and prospectively) the left itself has contributed to deepening divisions ... 'Unity' must be gradually built up upon the articulation of differences and individual experiences. (1990, p. 21)

244 Space, place and gender

Yet even while he recognizes the need to construct alliances in the search for unity, Harvey forces everyone into one mould: 'The very possibility of a genuine rainbow coalition defines a unified politics which inevitably speaks the tacit language of class, because this is precisely what defines the common experience within the differences' (p. 358). Any on-the-ground experience of trying to build alliances would demonstrate the inadequacy of this view. There is here no understanding of the need to recognize conflicts (remember *Blade Runner*?) and complexity and to deal with them in their own right, as unities which are articulations of genuine and often contradictory differences.

Milton Keynes
published in 1991

## Notes

1 But if modernist accounts such as Harvey's miss out resistance and political struggle, this is absolutely not to argue that the majority of postmodernists do the opposite. All those lists of dualist differences between modernism and postmodernism (or Fordism and post-Fordism) obscure the fact that an awful lot remains tediously the same. One of the problems of some postmodernism is its treatment of 'others' as titillating exotica and as primarily constituted, in effect, to affirm the identity of the central character. They are certainly only more rarely represented as active, and actively resisting (see next section; Bondi, 1990; Moore, 1988).

2 Gregory (1990) also makes this point, and analyses its effects, in relation to disciplines other than geography.

3 The critique of geography at that point was very much concerned with bringing in social processes as the explanation of spatial patterns. Various formulations of structural causality, including a structuralist Marxism, were important here. In that context, interestingly enough, introducing social process was emphatically not the same thing as introducing time/history. Indeed, Soja (p. 18) argues that structuralism has been 'one of the twentieth-century's most important avenues for the re-assertion of space in critical social theory'. This seems to me to be an equally problematic formulation. A 'configuration', in the terms in which Foucault and structuralism used it, may be synchronic; but that does not make it spatial. A structuralist perspective can of course be *used* to analyse both history and geography and to link the synchronic with the diachronic; but in some versions it might also be understood as challenging that very dichotomy.

4 To argue this is, in my view, absolutely not to be anti-Marxist, still less is it to be anti-materialist. The point is more that what we are offered in this analysis is a very unreconstructed Marxism.

5 This has already been pointed out in relation to the linear history in *Postmodern Geographies*, and it will be taken up again in later chapters.

6 Most obviously they are taken to task, as in 'mainstream' theory in a number of fields, for heralding now as major discoveries things which feminists have been saying for many years.

7 Interestingly, this sexism extends to the institutions of the art world as well as its practitioners as, argues Chadwick, there has been a reaction against postmodern pluralism. Thus: 'The pluralism of the 1970s has been viewed as a symptom of the disintegration of the set of practices ... through which Modernism was defined. By the late 1970s, a reaction against pluralism, and a backlash against women and minorities, could also be observed within the dominant institutions and discourses of the art world. Exhibitions celebrating the "return" to painting, and focusing on a new generation of male neoexpressionists – for example, David Salle, Julian Schnabel, and Francesco Clemente – were remarkable for their exclusion of virtually all women' (Chadwick, 1990, p. 347). It is also to be remarked that Harvey's selection of a postmodern painting is precisely by one of these artists, and from this period (1980).

8 In this context, it is surprising that Harvey does not even refer to the work of John Berger.

9 And looking at Salle's contribution one could make the same point, of course, about male *post*-modern artists.

10 Once again on references: this article by Pollock is about modernity and space, surely central to Harvey's concerns, yet he does not reference it – the full title is 'Modernity and the spaces of femininity'. She also discusses the presence of the black maid in Manet's painting.

11 Indeed, even if it produced a city for men in the ways enumerated, nineteenth-century urbanization was very important for women, especially for those wanting to live with other women. These impressions and possibilities also, of course, varied by class (see Pollock, 1985; and below), but I am assuming Harvey would readily accept this.

12 George Sand, determined to discover the streets of Paris for herself, had to dress up as a boy to do so (Wolff, 1985, p. 41).

13 But it probably *is* worth noting how similar they appear to be to Baudrillard's as he wanders New York (Baudrillard, 1988). It is something which the great men of modernism and postmodernism seem to share – yet both are held up to us as figures to admire.

14 Thus, the editorial of a recent edition of *Feminist Arts News* contained the following: 'This issue of FAN reveals the complexities and richness of women's work in modernism, practices which redefine modernism itself. The map of modernism as a progressive linear development is replaced with histories of its discontinuities and reformations. No longer a story of how New York replaced Paris, but a dissection of the wholesale theft of African cultures and images, of the silences on women's work, and a long overdue address to Black Women's creativity in, and deconstruction of, modernism' (vol. 3, no. 4).

15 The full quotation is: 'It [the preceding discussion of film] supports the idea that the experience of time–space compression in recent years, under the

pressures of the turn to more flexible modes of accumulation, has generated a crisis of representation in cultural forms, and that this is a subject of intense aesthetic concern, either *in toto* (as I think is the case in *Wings of Desire*) or in part (as would be true of everything from *Blade Runner* to Cindy Sherman's photographs and the novels of Italo Calvino or Pynchon).'

16  One might also ask some serious questions about the social meaning of some of the canonical works of modernism.

17  Indeed, as Kelly has pointed out, perhaps the most crucial aspect of *modernist* art theory is precisely its insistence on signifying 'authorial presence' (Kelly, 1981, cited in Elliott and Wallace, 1990).

18  Harvey has one reference to Hartsock (1987) which he uses simply to take an unsubstantiated swipe at postmodernism. Noting that some authors emphasize 'the opening given in postmodernism to understanding differences and otherness, as well as the liberatory potential it offers for a whole host of new social movements (women, gays, blacks, ecologists, regional autonomists, etc.)'[!] he goes on to assert: 'Curiously, most movements of this sort, though they have definitely helped change "the structure of feeling", pay scant attention to postmodernist arguments, and some feminists (e.g. Hartsock, 1987) are hostile . . .' (p. 48). This is grossly to misrepresent a complex debate. Moreover dissatisfaction with the answers of postmodernism, as I indicated above, does not mean that we are happy to tag along behind an exclusively masculine modernism such as Harvey's.

# References

Baudrillard, J., 1988, *America* (Verso, London).

Bauman, Z., 1988, 'Is there a postmodern sociology?', *Theory, Culture & Society*, 5, pp. 217–37.

Bondi, L., 1990, 'On gender tourism in the space age: a feminist response to *Postmodern Geographies*', paper presented to the panel: Author meets critic: Ed Soja's *Postmodern Geographies*, AAG, Toronto, April; copy available from the author, Department of Geography, University of Edinburgh, Edinburgh.

Bruno, G., 1987, 'Ramble city: postmodernism and *Blade Runner*', *October*, 41, pp. 61–74.

Chadwick, W., 1990, *Women, Art, and Society* (Thames & Hudson, London).

Chute, D., 1986, 'Out to Lynch', *Film Comment*, 22 (September/October), pp. 32–5.

Clifford, J. and Marcus, G.E. (eds), 1986, *Writing Culture: The Poetics and Politics of Ethnography* (University of California Press, Berkeley, CA).

Cosgrove, D., 1984, *Social Formation and Symbolic Landscape* (Croom Helm, London).

Cowie, E., 1978, 'Woman as sign', *m/f*, no. 1, pp. 49–63.

Crimp, D., 1982, 'Appropriating appropriation', in P. Marincola, ed., *Image Scavengers: Photography* (Institute of Contemporary Art, Philadelphia, PA).

——, 1985, 'On the museum's ruins', in H. Foster, ed., *Postmodern Culture* (Pluto Press, London), pp. 43–56.

Davidoff, L. and Hall, C., 1983, 'The architecture of public and private life: English middle-class society in a provincial town 1780–1850', in D. Fraser and A. Sutcliffe, eds, *The Pursuit of Urban History* (Edward Arnold, Sevenoaks, Kent).

Dear, M., 1990, '*Postmodern Geographies*: review', *Annals of the Association of American Geographers*, 80, pp. 649–54.

Denzin, N., 1988, '*Blue Velvet*: postmodern contradictions', *Theory, Culture & Society*, 5, pp. 461–73.

Deutsche, R., 1990, 'Men in space', *Artforum*, February, pp. 21–3.

Duffy, C.A., 1985, *Standing Female Nude* (Anvil Press Poetry, London).

Duncan, C., 1990, 'The MoMA's hot mamas', *Feminist Arts News*, 3(4), pp. 15–19.

Elliott, B. and Wallace, J.A., 1990, 'Modernist anomalies: Bloomsbury and gender', *Feminist Arts News*, 3(4), pp. 21–4.

Flax, J., 1986, 'Gender as a social problem: in and for feminist theory', *American Studies/Amerika Studien* (June).

Fraser, N. and Nicholson, L., 1988, 'Social criticism without philosophy: an encounter between feminism and postmodernism', *Theory, Culture & Society*, 5, pp. 373–94.

Gledhill, C., 1978, '*Klute*: part I: a contemporary film noir and feminist criticism', in E.A. Kaplan, ed., *Women in Film Noir* (British Film Institute, London).

Gregory, D., 1990, 'Chinatown, part three? Soja and the missing spaces of social theory', *Strategies*, 3, pp. 40–104.

Grossberg, L., 1986, 'Reply to the critics', *Critical Studies in Mass Communication*, 3, pp. 86–95.

Grover, J.Z., 1989, 'The misrepresentation of misrepresentation', *The Women's Review of Books*, 6(10–11), pp. 13–14.

Hadjimichalis, C. and Vaiou, D., 1990, 'Flexible labour markets and regional development in northern Greece', *International Journal of Urban and Regional Research*, 14, pp. 1–24.

Hall, C., 1981, 'Gender divisions and class formation in the Birmingham middle class, 1780–1850', in R. Samuel, ed., *People's History and Socialist Theory* (Routledge & Kegan Paul, London).

Haraway, D., 1983, 'A manifesto for cyborgs: science, technology and socialist feminism in the 1980s', *Socialist Review*, 80, pp. 65–107.

Harding, S., 1986, *The Science Question in Feminism* (Cornell University Press, Ithaca, NY).

——, (ed.), 1987, *Feminism and Methodology* (Indiana University Press, Bloomington, IN).

Hart, N., 1989, 'Gender and the rise and fall of class politics', *New Left Review*, no. 175, pp. 19–47.

Hartsock, N., 1987, 'Rethinking modernism: minority vs majority theories', *Cultural Critique*, 7, pp. 187–206.

Harvey, D., 1985, *Consciousness and the Urban Experience: Studies in the History and Theory of Capitalist Urbanization* (Basil Blackwell, Oxford).

——, 1989, *The Condition of Postmodernity* (Basil Blackwell, Oxford).

Hewison, R., 1990, *Future Tense: A New Art for the Nineties* (Methuen, London).

Irigaray, L., 1978, Interview, in M.F. Hans and G. Lapouge, eds, *Les Femmes, La Pornographie, L'Erotisme*.

Jameson, F., 1989, 'Marxism and postmodernism', *New Left Review*, no. 176, pp. 31–45.

Jardine, A., 1985, *Gynesis: Configurations of Women and Modernity* (Cornell University Press, Ithaca, NY).

Kelly, M., 1981, 'Re-viewing modernist criticism', *Screen*, 22(3), p. 51.

Lennox, S., 1987, 'Anthropology and the politics of deconstruction', paper presented at the ninth annual conference of the National Women's Studies Association, Atlanta, GA, June; copy available from the author.

McGuigan, C. and Huck, J., 1986, 'Black and blue is beautiful? Review of *Blue Velvet*', *Newsweek*, 108 (27 October), pp. 65–7.

Mascia-Lees, F.E., Sharpe, P. and Cohen, C.B., 1989, 'The postmodernist turn in anthropology: cautions from a feminist perspective', *Signs*, 15(1), pp. 7–33.

Massey, D., 1984, *Spatial Divisions of Labour: Social Structures and the Geography of Production* (Macmillan, Basingstoke).

——, 1991, 'The political place of locality studies', *Environment and Planning, A* 23, pp. 267–81; this vol. ch. 5.

Moore, S., 1988, 'Getting a bit of the Other – the pimps of postmodernism', in R. Chapman and J. Rutherford, eds, *Male Order: Unwrapping Masculinity* (Lawrence & Wishart, London), pp. 165–92.

Morgan, J., 1990, 'Speaking in tongues: women artists and modernism 1900–1930', *Feminist Arts News*, 3(4), pp. 12–14.

Morris, M., 1988, *The Pirate's Fiancée* (Verso, London).

Nicholson, L.J. (ed.), 1990, *Feminism/Postmodernism* (Routledge, London).

Owens, C., 1985, 'The discourse of others: feminists and postmodernism', in H. Foster, ed., *Postmodern Culture* (Pluto Press, London) pp. 57–82.

Pollock, G., 1988, *Vision and Difference: Femininity, Feminism and Histories of Art* (Routledge, London).

Rabkin, W., 1986, 'Deciphering *Blue Velvet*: interview with David Lynch', *Fangoria*, 58 (October), pp. 52–6.

Rorty, R., 1979, *Philosophy and the Mirror of Nature* (Princeton University Press, Princeton, NJ).

Sangren, S., 1988, 'Rhetoric and the authority of ethnography', *Current Anthropology*, 29, pp. 405–24.

Soja, E., 1989, *Postmodern Geographies: The Reassertion of Space in Critical Social Theory* (Verso, London).

Swain, S., 1988, *Great Housewives of Art* (Grafton Books, London).

Taylor, B., 1987, *Modernism, Post-modernism, Realism: A Critical Perspective for Art* (Allen & Unwin, Winchester, MA).

Valentine, G., 1989, 'The geography of women's fear', *Area*, 21, pp. 385–90.

Wolff, J., 1985, 'The invisible flâneuse: women and the literature of modernity', *Theory, Culture & Society*, 2(3), pp. 37–46.

# 11

# Politics and Space/Time

'Space' is very much on the agenda these days. On the one hand, from a wide variety of sources come proclamations of the significance of the spatial in these times: 'It is space not time that hides consequences from us' (Berger); 'The difference that space makes' (Sayer); 'that new spatiality implicit in the postmodern' (Jameson); 'it is space rather than time which is the distinctively significant dimension of contemporary capitalism' (Urry); and 'All the social sciences must make room for an increasingly geographical conception of mankind' (Braudel). Even Foucault is now increasingly cited for his occasional reflections on the importance of the spatial. His 1967 Berlin lectures contain the unequivocal: 'The anxiety of our era has to do fundamentally with space, no doubt a great deal more than with time'. In other contexts the importance of the spatial, and of associated concepts, is more metaphorical. In debates around identity the terminology of space, location, positionality and place figures prominently. Homi Bhabha, in discussions of cultural identity, argues for a notion of a 'third space'. Jameson, faced with what he sees as the global confusions of postmodern times, 'the disorientation of saturated space', calls for an exercise in 'cognitive mapping'. And Laclau, in his own very different reflections on the 'new revolution of our time', uses the terms 'temporal' and 'spatial' as the major differentiators between ways of conceptualizing systems of social relations.

In some ways, all this can only be a delight to someone who has long worked as a 'geographer'. Suddenly the concerns, the concepts (or, at least, the *terms*) which have long been at the heart of our discussion are at the centre also of wider social and political debate.

And yet, in the midst of this gratification I have found myself uneasy about the way in which, by some, these terms are used. Here I want to examine just one aspect of these anxieties about some of the current use of spatial terminology – the conceptualization (often implicit) of the term 'space' itself.

In part this concern about what the term 'space' is meant to mean arises simply from the multiplicity of definitions adopted. Many authors rely heavily on the terms space/spatial, and each assumes that their meaning is clear and uncontested. Yet in fact the meaning which different authors assume (and therefore – in the case of metaphorical usage – the import of the metaphor) varies greatly. Buried in these unacknowledged disagreements is a debate which never surfaces; and it never surfaces because everyone assumes we already know what these terms mean. Henri Lefebvre, in the opening pages of his book *The Production of Space*, commented on just this phenomenon: the fact that authors who in so many ways excel in logical rigour will fail to define a term which functions crucially in their argument: 'Conspicuous by its absence from supposedly epistemological studies is ... the idea ... of space – the fact that "space" is mentioned on every page notwithstanding'.[1] At least there ought to be a debate about the meaning of this much-used term.

None the less, had this been all I would probably not have been exercised to write a paper about it. But the problem runs more deeply than this. For among the many and conflicting definitions of space which are current in the literature there are some – and very powerful ones – which deprive it of politics and of the possibility of politics: they effectively de-politicize the realm of the spatial. By no means all authors relegate space in this way. Many, drawing on terms such as centre/periphery/margin, and so on, and examining the 'politics of location', for instance, think of spatiality in a highly active and politically enabling manner. But for others space is the sphere of the lack of politics.

Precisely because the use of spatial terminology is so frequently unexamined this use of the term is not always immediately evident. It dawned fully on me when I read a statement by Ernesto Laclau in his *New Reflections on the Revolution of our Time*. 'Politics and space,' he writes, 'are antinomic terms. Politics only exist insofar as the spatial eludes us'.[2] For someone who, as a geographer, has for years been arguing, along with many others, for a dynamic and politically progressive way of conceptualizing the spatial, this was clearly provocative!

Because my own inquiries were initially stimulated by Laclau's book, and because unearthing the implicit definitions at work implies a detailed reading (which restricts the number of authors who can be considered) this discussion takes *New Reflections* as a starting point, and considers it in most detail. But, as will become clear, the implicit definition used by Laclau, and which de-politicizes space, is shared by many other authors. In its simpler forms it operates, for instance, in the debate over the nature of structuralism, and is an implicit reference point in many a text. It is, moreover, in certain of its fundamental aspects shared by authors, such as Fredric Jameson, who in other ways are making arguments very different from those of Laclau.

To summarize it rather crudely, Laclau's view of space is that it is the realm of stasis. There is, in the realm of the spatial, no true temporality and thus no possibility of politics. It is on this view, and on a critique of it, that much of the initial discussion will be concentrated. But in other parts of the debate about the nature of the current era, and in particular in relation to 'postmodernity', the realm of the spatial is given entirely different associations from those ascribed to it by Laclau. Thus Jameson, who sees postmodern times as being particularly characterized by the importance of spatiality, interprets it in terms of an unnerving multiplicity: space is chaotic depthlessness.[3] This is the opposite of Laclau's characterization, yet for Jameson it is – once again – a formulation which deprives the spatial of any meaningful politics.

A caveat must be entered from the start. This discussion will be addressing only one aspect of the complex realm which goes by the name of the spatial. Lefebvre, among others, insisted on the importance of considering not only what might be called 'the geometry' of space but also its lived practices and the symbolic meaning and significance of particular spaces and spatializations. Without disagreeing with that, the concentration here will none the less be on the view of space as what I shall provisionally call 'a dimension'. The argument is that different ways of conceptualizing this aspect of 'the spatial' themselves provide very different bases (or in some cases no basis at all) for the politicization of space. Clearly, anyway, the issue of the conceptualization of space is of more than technical interest; it is one of the axes along which we experience and conceptualize the world.

## Space and time

An examination of the literature reveals, as might be expected, a variety of uses and meanings of the term 'space', but there is one characteristic of these meanings which is particularly strong and widespread. This is the view of space which, in one way or another, defines it as stasis, and as utterly opposed to time. Laclau, for whom the contrast between what he labels temporal and what he calls spatial is key to his whole argument, uses a highly complex version of this definition. For him, notions of time and space are related to contrasting methods of understanding social systems. In his *New Reflections on the Revolution of our Time*, Laclau posits that 'any repetition that is governed by a structural law of successions is space' and 'spatiality means coexistence within a structure that establishes the positive nature of all its terms'.[4] Here, then, any postulated causal structure which is complete and self-determining is labelled 'spatial'. This does not mean that such a 'spatial' structure cannot change – it may do – but the essential characteristic is that all the causes of any change which may take place are internal to the structure itself. On this view, in the realm of the spatial there can be no surprises (provided that we are analytically well equipped). In contrast to the closed and self-determining systems of the spatial, time (or temporality) for Laclau takes the form of dislocation, a dynamic which disrupts the predefined terms of any system of causality. The spatial, because it lacks dislocation, is devoid of the possibility of politics.

This is an importantly different distinction between time and space from that which simply contrasts change with an utter lack of movement. In Laclau's version, there can be movement and change within a so-called spatial system; what there cannot be is real dynamism in the sense of a change in the terms of 'the system' itself (which can therefore never be a simply coherent closed system). A distinction is postulated, in other words, between different types of what would normally be called time. On the one hand, there is the time internal to a closed system, where things may change yet without really changing. On the other hand, there is genuine dynamism, Grand Historical Time. In the former is included cyclical time, the times of reproduction, the way in which a peasantry represents to itself (says Laclau) the unfolding of the cycle of the seasons, the turning of the earth. To some extent, too, there is 'embedded time', the time in which our daily lives are set.[5] These times, says Laclau, this kind of 'time' is space.

Laclau's argument here is that what we are inevitably faced with in the world are 'temporal' (by which he means dislocated) structures: dislocation is intrinsic and it is this – this essential openness – which creates the possibility of politics. Any attempt to represent the world 'spatially', including even the world of physical space, is an attempt to ignore that dislocation. Space therefore, in his terminology, is representation, is any (ideological) attempt at closure: 'Society, then, is unrepresentable: any representation – *and thus any space* – is an attempt to constitute society, not to state what it is'. Pure spatiality, in these terms, cannot exist: 'The ultimate failure of all hegemonization [in Laclau's term, spatialization], then, means that the real – including physical space – is in the ultimate instance temporal'; or again: 'the mythical nature of any space'.[6] This does not mean that the spatial is unimportant. This is not the point at issue, nor is it Laclau's intent. For the 'spatial' as the ideological/mythical is seen by him as itself part of the social and as constitutive of it: 'And insofar as the social is impossible without some fixation of meaning, without the discourse of closure, the ideological must be seen as constitutive of the social'.[7] The issue here is not the relative priority of the temporal and the spatial, but their definition. For it is through this logic, and its association of ideas with temporality and spatiality, that Laclau arrives at the de-politicization of space. 'Let us begin', writes Laclau, 'by identifying three dimensions of the relationship of dislocation that are crucial to our analysis. The *first* is that dislocation is the very form of temporality. And temporality must be conceived as the exact opposite of space. The "spatialization" of an event consists of eliminating its temporality'.[8]

The second and third dimensions of the relationship of dislocation take the logic further: 'The *second* dimension is that dislocation [which, remember, is the antithesis of the spatial] is the very form of possibility' and 'The *third* dimension is that dislocation is the very form of freedom. Freedom is the absence of determination'.[9] This leaves the realm of the spatial looking like unpromising territory for politics. It is lacking in dislocation, the very form of possibility (the form of temporality), which is also 'the very form of freedom'. Within the spatial, there is only determination, and hence no possibility of freedom or of politics.

Laclau's characterization of the spatial is, however, a relatively sophisticated version of a much more general conception of space and time (or spatiality and temporality). It is a conceptualization in which the two are opposed to each other, and in which time is the one which matters and of which History (capital H) is made. Time Marches On but space is a kind of stasis, where nothing really happens.

There are a number of ways in which, it seems to me, this manner of characterizing space and the realm of the spatial is questionable. Three of them, chosen precisely because of their contrasts, because of the distinct light they each throw on the problems of this view of space, will be examined here. The first draws on the debates which have taken place in 'radical geography' over the last two decades and more; the second examines the issue from the point of view of a concern with gender; and the third examines the view from physics.

## Radical geography

In the 1970s, the discipline of geography experienced the kinds of developments described by Anderson in 'A culture in contraflow' for other social sciences.[10] The previously hegemonic positivist 'spatial science' was increasingly challenged by a new generation of Marxist geographers. The argument turned intellectually on how 'the relation between space and society' should be conceptualized. To caricature the debate, the spatial scientists had posited an autonomous sphere of the spatial in which 'spatial relations' and 'spatial processes' produced spatial distributions. The geography of industry, for instance, would be interpreted as simply the result of 'geographical location factors'. Countering this, the Marxist critique was that all these so-called spatial relations and spatial processes were actually social relations taking a particular geographical form. The geography of industry, we argued, could therefore not be explained without a prior understanding of the economy and of wider social and political processes. The aphorism of the seventies was 'space is a social construct'. That is to say – though the point was perhaps not made clearly enough at the time – space is constituted through social relations and material social practices.

But this, too, was soon to seem an inadequate characterization of the social/spatial relation. For while it is surely correct to argue that space is socially constructed, the one-sidedness of that formulation implied that geographical forms and distributions were simply outcomes, the endpoint of social explanation. Geographers would thus be the cartographers of the social sciences, mapping the outcomes of processes which could only be explained in other disciplines – sociology, economics, and so forth. What geographers mapped – the spatial form of the social – was interesting enough, but it was simply an end-product: it had no material effect. Quite apart from any demeaning disciplinary implications, this was plainly not the case. The events taking place all around us in the 1980s – the massive spatial restructuring both intra-nationally and internationally as an integral part of the social and economic changes – made it plain that, in one way or another, 'geography matters'. And so, to the aphorism of the 1970s – that space is socially constructed – was added in the 1980s the other side of the coin: that the social is spatially constructed too, and that makes a difference. In other words, and in its broadest formulation, society is necessarily constructed spatially, and that fact – the spatial organization of society – makes a difference to how it works.

But if spatial organization makes a difference to how society works and how it changes, then, far from being the realm of stasis, space and the spatial are also implicated (*contra* Laclau) in the production of history – and thus, potentially, in politics. This was not an entirely new thought; Henri Lefebvre, writing in 1974, was beginning to argue a very similar position:

> The space of capitalist accumulation thus gradually came to life, and began to be fitted out. This process of animation is admiringly referred to as

history, and its motor sought in all kinds of factors: dynastic interests, ideologies, the ambitions of the mighty, the formation of nation states, demographic pressures, and so on. This is the road to a ceaseless analysing of, and searching for, dates and chains of events. Inasmuch as space is the locus of all such chronologies, might it not constitute a principle of explanation at least as acceptable as any other?[11]

This broad position – that the social and the spatial are inseparable and that the spatial form of the social has causal effecticity – is now accepted increasingly widely, especially in geography and sociology,[12] though there are still those who would disagree, and beyond certain groups even the fact of a debate over the issue seems to have remained unrecognized (Anderson, for example, does not pick it up in his survey).[13] For those familiar with the debate, and who saw in it an essential step towards the politicization of the spatial, formulations of space as a static resultant without any effect – whether the simplistic versions or the more complex definitions such as Laclau's – seem to be very much a retrograde step.

However, in retrospect, even the debates within radical geography have still fully to take on board the implications of our own arguments for the way in which space might be conceptualized.

## Issues of gender

For there are also other reservations, from completely different directions, which can be levelled against this view of space and which go beyond the debate which has so far taken place within radical geography. Some of these reservations revolve around issues of gender.

First of all, this manner of conceptualizing space and time takes the form of a dichotomous dualism. It is neither a simple statement of difference (A, B, . . .) nor a dualism constructed through an analysis of the interrelations between the objects being defined (capital: labour). It is a dichotomy specified in terms of a presence and an absence; a dualism which takes the classic form of A/not-A. As was noted earlier, one of Laclau's formulations of a definition is: 'temporality must be conceived as the exact opposite of space'.[14] Now, apart from any reservations which may be raised in the particular case of space and time (and which we shall come to later), the mode of thinking which relies on irreconcilable dichotomies of this sort has in general recently come in for widespread criticism. All the strings of these kinds of opposition with which we are so accustomed to work (mind–body, nature–culture, reason–emotion, and so forth) have been argued to be at heart problematical and a hindrance to either understanding or changing the world. Much of this critique has come from feminists.[15]

The argument is twofold. First, and less importantly here, it is argued that this way of approaching conceptualization is, in western societies and more generally in societies where child-rearing is performed overwhelmingly by members of one sex (women), more typical of males than of females. This is an argument which generally draws on object-relations theory approaches to identity-formation. Second, however, and of more immediate significance for the argument being constructed here, it has been contended that this kind of dichotomous thinking, together with a whole range of the sets of dualisms which take this form (we shall look at some of these in more detail below) are related to the construction of the radical distinction between genders in our society, to the characteristics assigned to each of them, and to the power relations maintained between them. Thus, Nancy Jay, in an article entitled 'Gender and dichotomy' examines the social conditions and consequences of the use of logical dichotomy. She argues not only that logical dichotomy and radical gender distinctions are associated but also, more widely, that such a mode of constructing difference works to the advantage of certain (dominant) social groups, 'that almost any ideology based on A/Not-A dichotomy is effective in resisting change. Those whose understanding of society is ruled by such ideology find it very hard to conceive of the possibility of alternative forms of social order (third possibilities). Within such thinking, the only alternative to the *one* order is disorder'.[16] Genevieve Lloyd, too, in a sweeping history of 'male' and 'female' in western philosophy, entitled *The Man of Reason*, argues that such dichotomous conceptualizations, and – what we shall come to later – the prioritization of one term in the dualism over the other, are not only central to much of the formulation of concepts with which western philosophy has worked but that they are dependent upon, and is instrumental in the conceptualization of, among other things, a particular form of radical distinction between female and male genders.[17] Jay argues that 'Hidden, taken for granted, A/Not-A distinctions are dangerous, and because of their peculiar affinity with gender distinctions, it seems important for feminist theory to be systematic in recognizing them'.[18] The argument is that the definition of 'space' and 'time' under scrutiny here is precisely of this form, and on that basis alone warrants further critical investigation.

But there is also a further point. For within this kind of conceptualization, only one of the terms (A) is defined positively. The other term (not-A) is conceived only in relation to A, and as lacking in A. A fairly thorough reading of some of the recent literature which uses the terminology of space and time, and which employs this form of conceptualization, leaves no doubt that it is time which is conceived of as in the position of 'A', and space which is 'not-A'. Over and over again, time is defined by such things as change, movement, history, dynamism; while space, rather lamely by comparison, is simply the absence of these things. There are two aspects to this. First, this kind of definition means that it is time, and the characteristics associated with time, which are the primary constituents of both space and time; time is the nodal point, the privileged signifier. And second, this kind of definition means that space is defined by absence, by lack. This is clear in the simple (and often implicit) definitions (time equals change/movement, space equals the lack of these things), but it can also be argued to be the case with more complex definitions such as those put forward by Laclau. For although in a formal sense it is the spatial which in Laclau's formulation is complete and the temporal which marks the lack (the absence of representation, the impossibility of closure), in the whole tone of the argument it is in fact space which is associated with negativity and absence. Thus: 'temporality must be conceived as the exact opposite of space. The "spatialization" of an event consists of eliminating its temporality'.[19]

Now, of course, in current western culture, or in certain of its dominant theories, woman too is defined in terms of lack. Nor, as we shall see, is it entirely a matter of coincidence that space and the feminine are frequently defined in terms of dichotomies in which each of them is most commonly defined as not-A. There is a whole set of dualisms whose terms are commonly aligned with time and space. With time are aligned History, Progress, Civilization, Science, Politics and Reason, portentous things with gravitas and capital letters. With space on the other hand are aligned the other poles of these concepts: stasis, ('simple') reproduction, nostalgia, emotion, aesthetics, the body. All these dualisms, in the way that they are used, suffer from the criticisms made above of dichotomies of this form: the problem of mutual exclusivity and of the consequent impoverishment of both of their terms. Other dualisms could be added which also map on to that between time and space. Jameson, for instance, as do a whole line of authors before him, clearly relates the pairing to that between transcendence and immanence, with the former connotationally associated with the temporal and immanence with the spatial. Indeed, in this and in spite of their other differences, Jameson and Laclau are very similar. Laclau's distinction between the closed, cyclical time of simple reproduction (spatial) and dislocated, changing history (temporal), even if the latter has no inevitability in its progressive movement, is precisely that. Jameson, who bemoans what he characterizes as the tendency towards immanence and the flight from transcendence of the contemporary period, writes of 'a world peculiarly without transcendence and without perspective . . . and indeed without plot in any traditional sense, since all choices would be equidistant and on the same level'[20] – and this is a world where, he believes, a sense of the temporal is being lost and the realm of the spatial is taking over.

Now, as has been pointed out many times, these dualisms which so easily map on to each other also map on to the constructed dichotomy between female and male. From Rousseau's seeing woman as a potential source of disorder, as needing to be tamed by Reason, to Freud's famous pronouncement that woman is the enemy of civilization, to the many subsequent critics and analysts of such statements of the 'obviousness' of dualisms, of their interrelation one with another, and of their connotations of male and female – such literature is now considerable.[21] And space, in this system of interconnected dualisms, is coded female. ' "Transcendence", in its origins, is a transcendence *of* the feminine,' writes Lloyd, for instance.[22] Moreover, even where the transcodings between dualisms have an element of inconsistency, this rule still applies. Thus where time is dynamism, dislocation and History, and space is stasis, space is coded female and denigrated. But where space is chaos (which you would think was quite different from stasis; more indeed like dislocation), then time is Order . . . and space is *still* coded female, only in this context interpreted as threatening.

Elizabeth Wilson, in her book *The Sphinx in the City*, analyses this latter set of connotations.[23] The whole notion of city culture, she argues, has been developed as one pertaining to men. Yet within this context women present a threat, and in two ways. First there is the fact that in the metropolis we are freer, in spite of all the also-attendant dangers, to escape the rigidity of patriarchal social controls which can be so powerful in a smaller community. Second, and following from this, 'women have fared especially badly in western visions of the metropolis because they have seemed to represent disorder. There is fear of the city as a realm of uncontrolled and chaotic sexual licence, and the rigid control of women in cities has been felt necessary to avert this danger'. 'Woman represented feeling, sexuality and even chaos, man was rationality and control'.[24] Among male modernist writers of the early twentieth century, she argues – and with the exception of Joyce – the dominant response to the burgeoning city was to see it as threatening, while modernist women writers (Woolf, Richardson) were more likely to exult in its energy and vitality. The male response was perhaps more ambiguous than this, but it was certainly a mixture of fascination and fear. There is an interesting parallel to be drawn here with the sense of panic in the midst of exhilaration which seems to have overtaken some writers at what they see as the ungraspable (and therefore unbearable) complexity of the post-modern age. And it is an ungraspability seen persistently in spatial terms, whether through the argument that it is the new (seen-to-be-new) time–

space compression, the new global–localism, the breaking down of borders, which is the cause of it all, or through the interpretation of the current period as somehow in its very character intrinsically more spatial than previous eras. In Jameson these two positions are brought together, and he displays the same ambivalence. He writes of 'the horror of multiplicity', of 'all the web threads flung out beyond my "situation" into the unimaginable synchronicity of other people'.[25] It is hard to resist the idea that Jameson's (and others') apparently vertiginous terror (a phrase they often use themselves) in the face of the complexity of today's world (conceived of as social but also importantly as spatial) has a lot in common with the nervousness of the male modernist, nearly a century ago, when faced with the big city.

It is important to be clear about what is being said of this relationship between space/time and gender. It is not being argued that this way of characterizing space is somehow essentially male; there is no essentialism of feminine/masculine here. Rather, the argument is that the dichotomous characterization of space and time, along with a whole range of other dualisms which have been briefly referred to, and with their connotative interrelations, may both reflect and be part of the constitution of, among other things, the masculinity and femininity of the sexist society in which we live. Nor is it being argued that space should simply be reprioritized to an equal status with, or instead of, time. The latter point is important because there have been a number of contributions to the debate recently which have argued that, especially in modernist (including Marxist) accounts, it is time which has been considered the more important. Ed Soja, particularly in his book *Postmodern Geographies*, has made an extended and persuasive case to this effect (but see the critique by Gregory).[26] The story told earlier of Marxism within geography – supposedly the spatial discipline – is indicative of the same tendency. In a completely different context, Terry Eagleton has written in his foreword to Kristin Ross's *The Construction of Social Space* that 'Ross is surely right to claim that this idea [the concept of space] has proved of far less glamorous appeal to radical theorists than the apparently more dynamic, exhilarating notions of narrative and history'.[27] It is interesting to speculate on the degree to which this deprioritization might itself have been part and parcel of the system of gender connotations. Ross herself writes: 'The difficulty is also one of vocabulary, for while words like "historical" and "political" convey a dynamic of intentionality, vitality, and human motivation, "spatial", on the other hand, connotes stasis, neutrality, and passivity';[28] and in her analysis of Rimbaud's poetry and of the nature of its relation to the Paris Commune she does her best to counter that essentially negative view of spatiality. (Jameson, of course, is arguing pretty much the same point about the past prioritization of time, but his mission is precisely the opposite of Ross's and Soja's; it is to hang on to that prioritization.)

The point here however is not to argue for an upgrading of the status of space within the terms of the old dualism (a project which is arguably inherently difficult anyway, given the terms of that dualism), but to argue that what must be overcome is the very formulation of space/time in terms of this kind of dichotomy. The same point has frequently been made by feminists in relation to other dualisms, most particularly perhaps – because of the debate over the writings of Simone de Beauvoir – the dualism of transcendence and immanence. When de Beauvoir wrote, 'Man's design is not to repeat himself in time: it is to take control of the instant and mould the future. It is male activity that in creating values has made of existence itself a value; this activity has prevailed over the confused forces of life; it has subdued Nature and Woman',[29] she was making precisely that distinction between cyclicity and 'real change' which is not only central to the classic distinction between immanence and transcendence but is also part of the way in which Laclau distinguishes between what he calls the spatial and the temporal. De Beauvoir's argument was that women should grasp the transcendent. A later generation of feminists has argued that the problem is the nature of the distinction itself. The position here is both that the two dualisms (immanence/transcendence and space/time) are related and that the argument about the former dualism could and should be extended to the latter. The next line of critique, the view from physics, provides some further hints about the directions which that reformulation might take.

## The view from physics

The conceptualization of space and time under examination here also runs counter to notions of space and time within the natural sciences, and most particularly in physics. Now, in principle, this may not be at all important; it is not clear that strict parallels can or should be drawn between the physical and the social sciences. And indeed there continue to be debates on this subject in the physical sciences. The point is, however, that the view of space and time outlined above already does have, as one of its roots at least, an interpretation drawn – if only implicitly – from the physical sciences. The problem is that it is an outmoded one.

The viewpoint, as used for instance by Laclau, accords with the viewpoint of classical, Newtonian, physics. In classical physics, both space and time exist in their own right, as do objects. Space is a passive arena, the setting for objects and their interaction. Objects, in turn, exist prior to their interactions and affect one another through force-fields. The observer, similarly, is detached from the observed world. In modern physics, on the other hand, the identity of things is *constituted through* interactions. In modern physics, while velocity, acceleration, and so forth are defined, the basic ontological categories, such as space and time, are not. Even more significantly from the point of view of the argument here, in modern physics, physical reality is conceived of as a 'four-dimensional existence instead of . . . the evolution of a three-dimensional existence'.[30] Thus: 'According to Einstein's theory . . . space and time are not to be thought of as separate entities existing in their own right – a three-dimensional space, and a one-dimensional time. Rather, the underlying reality consists of a four-dimensional space–time'.[31] Moreover the observer, too, is part of the observed world.

It is worth pausing for a moment to clarify a couple of points here. The first point is that the argument here is not in favour of a total collapse of the differences between something called the spatial and the temporal dimensions. Nor, indeed, would that seem to be what modern physics is arguing either. Rather, the point is that space and time are inextricably interwoven. It is not that we cannot make any distinction at all between them but that the distinction we do make needs to hold the two in tension, and to do so within an overall, and strong, concept of four-dimensionality.

The second point is that the definitions of both space and time in themselves must be constructed as the result of interrelations. This means that there is no question of defining space simply as not-time. It must have a positive definition, in its own terms, just as does time. Space must not be consigned to the position of being conceptualized in terms of absence or lack. It also means, if the positive definitions of both space and time must be interrelational, that there is no absolute dimension, space. The existence of the spatial depends on the interrelations of objects: 'In order for "space" to make an appearance there needs to be at least two fundamental particles'.[32] This is, in fact, saying no more than what is commonly argued, even in the social sciences – that space is not absolute, it is relational. Perhaps the problem at this point is that the implications of this position seem not to have been taken on board.

Now, in some ways all this does seem to have some similarities with Laclau's use of the notion of the spatial, for his definition does refer to forms of social interaction. As we have seen, however, he designates them (or the concepts of them) as spatial only when they form a closed system, where there is a lack of dislocation which can produce a way out of the postulated (but impossible) closure. However, such use of the term is anyway surely metaphorical. What it represents is evidence of the connotations which are being attached to the terms space and spatial. It is not directly talking of 'the spatial' itself. Thus, to take up Laclau's usage in more detail: at a number of points as we have seen he presents definitions of space in terms of possible (in fact, he would argue, impossible) causal structures – 'any repetition that is governed by a structural law of successions is space'; or, 'spatiality means coexistence within a structure that establishes the positive nature of all its terms'.[33] My question of these definitions and of other related ones, both elsewhere in this book and more widely – for instance in the debate over the supposed 'spatiality' of structuralism – is, 'says who?' Is not this appellation in fact pure assertion? Laclau agrees in rejecting the possibility of the actual existence of pure spatiality in the sense of undislocated stasis. A further question must therefore be: why postulate it? Or, more precisely, why postulate it as 'space'? As we have just seen, an answer which proposes an absolute spatial dimension will not do. An alternative answer might be that this ideal pure spatiality, which only exists as discourse/myth/ideology is in fact a (misjudged) metaphor. In this case it is indeed defined by interrelations – this is certainly not 'absolute space', the independently existing dimension – and the interrelations are those of a closed system of social relations, a system outside of which there is nothing and in which nothing will dislocate (temporalize) its internally regulated functioning. But then my question is: why call it space? The use of the term 'spatial' here would seem to be purely metaphorical. In so far as such systems do exist – and even in so far as they are merely postulated as an ideal – they can in no sense *be* simply spatial nor exist only *in* space. In themselves they *constitute* a particular form of space–time.[34]

Moreover, as metaphors the sense of Laclau's formulations goes against what I understand by – and shall argue below would be more helpful to understand by – space/the spatial. 'Any repetition that is governed by a structural law of successions'? – but *is* space so governed? As was argued above, radical geographers reacted strongly in the 1970s precisely against a view of 'a spatial realm', a realm, posited implicitly or explicitly by a wide range of then-dominant practitioners, from mathematicized 'regional scientists' to data-bashers armed with ferociously high regression-coefficients, in which there were spatial processes, spatial laws and purely spatial explanations. In terms of causality, what was being argued by those of us who attacked this view was that the spatial is externally determined. A formulation like the one above, because of the connotations it attaches to the words space/spatial in terms of the nature of causality, thus takes us back a good two decades. Or again, what of the second of Laclau's definitions given above? – that the spatial is the 'coexistence within a structure that establishes the positive nature of all its terms'? What then of the paradox of simultaneity and the causal chaos of happenstance juxtaposition which are, as we shall argue below (and as Jameson sees), integral characteristics of relational space?

In this procedure, any sort of stasis (for instance a self-regulating structural coherence which cannot lead to any transformation outside its own terms) gets called space/spatial. But there is no reason for this save the prior definition of space as lacking in (this kind of) transformative dynamic *and*, equally importantly, an assumption that anything lacking in (this kind of) dynamism is spatial. Instead, therefore, of using the terms space (and time) in this metaphorical way to refer to such structures why do we not remain with definitions (such as dislocated/undislocated) which refer to the nature of the causal structures themselves? Apart from its greater clarity, this would have the considerable advantage of leaving us free to retain (or maybe to develop) a more positive concept of space.

Indeed, conceptualizing space and time more in the manner of modern physics would seem to be consistent with Laclau's general argument. His whole point about radical historicity is this: 'any effort to spatialize time ultimately fails and space itself becomes an event'. Spatiality in this sense is agreed to be impossible. ' "Articulation" ... is the primary ontological level of the constitution of the real', writes Laclau.[35] This is a fundamentally important statement, and one with which I agree. The argument here is thus not opposed to Laclau; rather it is that exactly the same reasoning, and manner of conceptualization, which he applies to the rest of the world, should be applied to space and time as well. It is not that the interrelations between objects occur *in* space and time; it is these relationships themselves which *create/define* space and time.[36]

It is not of course necessary for the social sciences simply to follow the natural sciences in such matters of conceptualization.[37] In fact, however, the views of space and time which are being examined here do, if only implicitly, tend to lean on versions of the world derived from the physical sciences; but the view they rely on is one which has been superseded theoretically. Even so, it is still the case that even in the natural sciences it is possible to use different concepts/theories for different purposes. Newtonian physics is still perfectly adequate for building a bridge. Moreover, there continue to be debates between different parts of physics. What is being argued here is that the social issues which we currently need to understand, whether they be the high-tech postmodern world or questions of cultural identity, require something that would look more like the 'modern physics' view of space. It would, moreover, precisely by introducing into the concept of space that element of dislocation/freedom/possibility, enable the politicization of space/space–time.

## An alternative view of space

A first requirement of developing an alternative view of space is that we should try to get away from a notion of society as a kind of 3-D (and indeed more usually 2-D) slice which moves through time. Such a view is often, even usually, implicit rather than explicit, but it is remarkably pervasive. It shows up in the way people phrase things, in the analogies they use. Thus, just briefly to cite two of the authors who have been referred to earlier, Foucault writes: 'We are at a moment, I believe, when our experience of the world is less that of a long life developing through time than that of a network that connects points and intersects with its own skein'[38] and Jameson contrasts 'historiographic deep space or perspectival temporality' with a (spatial) set of connections which 'lights up like a nodal circuit in a slot machine'.[39] The aim here is not to disagree in total with these formulations, but to indicate what they imply. What they both point to is, on the one hand, a contrast between temporal movement and, on the other, a notion of space as instantaneous connections between things at one moment. For Jameson, the latter type of (inadequate) history-telling has replaced the former. And if this is true then it is indeed inadequate. But while the contrast – the shift in balance – to which both authors are drawing attention is a valid one, in the end the notion of space as *only* systems of simultaneous relations, the flashing of a pin-ball machine, is inadequate. For, of course, the temporal movement is also spatial; the moving elements have spatial relations to one another. And the 'spatial' interconnections which flash across can only be constituted temporally as well. Instead of linear process counterposed to flat surface (which anyway reduces space from three to two dimensions), it is necessary to insist on the irrefutable four-dimensionality (indeed n-dimensionality) of things. Space is not static, nor time spaceless. Of course spatiality and temporality are different from each other but neither can be conceptualized as the absence of the other. The full implications of this will be elaborated below, but for the moment the point is to try to think in terms of all the dimensions of space–time. It is a lot more difficult than at first sight it might seem.

Second, we need to conceptualize space as constructed out of interrelations, as the simultaneous coexistence of social interrelations and interactions at all spatial scales, from the most local level to the most global. Earlier it was reported how, in human geography, the recognition that the spatial is socially constituted was followed by the perhaps even more powerful (in the sense of the breadth of its implications) recognition that the social is necessarily spatially constituted too. Both points (though perhaps in reverse order) need to be grasped at this moment. On the one hand, all social (and indeed physical) phenomena/activities/relations have a spatial form and a relative spatial location. The relations which bind communities, whether they be 'local' societies or worldwide organizations; the relations within an industrial corporation; the debt relations between the South and the North; the relations which result in the current popularity in European cities of music from Mali. The spatial spread of social relations can be intimately local or expansively global, or anything in between. Their spatial extent and form also changes over time (and there is considerable debate about what is happening to the spatial form of social relations at the moment). But, whatever way it is, there is no getting away from the fact that the social is inexorably also spatial.

The proposition here is that this fact be used to define the spatial. Thus, the spatial is socially constituted. 'Space' is created out of the vast intricacies, the incredible complexities, of the interlocking and the non-interlocking, and the networks of relations at every scale from local to global. What makes a particular view of these social relations specifically spatial is their simultaneity. It is a simultaneity, also, which has extension and configuration. But simultaneity is absolutely not stasis. Seeing space as a moment in the intersection of configured social relations (rather than as an absolute dimension) means that it cannot be seen as static. There is no choice between flow (time) and a flat surface of instantaneous relations (space). Space is not a 'flat' surface in that sense because the social relations which create it are themselves dynamic by their very nature. It is a question of a manner of thinking. It is not the 'slice through time' which should be the dominant thought but the simultaneous coexistence of social relations that cannot be conceptualized as other than dynamic. Moreover, and again as a result of the fact that it is conceptualized as created out of social relations, space is by its very nature full of power and symbolism, a complex web of relations of domination and subordination, of solidarity and co-operation. This aspect of space has been referred to elsewhere as a kind of 'power-geometry'.[40]

Third, this in turn means that the spatial has *both* an element of order *and* an element of chaos (or maybe it is that we should question that dichotomy also). It cannot be defined on one side or the other of the mutually exclusive dichotomies discussed earlier. Space has order in two senses. First, it has order because all spatial locations of phenomena are caused; they can in principle be explained. Second, it has order because there are indeed spatial systems, in the sense of sets of social phenomena in which spatial arrangement (that is, mutual relative positioning rather than 'absolute' location) itself is part of the constitution of the system. The spatial organization of a communications network, or of a supermarket chain with its warehousing and distribution points and retail outlets would both be examples of this, as would the activity space of a multinational company. There is an integral spatial coherence here, which constitutes the geographical distributions and the geographical form of the social relations. The spatial form was socially 'planned', in itself directly socially caused, that way. But there is also an element of 'chaos' which is intrinsic to the spatial. For although the location of each (or a set) of a number of phenomena may be directly caused (we know why X is here and Y is there) the spatial positioning of one in relation to the other (X's location in relation to Y) may not be directly caused. Such relative locations are produced out of the independent operation of separate determinations. They are in that sense 'unintended consequences'. Thus, the chaos of the spatial results from the happenstance juxtapositions, the accidental separations, the often paradoxical nature of the spatial arrangements which result from the operation of all these causalities. Both Mike Davis and Ed Soja, for instance, point to the paradoxical mixtures, the unexpected land uses side by side, within Los Angeles. Thus, the relation between social relations and spatiality may vary between that of a fairly coherent system (where social and spatial form are mutually determinant) and that where the particular spatial form is not directly socially caused at all.

This has a number of significant implications. To begin with, it takes further the debate with Ernesto Laclau. For in this conceptualization space is essentially disrupted. It is, indeed, 'dislocated' and necessarily so. The simultaneity of space as defined here in no way implies the internally coherent closed system of causality which is dubbed 'spatial' in his *Reflections*. There is no way that 'spatiality' in this sense 'means coexistence within a structure that establishes the positive nature of all its terms'.[41] The spatial, in fact, precisely *cannot* be so. And this means, in turn, that the spatial too is open to politics.

But, further, neither does this view of space accord with Fredric Jameson's which, at first sight, might seem to be the opposite of Laclau's. In Jameson's view the spatial does indeed, as we have seen, have a lot to do with the chaotic. While for Laclau spatial discourses are the attempt to represent (to pin down the essentially unmappable), for Jameson the spatial is precisely unrepresentable – which is why he calls for an exercise in 'mapping' (though he acknowledges the procedure will be far more complex than cartography as we have known it so far). In this sense, Laclau and Jameson, both of whom use the terms space/spatiality with great frequency, and for both of whom the concepts perform an important function in their overall schemas, have diametrically opposed interpretations of what the terms actually mean. Yet for both of them their concepts of spatiality work against politics. While for Laclau it is the essential orderliness of the spatial (as he defines it) which means the death of history and politics, for Jameson it is the chaos (precisely, the dislocation) of (his definition of) the spatial which apparently causes him to panic, and to call for a map.

So this difference between the two authors does not imply that, since the view of the spatial proposed here is in disagreement with that of Laclau, it concords with that of Jameson. Jameson's view is in fact equally problematical for politics, although in a different way. Jameson labels as 'space' what he sees as unrepresentable (thus the 'crisis of representation' and the 'increasing spatialization' are to him inextricably associated elements of postmodern society). In this, he perhaps unknowingly recalls an old debate within geography which goes by the name of 'the problem of geographical description'. Thus, thirty years ago H.C. Darby, an eminent figure in the geography of his day, ruminated:

> A series of geographical facts is much more difficult to present than a sequence of historical facts. Events follow one another in time in an inherently dramatic fashion that makes juxtaposition in time easier to convey through the written word than juxtaposition in space. Geographical description is inevitably more difficult to achieve successfully than is historical narrative.[42]

Such a view, however, depends on the notion that the difficulty of geographical description (as opposed to temporal story-telling) arises in part because in space you can go off in any direction and in part because in space things which are next to one another are not necessarily connected. However, not only does this reduce space to unrepresentable chaos, it is also extremely problematical in what it implies for the notion of *time*. And this would seem on occasions to be the case for Jameson too. For, while space is posed as the unrepresentable, time is thereby, at least implicitly and at those moments, *counterposed* as the comforting security of a story it is possible to tell. This of course clearly reflects a notion of the difference between time and space in which time has a coherence and logic to its telling, while space does not. It is the view of time which Jameson might, according to some of his writings, like to see restored: time/History in the form of the Grand Narrative.[43]

*However*, this is also a view of temporality, as sequential coherence, which has come in for much questioning. The historical in fact can pose similar problems of representation to the geographical. *Moreover*, and ironically, it is precisely this view of history which Laclau would term spatial:

> with inexorable logic it then follows that there can be no dislocation possible in this process. If everything that happens can be explained

*internally* to this world, nothing can be a mere event (which entails a radical temporality, as we have seen) and everything acquires an absolute intelligibility within the grandiose scheme of a pure spatiality. This is the Hegelian–Marxist moment.[44]

*Further still*, what is crucially wrong with both these views is that they are simply opposing space and time. For both Laclau and Jameson time and space are causal closure/representability on the one hand and unrepresentability on the other. They simply differ as to which is which! What unites them, and what I argue should be questioned, is the very counterposition in this way of space and time. It is a counterposition which makes it difficult to think the social in terms of the real multiplicities of space–time. This is an argument which is being made forcefully in debates over cultural identity: '. . . ethnic identity and difference are socially produced in the here and now, not archeologically salvaged from the disappearing past';[45] and Homi Bhabha inquires,

> Can I just clarify that what to me is problematic about the understanding of the 'fundamentalist' position in the Rushdie case is that it is *represented* as archaic, almost medieval. It may sound very strange to us, it may sound absolutely absurd to some people, but the point is that the demands over *The Satanic Verses* are being made *now*, out of a particular political state that is functioning very much in our time . . .[46]

Those who focus on what they see as the terrifying simultaneity of today, would presumably find such a view of the world problematical, and would long for such 'ethnic identities' and 'fundamentalisms' to be (re)placed in the past so that one story of progression between differences, rather than an account of the production of a number of different differences at one moment in time, could be told. That this cannot be done is the real meaning of the contrast between thinking in terms of three dimensions plus one and recognizing fully the inextricability of the four dimensions together. What used to be thought of as 'the problem of geographical description' is actually the more general difficulty of dealing with a world which is 4-D.

But all this leads to a fourth characteristic of an alternative view of space, as part of space–time. For precisely that element of the chaotic, or dislocated, which is intrinsic to the spatial has effects on the social phenomena which constitute it. Spatial form as 'outcome' (the happenstance juxtapositions and so forth) has emergent powers which can have effects on subsequent events. Spatial form can alter the future course of the very histories which have produced it. In relation to Laclau what this means, ironically, is that one of the sources of the dislocation, on the existence of which he (in my view correctly) insists, is precisely the spatial. The spatial (in my terms) is precisely one of the sources of the temporal (in his terms). In relation to Jameson the (at least partial) chaos of the spatial (which he recognizes) is precisely one of the reasons why the temporal is not, and cannot be, so tidy and monolithic a tale as he might wish. One way of thinking about all this is to say that the spatial is integral to the production of history, and thus to the possibility of politics, just as the temporal is to geography. Another way is to insist on the inseparability of time and space, on their joint constitution through the interrelations between phenomena; on the necessity of thinking in terms of space–time.

Mexico City
published in 1992

# Notes

1   H. Lefebvre, *The Production of Space* (Oxford, Blackwell 1991), p. 3.

2   E. Laclau, *New Reflections on the Revolution of our Time* (London, Verso, 1990), p. 68. Thanks to Ernesto Laclau for many long discussions during the writing of this article.

3   F. Jameson, *Postmodernism; or, the Cultural Logic of Late Capitalism* (London, Verso, 1991).

4   Laclau, *New Reflections*, pp. 41, 69.

5   Ibid., p. 42. See, for instance, the discussion in M. Rustin, 'Place and time in socialist theory', *Radical Philosophy*, no. 47, 1987, pp. 30–6.

6   Laclau, *New Reflections*, pp. 82 (my emphasis), 42, 68.

7   Laclau, *New Reflections*, p. 92. And in this sense, of course, it could be said that Laclau's space is 'political' because any representation is political. But this is the case only in the sense that *different* spaces, different 'cognitive map-pings', to borrow Jameson's terminology, can express different political stances. It still leaves each space – and thus the concept of space – as characterized by closure and immobility, as containing no sense of the open, creative possibilities for political action/effectivity. Space is the realm of the discourse of closure, of the fixation of meaning.

8   Laclau, *New Reflections*, p. 41 (my emphasis).

9   Ibid., pp. 42, 43 (my emphases).

10  P. Anderson, 'A culture in contraflow', *New Left Review*, no. 180, pp. 41–78; and no. 182, pp. 85–137.

11  Lefebvre, *The Production of Space*, p. 275.

12  See, for instance, D. Massey, *Spatial Divisions of Labour: Social Structures and the Geography of Production* (Basingstoke, Macmillan, 1984); D. Gregory and J. Urry (eds), *Social Relations and Spatial Structures* (Basingstoke, Macmillan, 1985); and E. Soja, *Postmodern Geographies: The Reassertion of Space in Critical Social Theory* (Verso, London, 1989).

13  It should be noted that the argument that 'the spatial' is particularly important in the current era is a different one from the one being made here. The argument about the nature of postmodernity is an empirical one about the characteristics of these times. The argument developed within geography was an in-principle position concerning the nature of explanation, and the role of the spatial within this.

14  Laclau, *New Reflections*, p. 41.

15  See, for instance, J. Flax, 'Political philosophy and the patriarchal unconscious: a psychoanalytic perspective on epistemology and metaphysics', in S. Harding and M.B. Hintikka (eds), *Discovering Reality: Feminist Perspectives on Epistemology, Metaphysics, Methodology, and Philosophy of Science* (Dordrecht, Reidel, 1983), pp. 245–81. And in the same volume, the Introduction by Harding and Hintikka (pp. ix–xix), and L. Lange, 'Woman is not a rational animal: on Aristotle's biology of reproduction', pp. 1–15. Also J. Flax, 'Postmodernism and gender relations in feminist theory', in L.J. Nicholson (ed.), *Feminism/Postmodernism* (London, Routledge, 1990), pp. 39–62 and N. Hartsock, 'Foucault on power: a theory for women?', in the same volume, pp. 157–75.

16  N. Jay, 'Gender and dichotomy', *Feminist Studies*, 7, no. 1, 1981 (Spring), pp. 38–56, here p. 54.

17  G. Lloyd, *The Man of Reason: 'Male' and 'Female' in Western Philosophy* (London, Methuen, 1984).

18  Jay, 'Gender and dichotomy', p. 47.

19  Laclau, *New Reflections*, p. 41.

20  Jameson, *Postmodernism*, p. 269.

21  See, for instance, D. Dinnerstein, *The Rocking of the Cradle and the Ruling of the World* (London, Women's Press, 1987); M. le Dœuff, *Hipparchia's Choice: An Essay Concerning Women, Philosophy, etc.* (Oxford, Blackwell, 1991); and Lloyd, *The Man of Reason*.

22  Lloyd, *The Man of Reason*, p. 101.

23  E. Wilson, *The Sphinx in the City: Urban Life, the Control of Disorder, and Women* (London, Virago, 1991).

24  Wilson, *The Sphinx in the City*, pp. 157, 87.

25  Jameson, *Postmodernism*, pp. 363, 362.

26  Soja, *Postmodern Geographies*; and D. Gregory, 'Chinatown, part three? Soja and the missing spaces of social theory', *Strategies*, no. 3, 1990.

27  T. Eagleton, Foreword to K. Ross, *The Emergence of Social Space: Rimbaud and the Paris Commune* (Basingstoke, Macmillan, 1988), p. xii.

28  Ross, *The Emergence of Social Space*, p. 8.

29  S. de Beauvoir, *The Second Sex*, transl. H.M. Parshley (Harmondsworth, Penguin, 1972), p. 97.

30  R. Stannard, *Grounds for Reasonable Belief* (Edinburgh, Scottish Academic Press, 1989).

31  Ibid., p. 35.

32  Ibid., p. 33.

33  Laclau, *New Reflections*, pp. 41, 69.

34 An alternative explanation of why such structures are labelled spatial is available. Moreover it is an explanation which relates also to the much wider question (although in fact it is rarely questioned) of why structuralist thought, or certain forms of it, has so often been dubbed spatial. This is that, since such structures are seen to be non-dynamic systems, they are argued to be non-temporal. They are static, and thus lacking in a time dimension. So, by a knee-jerk response they are called spatial. Similarly with the distinction between diachrony and synchrony. Because the former is sometimes seen as temporal, its 'opposite' is automatically characterized as spatial (although in fact not by Laclau, for whom certain forms of diachrony may also be 'spatial' – see p. 42). This, however, returns us to the critique of a conceptualization of space simply and only in terms of a lack of temporality. Atemporality is not a sufficient, or satisfactory, definition of the spatial. Things can be static without being spatial – the assumption, noted earlier, that anything lacking a transformative dynamic is spatial can not be maintained in positive terms; it is simply the (unsustainable) result of associating transformation solely with time. Moreover, while a particular synchrony (synchronic form) may have spatial characteristics, in its extension and configuration, that does not mean that it is a sufficient definition of space/spatial itself.

35 Laclau, *New Reflections*, pp. 84, 184.
36 Stannard, *Grounds for Reasonable Belief*, p. 33.
37 However, the social sciences deal with physical space too. All material phenomena, including social phenomena, are spatial. Any definition of space must include reference to its characteristics of extension, exclusivity, juxtaposition, and so on. Moreover, not only do the relationships between these phenomena create/define space–time but also the spacing (and timing) of phenomena enables and constrains the relationships themselves. Thus, it *is* necessary for social science to be at least consistent with concepts of physical space, although a social-science concept could also have additional features. The implications for the analysis of 'natural' space – of physical geography – are similar. Indeed, as Laclau argues, even physical space is temporal and therefore in his own lexicon not spatial: 'the real – including physical space – is in the ultimate instance temporal' (pp. 41–2). While I disagree with the labelling as spatial and temporal I agree with the sense of this – but why only 'in the ultimate instance'?!
38 M. Foucault, 'Of other spaces', *Diacritics*, Spring, 1986, pp. 22–7, here p. 22.
39 Jameson, *Postmodernism*, p. 374.
40 D. Massey, 'Power-geometry and a progressive sense of place', in J. Bird, B. Curtis, T. Putnam, G. Robertson and L. Tickner (eds), *Mapping the Futures* (London, Routledge, 1993).
41 Laclau, *New Reflections*, p. 69.
42 H.C. Darby, 'The problem of geographical description', *Transactions of the Institute of British Geographers*, vol. 30, 1962, pp. 1–14; here p. 2.
43 I am hesitant here in interpreting Jameson because, inevitably, his position has developed over the course of his work. I am sure that he would not in fact see narrative as unproblematic. Yet the counterposition of it to his concept

of spatiality, and the way in which he formulates that concept, does lead, in those parts of his argument, to that impression being given.

44  Laclau, *New Reflections*, p. 75.

45  M.P. Smith, 'Postmodernism, urban ethnography, and the new social space of ethnic identity', forthcoming in *Theory and Society*.

46  In 'Interview with Homi Bhabha', in J. Rutherford (ed.), *Identity: Community, Culture, Difference* (London, Lawrence & Wishart, 1990), pp. 207–21, here p. 215. At this point, as at a number of others, the argument links up with the discussion by Peter Osborne in his 'Modernity is a qualitative, not a chronological, category', *New Left Review*, no. 192, pp. 65–84.

# Index